Understanding
Great
Expectations

Charles Dickens in 1859, painted by W. P. Frith, who thought he looked like a man "who had reached the topmost rung of a very high ladder and was perfectly aware of his position." To Dickens, the portrait made him look "as if my next-door neighbor were my deadly foe, uninsured, and I had just received tidings of his house being afire."

UNDERSTANDING

Great Expectations

A STUDENT CASEBOOK TO ISSUES, SOURCES, AND HISTORICAL DOCUMENTS

George Newlin

The Greenwood Press
"Literature in Context" Series
Claudia Durst Johnson, Series Editor

GREENWOOD PRESS
Westport, Connecticut • London

Library of Congress Cataloging-in-Publication Data

Newlin, George.
   Understanding Great expectations : a student casebook to issues,
sources, and historical documents / George Newlin.
      p.   cm.—(Greenwood Press "Literature in context" series,
ISSN 1074-598X)
   Includes bibliographical references and index.
   ISBN 0-313-29940-4 (alk. paper)
   1. Dickens, Charles, 1812–1870. Great expectations—Examinations—
Study guides.   2. Dickens, Charles, 1812–1870. Great expectations—
Sources.   I. Title.   II. Series.
PR4560.N38   2000
823'.8—dc21   99-32528

British Library Cataloguing in Publication Data is available.

Library of Congress Catalog Card Number: 99-32528
ISBN: 0-313-29940-4
ISSN: 1074-598X

First published in 2000

Greenwood Press, 88 Post Road West, Westport, CT 06881
An imprint of Greenwood Publishing Group, Inc.
www.greenwood.com

Printed in the United States of America

The paper used in this book complies with the
Permanent Paper Standard issued by the National
Information Standards Organization (Z39.48–1984).

10 9 8 7 6 5 4 3 2 1

Copyright Acknowledgment

The author and publisher gratefully acknowledge permission for the use of the following
material:

From THE DANGER OF BEING A GENTLEMAN by Harold J. Laski. Copyright 1940 by The
Viking Press, renewed © 1967 by Winifred Mary Laski. Used by permission of Viking Penguin, a division of Penguin Putnam Inc.

Every reasonable effort has been made to trace the owners of copyright materials in this
book, but in some instances this has proven impossible. The author and publisher will be
glad to receive information leading to more complete acknowledgments in subsequent
printings of the book and in the meantime extend their apologies for any omissions.

To Fred Kaplan
magisterial biographer, brilliant scholar,
constant and generous friend

Contents

Acknowledgments

I have not yet written a book connected with Charles Dickens without depending heavily on the aid of David Parker, former curator of the Dickens House Museum in London, who has been a perennial source of essential knowledge, insight, support, and good cheer. His efforts have benefited scholars and strengthened scholarship the world around. The Dickens House provided the Frith portrait of Dickens that is the frontispiece of this volume.

John Jordan, professor of English at the University of California at Santa Cruz and director of the Dickens Project, was promptly responsive to my inquiry concerning his wonderful talk on "Partings," which I first heard from him "live" on that campus at the opening of the 1996 "Dickens Universe" at Kresge College.

Dr. Tony (Anthony Ronald) Williams, whom I found through David, was a bountiful source of information, bibliography, and reference on the London stage in the early nineteenth century. He generously spent much more time than he should have to make sure I had everything I could possibly need. I look forward to the publication of his admirable Ph.D. dissertation, "Dramatic Interpretations of the Metropolis, 1821–1881," written under the aegis of another great old friend and staunch supporter, the distinguished Dickens scholar Professor Michael Slater, at Birkbeck College, University of London.

Abbreviations

The following abbreviations have been used for works that are cited frequently in the text of this book. Full citation information can be found in the "Suggested Readings and Works Cited" sections at the end of each chapter.

DF	Daniel Defoe, *The Complete English Tradesman*
EJ	Edgar Johnson, *Dickens: His Tragedy and Triumph*
FK	Fred Kaplan, *Dickens: A Biography*
FP	Frederick Page, Introduction to *Great Expectations* for The Oxford Illustrated Dickens
GKC	G. K. Chesterton, *Appreciations and Criticisms of the Works of Charles Dickens*
HP	Harold Perkin, *The Origins of Modern English Society, 1780–1880*
HP/HJ	Henry Potter, *Hanging in Judgment: Religion and the Death Penalty in England from the Bloody Code to Abolition*
JF	John Forster, *The Life of Charles Dickens*
JJ	John Jordan, "Partings Welded Together: Self-fashioning in *Great Expectations* and *Jane Eyre*"

JM	James E. Marlow, *Charles Dickens: The Uses of Time*
LH	Lee Holcombe, *Wives and Property: Reform of the Married Women's Property Law in Nineteenth Century England*
MS	Michael Slater, ed., *The Dent Uniform Edition of Dickens' Journalism*, Vol. 1
PA	Peter Ackroyd, *Dickens*
PF	Percy Fitzgerald, *Chronicles of Bow Street Police-Office*
PH	Patricia Hollis, ed., *Class and Conflict in Nineteenth Century England, 1815–1880*
RH	Robert Hughes, *The Fatal Shore: The Epic of Australia's Founding*
WLG	W. Laurence Gadd, *The Great Expectations Country*

Introduction

THE BACKGROUND

Great Expectations was Charles Dickens's thirteenth novel. It is a masterpiece, perhaps the author's best work in terms of structure and organization. It is a psychological novel, one of the greatest in all fiction, and it is much more, for it gives us plenty of comedy, tragedy, murderous violence, gentle benevolence, and sociological commentary.

The tale of how the book came to be written is well worth telling, for it demonstrates Dickens's amazing energy, versatility, and adaptability to circumstance. Besides being England's greatest novelist, Dickens was a fine actor: a stage performer and reader of almost unparalleled virtuosity, as well as a theatrical producer and director. He was also a great editor, one of the best and most diligent ever. It was his lifelong ambition to promulgate his ideas of social justice: to improve education for the common people and their health, morale, and general welfare.

During the last two decades of his life, which ended at age fifty-eight in 1870, Dickens edited and completely controlled two weekly magazines: first, *Household Words* from 1850 to 1859; and then *All the Year Round* from 1859 until his death. He gave boundlessly of his time and enthusiasm, vetting carefully every word that was printed on the nonfiction side to make sure he agreed with what was said. He published articles on subjects he cared about, written by himself and by staff members and stringers, and long and short works of fiction that he solicited from other authors and often contributed himself.

A Tale of Two Cities, the novel that directly preceded *Great Expectations*, appeared weekly in *All the Year Round* from April 30 to November 26, 1859, and cemented the successful establishment of the new magazine. The successor serialization was Wilkie Collins's *The Woman in White*, which also hit the jackpot. In an editorial announcement, Dickens had said, "It is our hope and aim, while we work hard at every other department of our journal, to produce, in this one, some sustained works of imagination that may become a part of English Literature." So far, so good.

The Collins work was followed by Charles Lever's *A Day's Ride, a Life's Romance*. Lever had had considerable novelistic success, but this effort was a turkey, and a damaging blow. Sales of the magazine plummeted. Dickens owned the publication and could not watch its value decline with equanimity. He acted at once. "I called a council of war at the office. It was perfectly clear that the one thing to be done was, for me to strike in" (EJ 964). He had originally planned *Great Expectations* as a monthly serial, to be published in twenty thirty-two-page instalments, but now he had to compress everything in order to fit the weekly format of *All the Year Round*. The instalments had to be brief and crisp, the overall length curtailed.

Dickens bounced the Lever work to the back of the book, and *Great Expectations* became the opener of each issue, beginning December 1, 1860, and ending August 3, 1861. It accomplished its intended goal. *All the Year Round* thrived for the rest of his life, its 300,000 circulation substantially exceeding that of the London *Times*.

At the core of the novel is a twist on the Horatio Alger theme, popular in all ages, of the poor boy who makes good. Pip (Philip) Pirrip is an orphan, raised harshly by his much older sister and benignly by the gentle giant, his brother-in-law. Unlike Alger's heroes, however, his translation to a higher sphere occurs through no effort of his own. He seems intended to be the prince and to marry the princess. Hubris sets in. Catastrophe follows. Humiliation leads to humility and thus to humanity. Debtor's prison threatens. The gentle giant is his rescuer. He gets a job and works for his living. At the end of the novel, he appears likely to get the girl after all.

Dickens had not intended that ending: he had written a stark, disciplined, quiet finish, with Pip still a bachelor encountering the now happily married, but sadly chastened, Estella briefly on a London street. Dickens showed his last number before publication to his friend, novelist Edward Bulwer-Lytton (*The Last Days of Pompeii*). Bulwer-Lytton protested. The public, he thought, would not stand for such an ending. He persuaded Dickens, whose astounding adaptability and ingenuity again came into play. The guardedly optimistic version Dickens came up with in four days of thought and writing is a masterpiece of elegiac subtlety: credible, poignant, and satisfying. While some critics have thought it a flaw and regretted Bulwer-Lytton's advice, others, notably John Jordan, have found it very much to the point. He prefers it because, whereas in the original ending Pip knows he has lost Estella and accepts the fact, in the revision there is ambiguity. Jordan says, "If Pip and Estella had remained together after they left the ruined garden, if they had subsequently married, and especially if they remained married 'now,' Pip would in all likelihood say so. The fact that he doesn't suggests that none of these things is the case" (JJ 29).

AUTOBIOGRAPHICAL ELEMENTS

In his latter days, Dickens lived at Gad's Hill, a house overlooking the "meshes" and not far from Rochester, where the original of Satis House, called Restoration House, was a prominent dwelling. He imbued *Great Expectations* with many elements of his childhood, but, while he drew heavily on his own life as he crafted the novel, he did not do so in the most literal sense. It is helpful to remember that, when he was about twelve, his father John Dickens was put in debtor's prison, and Charles was obliged to leave home and school and go to work pasting labels on bottles of bootblack, working at first in a noisome, rat-infested warehouse down by the London docks with humble associates named Fagin and "Mealy Potatoes." He was in utter despair for the several months of his exile, for he had great ambitions for himself and saw himself ruined for lack of education and some kind of professional standing.

At last, matters improved at home. His father came out of prison, and young Charles begged for rescue. Touched and probably ashamed, John insisted, over his wife's objections, on bringing Charles home and putting him back in school. The boy never forgave his mother, though from her point of view, with several other mouths to feed and a feckless husband to worry about, her attitude was understandable and should not have been surprising. Many children in those times were on their own, even at younger ages. There were no child labor laws.

But Charles had a strong sense of himself as a remarkable, gifted person who would do great things. Coming from a lower middle-class background (his father was a navy paymaster at Chatham in Kent, on the English coast southeast of London, where the little boy saw prison hulks in the river and gibbets on the shore), with all the sensitivities of that status, his worst fears were of slipping lower on the social scale and never being able to climb back. He wrote of these feelings passionately in later years and told his intimate friend John Forster about them. But he never, ever told his children, and probably not his wife, of his blacking house experience.

Young Charles was so clever and quick in his work that the manager of the warehouse set him in a window for the entertainment of passers-by. This exposure was humiliating. It may have angered his father and precipitated the quarrel that led to his returning home. When Pip is in the forge and imagining that Estella will turn up outside and see him through the window, there seems to be remembrance of Dickens's old embarrassment. Dickens freely stated to Forster that he was degraded by having to work with "common" boys, one of whom went by the sobriquet of Mealy Potatoes. "No words can express the secret agony of my soul as I sunk into this companionship," he wrote (JF I, 33).

Dickens's biographers have always emphasized the autobiographical aspects of *Great Expectations*, though not always in the same way. Edgar Johnson says, "Grown to youth, Pip toils in the sweat and soot of the *black*smith shop, a place in the social scale even lower than wrapping bottles in a *black*ing warehouse" (EJ 983). Peter Ackroyd stresses Dickens's psychological need to wrestle with his painful memories and pass them through a crucible, transforming them as he reworked them into fiction. The image of a blacksmith's forge, where metal is heated and then hammered molten into new shapes, seems a fair analogy of this fictional process. Ackroyd feels that *Great Expectations* is "a novel in which he is engaged in exorcising the influence of his past by rewriting it" (PA 881).

Miss Havisham is derived partly from a woman Dickens as a child used to see "dressed entirely in white, with a ghastly white plating round her head and face, inside her white bonnet" (PA 886). He had heard of a duchess murdered, who lived alone in a great house that was always shut up. She passed her time entirely in the dark. In the *Household Narrative of Current Events* for January 1850 there was a story of a certain Martha Joachim, a recluse who dressed entirely in white after her suitor blew his brains out in front of her. In the same issue, there is a description of the transportation of convicts to Australia, as well as the story of a woman whose gown is set on fire.

So there are these anecdotes, and they are relevant but not crucial. The main point is that the book, with great psychological accuracy, analyzes sexual passion, hypocrisy, meanness, snobbishness—all those things Pip eventually faces in himself. By making him do so Dickens tries to free himself of the inclination—the temptation—to feel, express, and exemplify those things himself. This is why George Bernard Shaw thought the novel "an apology to Mealy Potatoes." Peter Ackroyd insightfully summarizes the point:

In many ways therefore it is a much more frankly autobiographical work than *David Copperfield* and if this book does indeed reflect a fresh access of self-knowledge on Dickens's part . . . that self-knowledge had also opened up the doors of self-perception. That is why all the previously inchoate and shadowy fears of his childhood are allowed to emerge without impediment. Combining into strange shapes so that Dickens himself seems to be part Pip and part Magwitch, the convict representing all that is guilty and all that is beneficent, all that is "common" and all that is powerful. Creating strange currents of thwarted love and sexuality in Miss Havisham and Estella. Lamenting the hopeless search for love. Fashioning a self-made "gentleman" in Pip who has no real place in the world and whose own values, created out of self-love, are impossibly frail—what aspect of the author might we see in *that?* It is as if Dickens were in a fever which allows him to speak freely for the first time, just as Pip, in his own sickness, reverts helplessly to the state of a child—". . . I fancied I was little Pip again." And Dickens, writing in Wellington Street North, was only a few steps away from

Chandos Street where little Charles had tied up pots of blacking as
he sat in the window. Towards the end of *Great Expectations* Pip
waits beside the deathbed of Magwitch, and it is almost as if the
young Charles Dickens were sitting at the deathbed of the old
Charles Dickens. (PA 899–900)

NOTE

Because there are multiple editions of the works of Charles Dickens
and Anthony Trollope, the parenthetical citations following quotations
from them give chapter numbers, which do not change, and not page
numbers, which do.

This work includes no glossary, but a number of references to individuals and works will be found in the Index in somewhat expanded form
for added usefulness to the reader.

WORKS CITED

Ackroyd, Peter. *Dickens*. New York: HarperCollins, 1990.

Johnson, Edgar. *Charles Dickens: His Tragedy and Triumph*. 2 vols. New
York: Simon & Schuster, 1952.

Jordan, John. "Partings Welded Together: Self-fashioning in *Great Expectations* and *Jane Eyre*." *Dickens Quarterly* 13, no. 1 (March 1996).

Shaw, George Bernard. Preface to *Great Expectations*. New York: Limited
Editions Club, 1937.

1

A Literary Analysis of *Great Expectations*

Great Expectations is special. Commentators have almost universally rated it very highly, if not the highest, among the works of
Charles Dickens, who is generally considered the greatest of English novelists. The novel does not have much of the exuberance or
manic humor found in earlier works and revived in his last complete novel, *Our Mutual Friend*, but Dickens, as always, works
from a rich, subtle, and diversified palette. Let us consider each of
its several elements in turn.

Plot is central in classic fiction, and never more in Dickens than
in this novel. Related to it, the elements we might consider are:
structure, themes, characters, symbolism, and such ingredients as
atmosphere, mood, tone, language and descriptive power, and
point of view. Of course there is also "technique": the use of certain literary devices ("figures of speech") to achieve effects. Central
to this book, and uniquely so in Dickens, is the figure of speech
called "irony," important enough to rate a segment of this chapter
by itself.

PLOT

Great Expectations' status as one of the most popular, universally read novels of the last 140 years can be attributed largely to

Dickens's ingenious plot and his extraordinarily effective prose in telling the gripping story he conceived. Edgar Johnson, perhaps the greatest Dickens biographer of our times, called *Great Expectations* (barring the changed ending, which he thought a flaw) "the most perfectly constructed and perfectly written of all Dickens's works" (EJ 993).

Is the story far-fetched? Is it humanly plausible that a convict who has terrorized a little boy into fetching him food and file could be grateful to that little boy and remember him through years of struggle, ultimately rewarding him (if that is the term) with the fruits of his battle to succeed?

Do we believe in such goodness in so low a specimen? Victor Hugo, in *Les Misérables*, requires that we believe it: when Jean Valjean, a fugitive convict like Abel Magwitch, steals some altar furniture from a bishop, he is saved by the saintly bishop's absolution. The bishop scolds him, in the presence of the police, for forgetting to take away other silver intended for him. Valjean experiences a conversion and works for good for the rest of his life. (This great French novel, written in 1862, a year or so after *Great Expectations* appeared, has plot elements that resemble those in the Dickens novel to a startling degree. The connection between the inexorable Inspector Javert and the unstoppable Compeyson is only one of them.) Magwitch, gobbling his food desperately, realizes in his desolation that Pip pities him when in a moment of fellow feeling the boy says, " 'I am glad you enjoy it.' 'Thankee, my boy. I do' " (3). Dickens does not highlight this transfiguring moment in the least, but in truth it is the spring that starts the story. Magwitch tells of remembering it for years in the Australian outback.

It may also be the case that Magwitch was seeking to avenge himself on the society that had given him no chance, by perpetrating a "black joke" at its expense, creating a puppet "gentleman" to deceive and symbolically undermine that society from within. This is not a standard line of criticism of the novel, but it is given some validity by Magwitch's imaginary defiance of haughty colonists riding by him on the road: "All on you owns stock and land; which on you owns a brought-up London gentleman?" (39). Robert Hughes's idea (see Chapter 7) might have had resonance for Dickens, for he avoided most aristocrats until near the end of his life.

What a diabolical plot it is, on one level. Pip is seduced into betraying a man who loves him for a girl who does not, believing her to be representative of the society he thinks he is being fitted to join. And who, unbeknownst to him, are this girl's parents? A murderess and a convict. Think of that girl, Estella: how has she been readied for that society? By being schooled to become a recalcitrant misfit who invites and (one suspects) earns brutality and mistreatment at the hands of her mate. She is manipulated as diabolically as Pip, and her catastrophe is, if anything, even more devastating, for she has no good parent to rediscover.

STRUCTURE

As we noted in the Introduction, Dickens changed his plan for the novel radically when he found he had to conform it to the weekly format of his magazine *All the Year Round*. The results, far from betraying any sign of treatment on a procrustean bed, seem in such perfect balance it is hard to believe the scheme was not intended from the beginning. It is an example of the not infrequent experience we have in life (and writers have in literature) that revisiting an initial plan, no matter how carefully charted, can yield a greatly superior result, attributable, perhaps, to the increased depth and thoroughness of the effort and the emergence of ideas and relationships not previously imagined or thought through.

The structure of *Great Expectations* has formal, plot, character, and stylistic (language) elements. Uniquely among Dickens's works, the very table of contents reveals nothing about where to find a particular chapter (unless it is the first of a part): rather, we see "The First Stage of Pip's Expectations: Chapters I to XIX," "The Second Stage" with twenty chapters; and "The Third" with twenty. In many other novels, Dickens names his chapters, but not here. In the other cases where Dickens divides a novel into major sections, he calls them "Books" or nothing at all. Here, they are "Stages," the first one ending as Pip boards a *stage*coach for London.

Dickens wants us to see the novel as a life's journey, laid out in three chronological episodes of almost precisely equal text length. The first takes us through Pip's childhood and early youth to the moment when he leaves to discover where his newly announced "Expectations" will bring him. The second shows the working out of these "Expectations" to the moment of their shattering by the arrival of Magwitch (from his port of debarkation, Portsmouth, certainly by *stage*coach). The last leads Pip and Magwitch through struggle and catastrophe and so to death in Magwitch's case and near-death in Pip's. "Expectations" are demolished, and past and future are at last annealed in a sober, responsible present.

The deployment of his characters is another aspect of Dickens's structure. Pip's lack of filial loyalty to his benefactor Joe Gargery is set explicitly against Mr. Wemmick's devotion to the Aged P and Clara Barley's long-suffering service to her irascible father, old Gruffandgrim. Pip's thoughtless cruelty to Biddy contrasts with Herbert's patient devotion to his Clara and Wemmick's joy in his union with Miss Skiffins. We have two pairs of "parental" figures for this orphan boy: Joe Gargery and Magwitch are honest foster fathers; Mrs. Joe and Miss Havisham are destructive foster mothers. The pairings continue with Biddy and Estella as contrasting sirens, between whom Pip falls to the ground, and Pip's legal mentors Jaggers and Wemmick.

In terms of style or language, we can make a beginning here by noting that the story opens at twilight beside the misty marshes, with the river beyond and the wind rushing from the "distant savage lair" of the sea. Stage One ends in the little village with the light mists "solemnly rising, as if to show me the world" and Pip ensconced in the coach for London. Stage Two starts in bright daylight, with the optimistic Pip in a hackney-coach, headed for Jaggers. The climactic catastrophe occurs during a terrible storm, with street lamps blown out and barge fires carried away before the wind. Its last words are, "and the wind and rain intensified the thick black darkness" (39). Stage Three begins the morning after, with the wind "as fierce as ever" and no way to keep a lamp lit out of doors (permitting the lurking Orlick to elude detection). It passes again through the misty marshes where Pip nearly dies at Orlick's hands, and ends, "as the morning mists had risen long ago when I first left the forge, so, the evening mists were rising now," but with this difference, that they showed Pip a "broad expanse of tranquil light" and an omen for a better future, for he sees "no shadow of another parting" from the girl he has always longed for—if not "expected" any longer (58).

THEMES

Great novels operate on many levels, and none does so more satisfactorily than *Great Expectations*. Its themes are many. Every scholar has his own list. Frederick Page says, "The theme is Pip's discontent with his actual benefactors (cold word!): first with Joe, later with Provis; his innocent misattribution of his fortune to Miss Havisham; his supposition that she must intend Estella for him" (FP viii). Edgar Johnson emphasizes Dickens's depiction of a triumph of hardworking integrity over corrupt worldly values (EJ 988–89). Peter Ackroyd is primarily interested in Pip's passion and unrequited love, his sexual and emotional renunciation: "there is torture in love, and despair, and madness" (PA 898, 955). Pip himself refers to this "theme that so long filled my heart" (37), and his speech to Estella (44) is much the most passionate lover's avowal in Dickens. Badri Raina focuses on self-actualization: "The story of Pip is the achieving of an authentic self" (quoted in JM 15).

There is no question that in Pip Dickens achieves, for the first and only time in his fiction, a truly convincing evolution of character from simplicity through spurious, superficial success to a chastened, authentic self-reliance. "Selfhood" is a modern concept, and the novel's self-healing aspect for Dickens is dealt with in the Introduction of this book, along with the Horatio Alger theme of the poor boy who makes good, twisted here to undermine Alger's optimism.

For this author, Dickens announces his central idea with his title. I consider his core theme to be the illusoriness of "expectations" or assumptions about what the future holds. For Pip, the first intimation of this truth comes when he puts on his new suit, the second when he sees his new home, and a third when he lunches at his first London restaurant.

> My clothes were rather a disappointment, of course. Probably every new and eagerly expected garment ever put on since clothes came in, fell a trifle short of the wearer's expectation. (19)

> [H]ere we were at Barnard's Inn. . . . I had supposed that establishment to be a hotel kept by Mr Barnard, to which the Blue Boar in our town was a mere public-house. Whereas I now found Barnard to be a disembodied spirit, or a fiction, and his inn the dingiest collection of shabby buildings ever squeezed together in a rank corner as a club for Tom-cats. (21)

> [W]e went and had lunch at a celebrated house which I then quite venerated, but now believe to have been the most abject superstition in Europe. (22)

These are frivolous setbacks compared with what Pip experiences at the hands of Miss Havisham, Estella, and Magwitch. This subject is explored in greater detail later in this chapter (see the discussion of irony).

Pip's expectations are not the only illusory ones. Virtually every other character in the story experiences disappointment at one time or another. The first in point of time is Miss Havisham, devastated in her joyful expectation as she dresses for her wedding. This blow, and the crushing of Magwitch's hope for freedom, engender all that follows. Consider Joe Gargery's expectation of "what larks" with Pip as he grows to manhood; Mrs. Joe's hopes for benefit from Pip's connection with Miss Havisham; Pumblechook's fatuous confidence that his patronage of the now fortunate Pip will be rewarded; Wopsle's equally unrealistic belief in his future as an actor; Biddy's hopes for lifelong partnership with Pip; Herbert Pocket's parents' mutual disappointments; Miss Havisham's looking forward to an old age warmed by a grateful daughter; Magwitch's fond notion that Pip can be his "gentleman" and that he can see him at it; Compeyson's plans to turn Magwitch in, gain a revenge, and collect a reward; Herbert Pocket's naive belief, with his "wonderfully hopeful" general air, in the efficacy of "looking about me" (22); Bentley Drummle's baronetcy dream knocked in the head by a horse; Orlick's murderous plans frustrated; and, in a light-hearted, satisfying moment, the listing of Miss Havisham's legacies to her fawning relatives. Only the hard-working, hard-headed realists Jaggers and Wemmick, the sunny-minded Aged P, and the practical Miss Skiffins seem to escape the plague. There is a humorous expectation, too, in Herbert's description of his beloved Clara's irascible father: "Oh yes, I constantly expect to see him . . . because I never hear him, without expecting him to come tumbling through the ceiling. But I don't know how long the rafters may hold" (30).

These "expectations," confident, fatuous, or desperate as they may be, contrast sharply with Magwitch's philosophic mood, riding Pip's boat on the swell of the Thames:

> He had his boat-cloak on him, and looked, as I have said, a natural part of the scene. It was remarkable (but perhaps the wretched life he had led accounted for it), that he was the least anxious of any of us. He was not indifferent, for he told me that he hoped to live

to see his gentleman one of the best of gentlemen in a foreign country; he was not disposed to be passive or resigned, as I understood it; but he had no notion of meeting danger half-way. When it came upon him, he confronted it, but it must come before he troubled himself. (54)

Another theme is that wealth and position are corrupting and corrupt, inducing inertia and sycophancy. Whenever the highest value is placed on being a parasite—on the prestige of not having to work for a living (because, by implication or often enough in fact, one's income is derived from the rents on inherited land)— the reward is snobbism and an unearned superiority of "station" undignified by honest effort or success at something as demeaning as "trade." The corrupting influence of Miss Havisham's wealth is less on her (she is beyond it) than on her relatives, who toady and sneer, pander and posture. Herbert's goal is "making it" and then living on it: "When you have once made your capital, you have nothing to do but employ it" (22). The aristocratic, indulged, and self-indulgent Bentley Drummle is an extreme case of slothful arrogance and uselessness. Mrs. Pocket is corrupted by her false view of herself as a superior person unjustly deprived of her rightful station by the accidental failure of her grandfather to achieve ennoblement. Her complacent irresponsibility endangers her neglected children, but she does not notice. Her self-deceiving distinction is enough to attract the sycophantic Mrs. Coiler, who considers her "of so aristocratic a disposition . . . that it *is* hard . . . to have dear Mr Pocket's time and attention diverted from dear Mrs Pocket" (23).

A related theme is the derisive emptiness of social status. Can a convict make a gentleman out of the orphan dependant of a blacksmith? Can a criminal lawyer (Jaggers) make a lady out of the orphan castoff of a murderess? What is the status of the rich Miss Havisham, immured in wealth and dependent for recreation on a poor neighborhood boy? How respectable is the conniving, subhuman toad Bentley Drummle, next heir but one to a baronetcy? What good do Compeyson's ostensibly upper-class manners and attire ultimately achieve for him? Connected to this idea, Joe Gargery, in his finest moment up to that point, philosophizes on social differences and states two more themes of the work: that the tides of life can bring us together and move us apart; and that personal integrity is independent of station.

Pip, dear old chap, life is made of ever so many partings welded together, as I may say, and one man's a blacksmith, and one's a whitesmith, and one's a goldsmith, and one's a coppersmith. Diwisions among such must come, and must be met as they come. If there's been any fault at all to-day, it's mine. You and me is not two figures to be together in London; nor yet anywheres else but what is private, and beknown, and understood among friends. It ain't that I am proud, but that I want to be right, as you shall never see me no more in these clothes. I'm wrong in these clothes. I'm wrong out of the forge, the kitchen, or off th' meshes. You won't find half so much fault in me if, supposing as you should ever wish to see me, you come and put your head in at the forge window and see Joe the blacksmith, there, at the old anvil, in the old burnt apron, sticking to the old work. I'm awful dull, but I hope I've beat out something nigh the rights of this at last. (27)

One theme clearly is connected to parenthood, but it is not parenting as such: it is the converse. Let us call it "filiality," to make a word to suit our need. Pip is an orphan who is brutalized by his surrogate mother and very well parented, except when it comes to protecting him from Mrs. Joe, by the sweet-natured, straight and honest Joe Gargery. Pip fails to understand Joe until very late indeed. He does not know how to be a good parent's loving, appreciative, and loyal child—that is, he does not know what "filial piety" means. Herbert Pocket's example seems to escape him. Wemmick's goes right over his head. Any instinct Estella might have for filiality is deliberately crushed: she is richly brought up but trained to have a stony heart, so she has access to no human feelings even when her adoptive mother Miss Havisham tries at last to evoke them.

Another pattern observable in the book is expressed in the notion that people we thought we have said good-bye to, literally or figuratively, have a way of turning up again, when least expected. Pip thinks he has seen the last of Drummle when he ceases reading with Matthew Pocket, but nothing could be further from the truth. Orlick is the quintessential "bad penny," who reappears unsought again and again—even after his failed attempt to murder Pip. The housekeeper Molly's story at first appearance seems inconsequential, but she is seen as anything but that when her story is told and her motherhood revealed near the end of the book. Jaggers has a prelude appearance on the stairs at Miss Havisham's, then turns up with his portentous announcement of "great expectations" and a substantial presence in the story as Pip's guardian. The convict who delivers the two pound notes is discovered again sitting behind Pip in the stagecoach. Estella's materializing in the Satis House garden just when Pip goes there too after eleven years abroad is a surprise because of the unlikely coincidence, but inevitable in terms of the plot. Trabb's boy, who made Pip's departure from home so undignified, is no longer quite a boy when he guides Herbert Pocket and Startop to the shack where Pip would otherwise have died. Compeyson is seen once clearly in the graveyard but reappears thereafter several times in third-person narrative and then in person again at the story's climax, when he pays with his life. But the great fortissimo reappearance is the bolt-from-the-blue core of the plot: Magwitch returned from Australia, Pip's dreams all undone.

Revenge, primarily as engendered by injustice, is a pervasive theme in *Great Expectations*. Society's great injustice to Magwitch, described by him at length, may have been the trigger that induced him to play a "black joke" upon it by making a blacksmith's apprentice into a "gentleman." But there is a particularity in his thirst for vengeance against his treacherous, manipulating former partner, Compeyson, whom he captures for the pursuing militia at the cost of his own brief freedom and destroys at last at the cost of any chance to prolong his own life. Miss Havisham's determination to avenge herself on the traitorous male leads her to a pathetic extreme—destroying herself and sabotaging Estella. Orlick's revenge on Mrs. Joe for the beating she has insisted Joe inflict on him leads to an ultimately successful murder; his attempt to avenge slights he feels Pip has inflicted is nearly as successful. Compeyson's yen to punish his old colleague and enemy Magwitch runs through the last third of the book like an underground river. But perhaps the most pervasive and the most subtle revenge theme is implied in Pip's attitude toward the abusive Mrs. Joe: "I had no hope of deliverance through my all-powerful sister, who repulsed me at every turn" (2). "In the little world in which children have their existence, whosoever brings them up, there is nothing so finely perceived and so finely felt as injustice" (8). His yearning for deliverance impels him to London and his "expectations" even as he yearns to remain with Joe and Biddy, who he knows love him and whom he almost realizes he loves.

James E. Marlow, in his brilliant, difficult book *Charles Dickens: The Uses of Time*, persuasively argues for another underlying theme in *Great Expectations*. He reminds us that in the 1830s and 1840s (the time at which Pip's early life is set), famine, virtual and actual, was a fact of English life. It remained so (with a thunderous echo in Ireland as the potato crop failed) at least until the repeal of the Corn Laws in 1846. Dickens and his fellow authors "found themselves staring into the teeth of hunger. Stark, physical hunger stalked the land. The great majority of Britons seemed only a step ahead of starvation, and millions suffered from periodic famines" (JM 69–70). So we find the theme of starvation, physical and moral, and its cannibalistic converse at the core of *Great Expectations*, which of all Dicken's novels may have been the one "most completely structured by the themes of voracity and cannibalism. . . . From the first scene in which Magwitch looks longingly upon Pip's 'fat cheeks' " (JM 177–78), the book is replete with images and allusions to annihilation and being annihilated, of which the threat that little Pip's heart and liver will be "tore out, roasted and ate" (1) is only the most graphic and literal.

The "dread of being eaten" finds ample expression in almost every meal represented in the novel. Of all the meals described, only a few are free from the taint of figuring as a cannibal feast. The first such meal is the one that Pip brings to Magwitch on the marshes; in providing it, despite the initial coercion, Pip begins to learn to care for the well-being of another. Joe later expresses Pip's own nascent feelings: "We don't know what you have done, but we wouldn't have you starved to death for it, poor miserable fellow-creatur" (5). The second such meal is the one with which Herbert Pocket wishes to welcome Pip to Barnard's Inn—that desolate home for great expectations. The third is the Walworth dinner, at which Wemmick shares his Walworth sentiments. The fourth is the convalescent meal that Joe provides for Pip after the catastrophe. Otherwise—from the traditional Christmas dinner at which Pip is likened to an ungrateful pig . . . to his own later and reluctant feeding of the returned Magwitch—all the meals in the novel are spoiled by cannibalistic intentions or fears, at one remove or another. Estella, Pumblechook, Mrs Pocket, Miss Havisham, and even Jaggers—all provide food for Pip with the intention of also feeding on him. Orlick reveals himself only as the most literal cannibal when he tells Pip, "I won't have a rag of you, I won't have a bone of you, left on earth" (53). In no other novel by Dickens is the "dread of being eaten" driven home more convincingly. (JM 178)

Magwitch's terrifying table manners, if such a term can be applied to his mode of feeding himself, epitomize this theme of *Great Expectations*. The first time we see him at it, "He was already handling mincemeat down his throat in the most curious manner—more like a man who was putting it away somewhere in a violent hurry, than a man who was eating it" (3). His ravenous manner of eating is not improved by success in Australia: "as he turned his food in his mouth, and turned his head sideways to bring his strongest fangs to bear upon it, he looked terribly like a hungry old dog" (40).

Pip hands us another theme as he reflects on his visit to Newgate Prison:

> I consumed the whole time in thinking how strange it was that I should be encompassed by all this taint of prison and crime; that, in my childhood out on our lonely marshes on a winter evening I should have first encountered it; that, it should have reappeared on two occasions, starting out like a stain that was faded but not gone; that, it should in this new way pervade my fortune and advancement. (32)

Yet another theme articulated for us by Pip himself comes when he says, "Better . . . to have left her a natural heart, even to be bruised or broken" (49). Estella confirms the point in the last scene in the garden. When she says, "I have been bent and broken, but—I hope—into a better shape" (59), she evokes the idea—the metaphor (see below)—of the forge as the crucible of life: a furnace that both Pip and she have passed through and survived.

The last theme on our list is retribution, as inflicted by the Sultan Misnar in the *Arabian Nights*. This story, which caught the young Dickens's imagination and led to his first written work (now lost), is summarized at the end of Chapter 38. It tells of a long-prepared, devastating catastrophe, wreaked on an unsuspecting victim whose actions and choices have led to it. We can quickly see how the idea applies not only to Pip but to Miss Havisham, her half-brother Arthur and his colleague Compeyson, and, comically, to the detestable Pumblechook, invaded and for once silenced, his mouth stuffed with flowering annuals.

CHARACTERS

Readers of Dickens have often noticed that his most memorable characters tend to be the eccentrics, the "odd-balls" in his works. What a richness we find in *Great Expectations!* Miss Havisham is unforgettable, of a stature rivalling *David Copperfield*'s Mr. Micawber. Wopsle is hilarious, especially on the stage as the oblivious Waldengarver. The opportunistic hypocrite Pumblechook is delightfully odious. There are the formidable Jaggers, and Wemmick, an all-business law clerk in the office and proud householder and son when he gets to Walworth. Among the minor figures, everyone knows the Aged P, and there are the testy Bill Barley, whose every phrase Dickens has to clean up; toady Mrs. Coiler; the servile Sarah Pocket and her cousin Camilla, whose inheritances so perfectly match their deserts; the proud Belinda Pocket, brought up to be useless and determined to fulfill her destiny; the poised, politic, and professional sergeant of militia; the tailor Trabb, his arms always eager to measure; and the inimitable Trabb's boy—apotheosis of impudence and bounce, mirror and foil to Pip's ill-assumed new dignity and, of all people, the instrument of Pip's rescue from certain death.

Pip, of course, is the center. Edgar Johnson felt that with him Dickens, for the only time in all his work, was "entirely successful in painting a gradually changing character" (EJ 767). With Pip, Dickens pursues more deeply than anywhere else his own self-analysis, a matter discussed in the Introduction's comments on the autobiographical aspect of *Great Expectations*. For nearly the only time in his work we have a true anti-hero, with no special talents, ambition, or artistic ability. Fred Kaplan cogently describes him as "utterly unheroic, unromanticized, his sensibility and moral core free of the complications of talent and of authorial self-glorification. He is as close to the self stripped bare as Dickens could ever get" (FK 434).

Estella seems for most of the novel a hollow mannequin, her only early humanity shown when she rewards Pip with a kiss for besting Herbert Pocket in youthful combat. She has found Herbert unsympathetic, and he is not invited back. (The significance of this fact, and the comparative success of Pip in this regard, pass completely over Pip's head when Herbert tells him about it on their meeting again in London.) But she reveals herself at last, and tellingly, when she speaks of Pocket hypocrisy:

> "It is not easy for even you . . . to know what satisfaction it gives me
> to see those people thwarted, or what an enjoyable sense of the
> ridiculous I have when they are made ridiculous. For you were not
> brought up in that strange house from a mere baby.—I was. You
> had not your little wits sharpened by their intriguing against you,
> suppressed and defenceless, under the mask of sympathy and pity
> and what not, that is soft and soothing.—I had. You did not gradu-
> ally open your round childish eyes wider and wider to the discovery
> of that impostor of a woman who calculates her stores of peace of
> mind for when she wakes up in the night.—I did."
> It was no laughing matter with Estella now, nor was she sum-
> moning these remembrances from any shallow place. I would not
> have been the cause of that look of hers, for all my expectations in
> a heap. (33)

The Gargerys are indeed an odd couple: Joe, a gentle giant, under the thumb of his shrewish, violent wife to whom he allows full
rein, even in punishing Pip unfairly, because his own father had
brutalized his mother. Yet his dignity and simplicity are moving. A
foil to the worldly, hard-fisted Jaggers, a veritable prince of the
city, he is a true countryman. He is by no means unsuccessful in
his vocation of blacksmith, which was an occupation of importance
and some prestige in preindustrial England. Those who jump to
the conclusion (as Pip did) that his is a lowly life miss the fact that
on short notice Joe is able to pay Pip's debts and keep him from
prison.

SYMBOLISM

To most students of Dickens, *Great Expectations* is full of symbols. But it must be remembered that symbols are in the eye of
the beholder: every work of some complexity and sophistication
will contain elements that present symbolic significance to readers
interested in parsing them in such terms. Some are so frequently
noted that it is difficult to find freshness in them: the river, for
example. Dickens often uses a river to stand for life, flowing even-

tually into the eternal ocean: "the swift stream of my life fast running out to sea!" (53); and "the moving river itself—the road that ran with us, seeming to sympathise with us, animate us, and encourage us on" (54), misleadingly as it turns out. Dickens gives us a telling juxtaposition of river and sea intersecting for Pip and Magwitch, as they wait for a steamer to bear the convict to safety. The sea in this case brings death to a traitor, whose eternity, one might speculate, will be uncomfortable.

What of the marshes—flat, deadly in their miasmic effluvia (like the contagion of crime), treacherous to any who do not know the routes through them thoroughly? What of the wind, an almost perpetual presence throughout the novel? What of water generally—sometimes a trap to drown, sometimes a mode of cleansing away evil, sometimes a way to prison, sometimes a way to life—or death? (Note the last paragraph of Chapter 46.) There is a telling symbol in the vapour rising from the marsh, into which Pip foresees himself changed by operation of the lime-kiln and which he imagines had already been "my own warning ghost" (53).

The mist, that "heavy veil from the East," recurs again and again at crucial inflection points in the story, and perhaps most significantly at the moments when it rises and so seems to offer hope. Dickens uses it almost cruelly, beguiling the reader seeking helpful omens and seeming to validate hopeful expectations just before the long-planned effort to save Magwitch from the hangman: "As I looked along the clustered roofs, with church towers and spires shooting into the unusually clear air, the sun rose up, and a veil seemed to be drawn from the river, and millions of sparkles burst out upon its waters. From me, too, a veil seemed to be drawn, and I felt strong and well" (53).

What of the hulks, those ghostly prison-ships, evoking thoughts of hopelessness, alienation, and man's callousness and inhumanity to man? And, for that matter, what of Newgate? Dickens's life-long concern, indeed preoccupation, with prisons, figurative and literal, can be seen as another ground of *Great Expectations*. In the introduction, we note that the forge and the work done in it may symbolize the process of making fiction itself, and particularly the psychological study of an evolving Pip as presented in this novel.

ATMOSPHERE

Great Expectations is, among many fine examples in Dickens, a supreme exemplar of his gift for "atmosphere": the instilling in the reader of an inchoate sense of fear or fun, foreboding or discomfort, hilarity or happiness. His descriptive power appears in scene painting like the following, which will come alive if read aloud:

> The marshes were just a long black horizontal line then, as I stopped to look after him; and the river was just another horizontal line, not nearly so broad nor yet so black; and the sky was just a row of long angry red lines and dense black lines intermixed. On the edge of the river I could faintly make out the only two black things in all the prospect that seemed to be standing upright; one of these was the beacon by which the sailors steered—like an un-hooped cask upon a pole—an ugly thing when you were near it; the other a gibbet, with some chains hanging to it which had once held a pirate. The man was limping on towards this latter, as if he were the pirate come to life, and come down, and going back to hook himself up again. (1)

In a few words, Dickens gives us the tranquillity of a graveyard and a turbulent life at last at peace: "And there, my sister was laid quietly in the earth while the larks sang high above it, and the light wind strewed it with beautiful shadows of clouds and trees" (35).

The moment of Magwitch's most unwelcome reappearance must surely be the epitome of the "dark and stormy night" of Gothic tales:

> It was wretched weather; stormy and wet, stormy and wet; mud, mud, mud, deep in all the streets. Day after day, a vast heavy veil had been driving over London from the East, and it drove still, as if in the East there were an eternity of cloud and wind. So furious had been the gusts, that high buildings in town had had the lead stripped off their roofs; and in the country, trees had been torn up, and sails of windmills carried away; and gloomy accounts had come in from the coast, of shipwreck and death. Violent blasts of rain had accompanied these rages of wind, and the day just closed as I sat down to read had been the worst of all.
>
>   . . . [T]he wind rushing up the river shook the house that night, like discharges of cannon, or breakings of a sea. When the rain came

with it and dashed against the windows, I thought, raising my eyes to them as they rocked, that I might have fancied myself in a storm-beaten lighthouse. (39)

MOOD

Great Expectations is a study in closely juxtaposed mood swings. The opening moments in the churchyard, quiet and contemplative at first, are broken to bits by the apparition of a convict breathing blood and death. The scenes in the Gargery forge and humble home are tranquil when not being harrowed by the hysteric termagant, Mrs. Joe. The interludes at elegant, decadent Satis House shift for Pip from boredom to desperate longing and back again. The niggling worries Pip has about his debts and his "margin" are annihilated by the dark, stormy night of Magwitch's return. The tension and broodingly ominous buildup to Pip's dealing with the problem of Magwitch are overwhelmed suddenly by the crassest of brutal villains, the malevolent Orlick, and his nearly successful scheme for murder. Above all, there is the great, tense climax to Magwitch's career as a repatriate, when all Pip's planning and care, described with impeccable, relentless detail, are negated by a customs launch shooting out to grapple his little boat.

TONE

"Tone" is achieved by language, chosen to achieve certain kinds of psychological effects. There is the blood-chilling interruption of a lonely little boy's crying to himself in the first moments of conscious realization that his parents and his five little brothers are dead and buried and he is an orphan:

"Hold your noise!" cried a terrible voice, as a man started up from among the graves at the side of the church porch. "Keep still, you little devil, or I'll cut your throat!"
   A fearful man, all in coarse grey, with a great iron on his leg. A man with no hat, and with broken shoes, and with an old rag tied round his head. A man who had been soaked in water, and smothered in mud, and lamed by stones, and cut by flints, and stung by nettles, and torn by briars; who limped and shivered, and glared and growled; and whose teeth chattered in his head as he seized me by the chin. (1)

"The Terrible Stranger in the Churchyard" by F. W. Pailthorpe (1885).

Dickens was an absolute master at establishing tone, and different tones to suit different psychological situations. Wopsle's hapless *Hamlet*, one of the funniest scenes in Dickens, diverts Pip and Herbert enormously:

We made some pale efforts in the beginning to applaud Mr Wopsle; but they were too hopeless to be persisted in. Therefore we had sat, feeling keenly for him, but laughing, nevertheless, from ear to ear. I laughed in spite of myself all the time, the whole thing was so droll; and yet I had a latent impression that there was something decidedly fine in Mr Wopsle's elocution . . . because it was very slow, very dreary, very up-hill and down-hill, and very unlike any way in which any man in any natural circumstances of life or death ever expressed himself about anything. (31)

LANGUAGE AND DESCRIPTIVE POWER

Coming late in Dickens's life and art as it does, the novel has a certain autumnal feeling: "a quality of serene irony and even sadness, which puts it quite alone among his other works" (GKC 197), but on virtually every page there is an example of Dickens's prose mastery, funny or frightening. The description of Magwitch on his first appearance (above) is a fine example. Joe Gargery's foolish benignity shines out of "eyes of such a very undecided blue that they seemed to have somehow got mixed with their own whites" (2). When he is dressed up: "In his working clothes, Joe was a well-knit characteristic-looking blacksmith; in his holiday clothes, he was more like a scarecrow in good circumstances, than anything else" (4).

The deceptive Wemmick is irresistible:

> I found him to be a dry man, rather short in stature, with a square wooden face, whose expression seemed to have been imperfectly chipped out with a dull-edged chisel. There were some marks in it that might have been dimples, if the material had been softer and the instrument finer, but which, as it was, were only dints. The chisel had made three or four of these attempts at embellishment over his nose, but had given them up without an effort to smooth them off. (21)

We have noted Pip's disappointment when he arrived at his London address for the first time. The picture is a harrowing one:

> We entered . . . a melancholy little square that looked to me like a flat burying-ground. I thought it had the most dismal trees in it, and the most dismal sparrows, and the most dismal cats, and the most dismal houses (in number half a dozen or so), that I had ever seen. I thought the windows of the sets of chambers into which those houses were divided, were in every stage of dilapidated blind and curtain, crippled flower-pot, cracked glass, dusty decay, and miserable makeshift; while To Let To Let To Let, glared at me from empty rooms, as if no new wretches ever came there, and the vengeance of the soul of Barnard were being slowly appeased by the gradual suicide of the present occupants and their unholy interment under the gravel. A frouzy mourning of soot and smoke attired this forlorn creation of Barnard, and it had strewed ashes on its head, and was

undergoing penance and humiliation as a mere dust-hole. Thus far my sense of sight; while dry rot and wet rot and all the silent rots that rot in neglected roof and cellar—rot of rat and mouse and bug and coaching-stables near at hand besides—addressed themselves faintly to my sense of smell, and moaned, "Try Barnard's Mixture." (21)

Chapter 54 is all of a piece in maintaining tension and keen apprehension, but with nothing overwrought or exaggerated about it. In little more than ten pages Dickens gives us a complete arc of planning, hope, peril, catastrophe—and final despair. The chapter is widely considered to be one of the pinnacles of Dickens's genius in writing gripping prose, comparable to the hurricane scene in *David Copperfield*.

The novel well reflects Dickens's ability to coin a telling descriptive phrase, such as "this guileless confectioner" (20), "a certain conquered languor" (22), "general conversational condescension"(23), "a decent speechless paroxysm" (35), and many more; and his skill at limning a character in a sentence: "a large hard-breathing middle-aged slow man, with a mouth like a fish, dull staring eyes, and sandy hair standing upright on his head, so that he looked as if he had just been all but choked" (4); "I remember Mrs Hubble as a little curly sharp-edged person in sky-blue" (4); "She was . . . an indigestive single woman, who called her rigidity religion, and her liver love" (25).

POINT OF VIEW

An author can decide to tell a story from the point of view of a principal character, through whose eyes the reader sees all the action. Sometimes, this even takes the form of narration in the first person, and this is what happens in *Great Expectations*. Dickens's other quasi-autobiographical novel, *David Copperfield*, is a supreme example. At the other extreme is the "omniscient narrator," the impersonal storyteller who knows everyone's motives and what is happening everywhere.

One of the remarkable things about Pip's narration is the way Dickens lets us see him through his own words even when he cannot see himself. This is never more apparent than in his scenes with Biddy.

"You are one of those, Biddy," said I, "who make the most of every chance. You never had a chance before you came here, and see how improved you are!"

Biddy looked at me for an instant, and went on with her sewing. "I was your first teacher, though; wasn't I?" said she, as she sewed.

"Biddy!" I exclaimed, in amazement. "Why, you are crying!"

"No, I am not," said Biddy, looking up and laughing. "What put that in your head?" (17)

In this novel told entirely in the first person, and by a character who seems, most of the time, to lack understanding of himself and those around him, Dickens adroitly aids us by enlisting Pip's bosom friend Herbert Pocket to help flesh out the picture:

"I was a blacksmith's boy but yesterday; I am—what shall I say I am—today?"

"Say a good fellow, if you want a phrase . . . a good fellow, with impetuosity and hesitation, boldness and diffidence, action and dreaming, curiously mixed in him." (30)

In the novel there are rare, but telling, moments when narrator Pip is superseded by a kind of omniscience (perhaps called Charles Dickens):

Mrs Joe was a very clean housekeeper, but had an exquisite art of making her cleanliness more uncomfortable and unacceptable than dirt itself. Cleanliness is next to Godliness, and some people do the same by their religion. (4)

That was a memorable day to me, for it made great changes in me. But it is the same with any life. Imagine one selected day struck out of it, and think how different its course would have been. Pause you who read this, and think for a moment of the long chain of iron or gold, of thorns or flowers, that would never have bound you, but for the formation of the first link on one memorable day. (9)

TECHNIQUE

Dickens is the supreme humorist of the English language. He is irrepressible, even in the gloomiest circumstances. One way he uses his gift is for *comic relief,* the device every reader of *Macbeth* remembers exemplified by the "porter scene" directly following Duncan's murder. In Chapter 2, the state of mind of the little boy terrorized by threat of annihilation, while pitiable to any feeling person, lends all the greater hilarity (to the reader, not to any of the people in the story) when he conceals a piece of bread in his trouser leg and the results of his effort come to notice. His affectionate Joe is appalled: "Pip, old chap! You'll do yourself a mischief. It'll stick somewhere. You can't have chawed it, Pip. . . . If you can cough any trifle on it up, Pip, I'd recommend you to do it. . . . Manners is manners, but still your elth's your elth" (2). The scene is wildly funny just because Pip's plight is so macabre. He is accused of stuffing himself, but what he is trying to do is avoid having his insides torn out and eaten.

A fine example of *humor* in *Great Expectations* is Wopsle's *Hamlet* in the seedy theater in the Bow Street district, quoted in part above (31).

Dickens is an expert at *foreshadowing,* hinting now at what is to come.

As I saw him go, picking his way among the nettles, and among the brambles that bound the green mounds, he looked in my young eyes as if he were eluding the hands of the dead people, stretching up cautiously out of their graves, to get a twist upon his ankle and pull him in. (1)

I saw [Drummle] through the window, seizing his horse's mane, and mounting in his blundering brutal manner. (43)

Dickens's use of *apostrophe,* a figure of speech in which a speaker addresses an absent figure, is important in *Great Expectations,* for it tells the reader that the absence continues. One would not expect Pip to evoke Joe Gargery's name as he does, if Joe were currently in his life: "O dear good Joe, whom I was so ready to leave and so unthankful to, I see you again" (18). And yet in the cancelled ending, Pip is walking with Joe's little boy. One wonders what has happened since to separate them; perhaps Pip has written his life story while stationed in Cairo.

Dickens uses *personification* a great deal, increasing the vividness of his writing by attributing to inanimate things human feelings and motivations.

> every board upon the way, and every crack in every board, calling after me, "Stop thief!" and "Get up, Mrs Joe!" (2)

> The gates and dykes and banks came bursting at me through the mist, as if they cried as plainly as could be, "A boy with Somebody-else's pork pie! Stop him!" The cattle came upon me with like suddenness, staring out of their eyes, and steaming out of their nostrils, "Halloa, young thief!" (3)

> Mr Jaggers's room was lighted by a skylight only . . . eccentrically patched like a broken head, and the distorted adjoining houses looking as if they had twisted themselves to peep down at me through it. (20)

> A bell with an old voice—which I dare say in its time had often said to the house, Here is the green farthingale, Here is the diamond-hilted sword, Here are the shoes with red heels and the blue solitaire—sounded gravely in the moonlight. (33)

> the day came creeping on, halting and whimpering and shivering, and wrapped in patches of cloud and rags of mist, like a beggar. (43)

A special case, where Dickens personifies a central symbol, comes as he parts from Biddy after his sister's funeral: "Once more, the mists were rising as I walked away. If they disclosed to me as I suspect they did, that I should *not* come back, and that Biddy was quite right, all I can say is—they were quite right too" (35).

Another device Dickens uses when a certain kind of atmosphere is needed is *repetition*, a kind of sing-song. We see it in his first description of Magwitch (described in this chapter's section on tone), and there are others:

> No one seemed surprised to see him, or interested in seeing him, or glad to see him, or sorry to see him, or spoke a word. (5)

> Her chest had dropped, so that she stooped, and her voice had dropped, so that she spoke low, and with a dead lull upon her;

altogether, she had the appearance of having dropped, body and soul, within and without, under the weight of a crushing blow. (8)

and slimy stakes stuck out of the mud, and slimy stones stuck out of the mud, and red landmarks and tidemarks stuck out of the mud, and an old landing-stage and an old roofless building slipped into the mud, and all about us was stagnation and mud. (54)

Dickens often uses *simile*, where one thing is likened to another, dissimilar thing by the use of "like" or "as." He is adept at tailoring it to the situation to add flavor, sometimes for horror, at others for humor:

I had seen the damp lying on the outside of my little window, as if some goblin had been crying there all night, and using the window for a pocket-handkerchief. Now I saw the damp lying on the bare hedges and spare grass, like a coarser sort of spiders' webs; hanging itself from twig to twig and blade to blade. (3)

Cribbed and barred and moored by massive rusty chains, the prison-ship seemed in my young eyes to be ironed [wearing leg-irons] like the prisoners. (5)

So, Mr Trabb measured and calculated me in the parlour, as if I were an estate and he the finest species of surveyor. (19)

It was pleasant to observe that Mrs Wemmick no longer unwound Wemmick's arm when it adapted itself to her figure, but sat in a high-backed chair against the wall, like a violoncello in its case, and submitted to be embraced as that melodious instrument might have done. (55)

One of the commonest and most effective of all literary devices is the *metaphor*, where a similarity or quality is evoked without "like" or "as" but simply stated.

the small bundle of shivers growing afraid of it all and beginning to cry, was Pip. (1)

Mr Trabb had sliced his hot rolls into three feather beds, and was slipping butter in between the blankets, and covering it up. (19)

Heaven knows we need never be ashamed of our tears, for they are rain upon the blinding dust of earth, overlying our hard hearts. (19)

Wemmick's first appearance includes the description of his mouth: "His mouth was such a post-office of a mouth that he had a mechanical appearance of smiling. We had got to the top of Holborn Hill before I knew that it was merely a mechanical appearance, and that he was not smiling at all" (21). Having established this characteristic, Dickens uses its convenient shorthand again and again. It is the longest-running metaphor in all his work. Here are some of its manifestations:

Wemmick was at his desk, lunching—and crunching—on a dry hard biscuit; pieces of which he threw from time to time into his slit of a mouth, as if he were posting them. (23)

By degrees, Wemmick got dryer and harder as we went along, and his mouth tightened into a post-office again. (25)

I could have posted a newspaper in his mouth, he made it so wide after saying this. (36)

It occurs as well in Chapters 37, 48 (twice), and 55, among other places.

Wemmick engenders another metaphor when he visits Newgate, where he "walked among the prisoners, much as a gardener might walk among his plants. This was first put into my head by his seeing a shoot that had come up in the night" (32). At the end of the chapter, Pip refers to "Mr Wemmick's conservatory."

Dickens fuses metaphor, symbol, and simile as he sums up his story: "my great expectations had all dissolved, like our own marsh mists before the sun" (57).

IRONY

The Oxford English Dictionary defines "irony" as a figure of speech "in which the intended meaning is the opposite of that expressed by the words used. . . . A condition of affairs or events of a character opposite to what was, or might naturally be, expected; a contradictory outcome of events as if in mockery of the promise and fitness of things." The word comes from a Greek word for dissimulation or affected ignorance. G. K. Chesterton observes that, whereas all Dickens's books are "full of an airy and yet ardent expectation of everything; of the next person who shall happen to speak, of the next chimney that shall happen to smoke, of the next event, of the next ecstasy, of the next fulfilment of any eager human fancy . . . the only book to which he gave the name of Great Expectations was the only book in which the expectation was never realised" (GKC 200).

For there to be irony, someone must know or ultimately discover the true state of affairs. Sometimes at first this is the author alone, postponing his revelation of the truth of the matter until later and leaving the reader to put two and two together after the fact; or it may be that the reader comes to know something an actor in the story does not know. An example of the first case occurs when Pip meditates, after visiting Newgate, on the pervasiveness of crime and prison in the events surrounding him, and then goes on: "While my mind was thus engaged, I thought of the beautiful young Estella, proud and refined, coming towards me, and I thought with absolute abhorrence of the contrast between the jail and her" (32). As we and Pip discover later, Estella's father is a convict, her mother a murderess. Both were intimate with Newgate. This fact once revealed puts a whole new face on Pip's worries that his prison visit will "contaminate" Estella.

In the previous discussion of point of view was quoted some of Pip's conversation with Biddy about his infatuation with Estella. It is easy enough, from the clues Dickens gives us, to infer that Biddy is in love with Pip. We know, because Pip tells us even while he overlooks its significance, that Biddy is an extraordinary young lady, of mental acumen beyond the normal run. The reader is pained on Biddy's behalf by his obtuseness. Her qualifications to be a highly satisfactory wife make the entire passage ironical.

We take the view that disappointed expectations is the core theme of *Great Expectations*. But disappointment does not always have an ironical dimension: if Biddy had been an ignorant, slow country girl, there would be no irony in Pip's failure to consider her as a prospective mate. There is no irony in Miss Havisham's betrayal by Compeyson: it would have been expected by anyone knowing both parties. Nor is Magwitch's failure to escape the hulks ironical: it clearly was unavoidable all the time.

Jaggers's announcement that Pip has "great expectations," though sincerely meant, is a false prediction, made so by his client Magwitch's insistence on returning to England to see what he has wrought. "Great" is the irony, made so by the plot Dickens constructed. Here, if there ever was one, is a "contradictory outcome of events as if in mockery of the promise and fitness of things." And yet one might argue that not all Pip's expectations have the same ironic cast. He misunderstands Miss Havisham, and she does not disabuse him because he is a "man" who must be punished. Is this ironical? Perhaps it is just a mistake. Pip is a blacksmith's apprentice, transformed through no fault of his own. From the reader's point of view there is no inherent contradiction to the "fitness of things" in his failing to win Estella.

The central irony of the novel lies, we think, in Magwitch's establishing Pip's expectations and then destroying his own hopes (and expectations) and the "gentleman" he has made by the simple act of coming to see him. But Pip himself sees irony everywhere he looks by the end of the story: in Biddy's marrying Joe just when he, Pip, was ready at last; in the loss of his financial expectations through the operation of law; in Miss Havisham's repentance, so much too late; in Joe's bailing him out of debtor's prison despite his disloyalty; in the unintended consequence of his good action for Herbert being a job and some financial security for himself at last. (Irony can be benign as well as mocking.)

Remember the last words of the novel: "I saw no shadow of a further parting from her." But we are not told of a happy home and family, as we are in *David Copperfield*; if we pay close attention to these words, we might well infer that the incurable romantic in Pip has risen to the surface once more and that further disappointment lies ahead. Such would be the last irony, saved by Dickens in his back pocket and presented so deceptively that most readers and critics over the years have never seen it. (John Jordan, in his masterful piece on "Partings," points out that at the time Pip writes his memoir there is no mention of Estella in wifely or motherly mode, and Joe is absent as well: what happened to them?)

Great Expectations is a masterpiece, plotted expertly for maximum suspense, leavened with humor and juxtaposed horror and dread; a story told with the utmost imaginative skill, yet with a meticulous attention to the slightest detail of narrative description; and perhaps above all a psychologically subtle and perfectly nuanced drama of Pip's survival against great annihilative threats, and of the human development of a protagonist who, in coming to know himself as no classic hero, becomes a modern one in our eyes by achieving a state of sober realism (tinged, doubtless, with romance), autonomy, and self-respect.

TOPICS FOR WRITTEN AND ORAL DISCUSSION

1. Reflect on and discuss the questions asked in the section on plot. Have you read or seen *Les Misérables?* Do you think Victor Hugo might have been influenced by *Great Expectations?* What parallels between the stories can you think of?

2. Can you think of any reason why Dickens omits naming his chapters or even making them readily accessible by page references in his table of contents?

3. Who was Procrustes and what does his bed have to do with anything?

4. Does the link suggested between a "Stage" of Pip's expectations and a stagecoach make any sense to you? Why were some coaches called "stage" coaches?

5. In our discussion of structure in terms of the characters, we omit a good many, Pumblechook, Wopsle, and Matthew and Belinda Pocket, for example. Can you think of ways to use them or others in a discussion of the novel's structural form?

6. As discussed, structure may be impacted by style or language. Can you point out the ways in which references to weather (mist and wind, rain and storm) seem to recur at important points in the narrative structure of the novel? Choose one of the Stages for a careful, detailed analysis.

7. Find the description of Miss Havisham's legacies to her relatives and discuss them. Are they appropriate? Are they well tailored to each beneficiary? What impact has Pip had on them?

8. Can you cite one or more characters who are successful without being corrupted by their good fortune? Explain.

9. Discuss the questions asked in the paragraph on the theme of social status.

10. Pip accuses himself often in the novel of lacking appreciation for the sterling qualities of Joe Gargery. Can you think of any valid excuse for his dereliction?

11. Do you agree that Estella has no access to her human feelings? Why does she treat Pip as she does? Why did Pip become a favorite at Satis House when Herbert did not?

12. The notion of hunger and its converse, voracity, as a theme of *Great Expectations* is not an obvious one, though James Marlow makes a strong case for it. Do you see it in the novel? As an exercise, write an essay on the meals he discusses and set up a range of these and other

repasts on a scale running from the least exploitive to the most cannibalistic.

13. Discuss in an essay the symbolism of the junction of river and sea that occurs in the fateful Chapter 54.

14. Several elements in the story may have symbolic significance. Pick one of these and explore it from this standpoint in an essay.

15. Atmosphere, mood, and tone are closely related. As we use the terms, atmosphere might involve a part or all of a Stage, mood part or all of a chapter, tone a phrase or a sentence. Pick one of these elements and in an essay apply it to one of your favorite parts of the book.

16. Look carefully at the passage describing Barnard's Inn. Can you spot two of the literary devices discussed in this chapter?

17. Pick any chapter of the novel and go through it carefully, identifying each technical device you see. There are a great many more in every category than have been cited above. Or choose one device, such as *simile* or *personification*, and see how many you can spot over a Stage of the novel.

18. Look in the Theme segment at examples of various characters' disappointments. Analyze some of these in an essay to see which have ironic implications and which do not.

19. Write an essay on the way *Great Expectations* exemplifies "a contradictory outcome of events as if in mockery of the promise and fitness of things."

20. Publication of *Great Expectations* began shortly before Christmas in 1860. The story begins on Christmas Eve, and the Christmas dinner occurs in Chapter 4. It has been suggested that the first six chapters, which were published over three weeks through December 15, constitute a free-standing Christmas story. (Dickens wrote many such over the last two decades of his life.) A Christmas story in the mid-Victorian era was not necessarily sentimental or imbued with the "Christmas spirit." Discuss.

SUGGESTED READINGS AND WORKS CITED

Ackroyd, Peter. *Dickens*. New York: HarperCollins, 1990.

Chesterton, G. K. *Appreciations and Criticisms of the Works of Charles Dickens*. London: J. M. Dent & Sons, 1911.

Davis, Paul. *Charles Dickens A to Z*. New York: Facts on File, 1998.

Himmelfarb, Gertrude. *The Idea of Poverty: England in the Early Industrial Age*. New York: Knopf, 1984.

Johnson, Edgar. *Charles Dickens: His Tragedy and Triumph*. 2 vols. New York: Simon & Schuster, 1952.

Jordan, John. "Partings Welded Together: Self-fashioning in *Great Expectations* and *Jane Eyre*." *Dickens Quarterly* 13, no. 1 (March 1996).

Kaplan, Fred. *Dickens: A Biography*. New York: Avon Books, 1988.

Marlow, James E. *Charles Dickens: The Uses of Time*. Cranbury, NJ, and London: Associated University Presses, 1994.

Page, Frederick. Introduction to *Great Expectations* in The Oxford Illustrated Dickens. New York and Oxford: Oxford University Press, 1953.

Raina, Badri. *Dickens and the Dialectic of Growth*. Madison: University of Wisconsin Press, 1986.

Shaw, George Bernard. Preface to *Great Expectations*. New York: Limited Editions Club, 1937.

2

What Was a "Gentleman" in the Early Nineteenth Century?

Yes, Pip, dear boy, I've made a gentleman on you!
It's me wot has done it! (39)

1066 AND ALL THAT

The question of social status, social station, social class, while it is a universal in all societies that have evolved past chief and tribe, has been a particularly prominent fact in the consciousness of England, at least ever since 1066. When the Normans defeated the Saxons, they took their lands, their castles, their country. From that day to this, this fact has governed the mind-set of "Society" in Great Britain. Generally speaking, French-influenced language and naming has had a presumption of relative prestige (a French word) by comparison with earthy Saxon words and nomenclature. (After the American Revolution, Noah Webster and others codified American defiance of snobbish class influences by getting the "Frenchness" out of such words as "honour" ["honor"] "neighbour" ["neighbor"], "emphasise" ["emphasize"], and "theatre" ["theater"]. The Saxons had to herd the "sheep," the "cows," and the "pigs" while their Norman masters ate "mutton" (French *mouton*), "beef" (*boeuf*), and "pork" (*porc*). Distinctions reflected in language of course both reflect and permeate thought and so profoundly color (in England, "colour") British consciousness to this day.

Since the Normans lived high and the Saxons lived low, it was naturally the case that the Normans did not "work" for their living. They did work hard, but they worked at playing: hunting deer and wild boar, hawking, jousting, duelling, riding to hounds. The best of them also worked at governing some of the time. The Saxons tilled the soil, watched flocks and herds, waited on table, washed floors. Therefore, by definition and pervasively, for centuries after the Norman conquest one who "worked" was descended from the defeated; one who did not work was presumptively descended from the victors. Living on land and the rents from it necessarily imported this latter presumption; hence, it was fundamental, to have status in the world, that one be perceived as not having to engage in trade or commerce, let alone having to work with one's hands, or even one's brains, as a day laborer, a bricklayer, a blacksmith, or a teacher. "Gentle" comes from the Old French *gentil*, and there it is, in a nutshell.

THE "OLD SOCIETY"

To understand the meaning of social status in England in the days of Pip's apprenticeship, it is essential to recall that the story Dickens tells in *Great Expectations* is laid several decades before he wrote it in 1860–61 at the age of forty-eight. Pip, at the time he narrates his life, must also be in his forties, as he was twenty-three when Magwitch reappeared in England, and after all his travails, the convict's death, his long illness, and his going out to Egypt, a period of eleven years elapsed before his return. His memoir would have had to be written some years after his encounter with Estella in the Satis House garden, so it is probable that he would have been forty-five or older in 1860, hence was born no later than 1815 (Dickens was born in 1812), in the earliest stages of the Industrial Revolution. We believe Dickens envisioned Pip as being just his age, as there are many details in the novel that are lifted word for word from his autobiographical writings, and the descriptions of the marshes, the gibbet, the hulks, the river, and Satis House seem to come from his childhood recollections. On this theory, Pip signed his indentures for the blacksmith's trade in 1826, at the age of fourteen, if the normal pattern was followed (see Chapter 4). Magwitch, having been transported sometime before 1820, gained freedom some years later and probably began repatriating funds to make his "gentleman" in the late 1820s. This is just when a new class consciousness began to come into being in England, the result of early industrialization and political change.

The point of this emphasis on timing is that both Magwitch and Pip were living, psychologically, under the old order of society. "The most profound and far-reaching consequence of the Industrial Revolution was the birth of a new class society" (HP 165). That society was *not* Pip's, nor Magwitch's, nor Jaggers's. For that matter, it was not Dickens's in nearly all of his work. Only *Hard Times* (1854) of all his novels depicts life under the new scheme of things. What, then, was the old order?

"The old society which spontaneously generated the Industrial Revolution was *an open aristocracy based on property and patronage*" (HP 17). Like other preindustrial but civilized societies, it was hierarchical. Men's places were set by an accepted order of precedence, with the rich, landed minority at the top. The structure was not quite the pyramid it later became: the middle ranks were proportionally a much larger share of the whole than the Victorian "middle class," and the "laboring poor" were much fewer proportionately than they became with industrialization. As we noted in Chapter 1 in the discussion of hunger at the time, it was a poor society, in which life for the great majority was a struggle to stay alive.

The laboring poor were the roadmenders, hodcarriers, brickmakers, and other unskilled laborers, cottagers, seamen, and soldiers, together with the (nonlaboring) paupers and the vagrants— all lacking property or special skills. In 1688 they had been over half the population and received one-fifth of the income; in 1803 they were just above a third of the total and collected one-sixth of the income. In that year, one-ninth of the population, over one million people, were on relief. "At both dates poverty was an inescapable fact of life, and the distance between the rich and the poor almost oriental" (HP 22).

The middle ranks in England were rather rapturously described by David Robinson in an 1824 issue of *Blackwood's* magazine: "the space between the ploughman and the peer, is crammed with circle after circle, fitted in the most admirable manner for sitting upon each other, for connecting the former with the latter, and for rendering the whole perfect in cohesion, strength and beauty" (quoted in HP 22). These ranks were distinguished from the nobility and gentry above them not so much by income differentials as by the fact that they had to earn a living, while those above them did not. They differed from those below them by possessing capital, in the form of livestock, tools, trade goods, or an investment in education. They ranged from great overseas merchants and officials down to wretchedly paid curates, small farmers, and semi-independent craftsmen who might be as hard-pressed as were the laboring poor. Joe Gargery, an independent blacksmith with two employees, would have stood relatively high in the lower end of this group, since he had not only independence and a level of practical education, but owned the tools of his trade, not an insignificant consideration, as Chapter 4 makes clear.

The middle ranks, between the extremes, were constituted of parallel business and professional hierarchies, their statuses finely graduated. One scholar identified forty status levels. Even domestic service had its pecking order, from great stewards on large estates down to scullery maids and stable boys. (Dickens's paternal grandparents were steward and servant, later housekeeper, respectively, to a peer; he did not advertise the fact.) Each occupation was marked by internal status ranges greater than any that separated it from those outside. The 'old society' was thus a set of vertically organized, finely graded hierarchies, in which individuals were acutely aware of those immediately above and below them.

The status of an individual was something into which he was born, and he announced his standing to the world in his manner, his speech, his deportment, his dress, his carriage if any, his house and servants, and the food he and his family and retainers ate. Charity schoolchildren were marked by uniforms to distinguish them from their more fortunate contemporaries. The great lexicographer Samuel Johnson, in the preface to his Dictionary (1755), said the English were "a people polished by art, and classed by subordination . . . [by] the fixed, invariable external rules of distinction of rank, which create no jealousy, since they are held to be accidental."

THE "GENTLEMAN" IN THE EIGHTEENTH CENTURY: LORD CHESTERFIELD'S LETTERS TO HIS SON

There was, however, one very important division: that between the "gentleman" and the "common people." This distinction was not definable in economic terms. The most popular handbook on British society pontificated that "All are accounted gentlemen in England who maintain themselves without manual labour" (quoted in HP 24), but clearly, it was not intended that the definition include vagrants or other idlers not somehow connected with the upper echelons of society.

Social consciousness was formalized, and behavior was prescribed, by no one more thoroughly than by Lord Chesterfield. Philip Dormer Stanhope, fourth Earl of Chesterfield (1694–1773) was a prominent landowner and government official who gained preeminence in diplomacy during a wide-ranging career. His lasting legacy is his letters to his illegitimate son, whom he fervently sought to guide to worldly success and so help overcome his problematic birth, and later to the successor heir, on the subject of manners, deportment, and conduct appropriate for a gentleman. His letters are voluminous—it is hard to imagine how he found the time—and they display a great deal of loving care (wasted, it would appear, on his "dear boy," who may have been crushed by the weekly or more frequent admonitions his sire pursued him with wherever he went and who died five years before his father).

Reading through them, it is strikingly obvious to this editor that Lord Chesterfield has had a very bad rap from his posterity, which believes him to have encouraged in his son a cynical, manipulative, hard-hearted, hypocritical view of the world. Dickens believed it, as Chapter 23 of his novel *Barnaby Rudge* makes clear. But the letters contradict this. In one of the earliest, Chesterfield says, noting the boy's lack of rank and fortune, "What, then, will you have to rely on but your own merit? That alone must raise you, and that alone will raise you, if you have but enough of it. . . . By merit I mean the moral virtues, knowledge, and manners; as to the moral virtues, I say nothing to you, they speak best for themselves." He urges energetic study of the classics, rhetoric, logic, geometry, astronomy, modern languages, modern history, and geography.

Chesterfield's comments on manners, deportment, and conduct are the most characteristic and historically interesting features of his writings. They have made the letters famous, and they are the aspects relevant for us now. It is impossible in this space to do more than hint at the range and specificity of his advice. Here are some extracts, with side captions supplied for convenience, from the first year and a half (out of nearly twenty) of correspondence.

FROM PHILIP DORMER STANHOPE, EARL OF CHESTERFIELD,
*THE LETTERS OF PHILIP DORMER STANHOPE, EARL OF
CHESTERFIELD, WITH THE CHARACTERS* (1748–49)
(John Bradshaw, ed. New York: Scribner, 1892)

Conversation. The characteristic of a well-bred man is, to converse with his inferiors without insolence, and with his superiors with respect and ease. He talks to kings without concern; he trifles with women of the first condition, with familiarity, gaiety, but respect; and converses with his equals, whether he is acquainted with them or not, upon general, common topics, that are not, however, quite frivolous, without the least concern of mind, or awkwardness of body; neither of which can appear to advantage, but when they are perfectly easy. (May 17, 1748)

Talk often, but never long; in that case, if you do not please, at least you are sure not to tire your hearers. . . .

Tell stories very seldom, and absolutely never but where they are very apt, and very short. Omit every circumstance that is not material, and beware of digressions. To have frequent recourse to narrative betrays great want of imagination.

Never hold anybody by the button, or the hand, in order to be heard out; for, if people are not willing to hear you, you had much better hold your tongue than them. . . .

Take, rather than give, the tone of the company you are in. If you have parts, you will show them, more or less, upon every subject; and, if you have not, you had better talk sillily upon a subject of other people's than of your own choosing.

Avoid as much as you can, in mixed companies, argumentative polemical conversations . . . and, if the controversy grows warm and noisy, endeavour to put an end to it by some genteel levity or joke. . . .

Above all things, and upon all occasions, avoid speaking of yourself, if it be possible. Such is the natural pride and vanity of our hearts, that it perpetually breaks out, even in people of the best parts, in all the various modes and figures of the egotism. . . .

Always look people in the face when you speak to them; the not doing it is thought to imply conscious guilt; besides that, you lose the advantage of observing by their countenances what impression your discourse makes upon them. . . .

Neither retail nor receive scandal willingly; for though the defamation of others may for the present gratify the malignity of the pride of our hearts, cool reflection will draw very disadvantageous conclusions from such a disposition. (October 19, 1748)

Manners. Manners, though the last, and it may be the least ingredient of real merit, are, however, very far from being useless in its composition; they adorn and give an additional force and lustre to both virtue and knowledge. They prepare and smooth the way for the progress of both; and are, I fear, with the bulk of mankind, more engaging than either. Remember, then, the infinite advantage of manners; cultivate and improve your own to the utmost; good sense will suggest the great rules to you, good company will do the rest. (May 27, 1748)

Circumspection. Carry with you, and welcome, into company all the gaiety and spirits, but as little of the giddiness of youth as you can. The former will charm, but the latter will often, though innocently, implacably offend. Inform yourself of the characters and situations of the company before you give way to what your imagination may prompt you to say. . . .

Cautiously avoid talking of either your own or other people's domestic affairs. Yours are nothing to them, but tedious; theirs are nothing to you. (October 29, 1748)

Dress. Any affectation whatsoever in dress, implies, in my mind, a flaw in the understanding. Most of our young fellows here display some character or other by their dress; some affect the tremendous, and wear a great and fiercely-cocked hat, an enormous sword, a short waistcoat, and a black cravat; these I should be almost tempted to swear the peace against, in my own defence, if I were not convinced that they are but meek asses in lions' skins. Others go in brown frocks, leather breeches, great oaken cudgels in their hands, their hats uncocked, and their hair unpowdered; and imitate grooms, stage-coachmen, and country bumpkins so well in their outsides, that I do not make the least doubt of their resembling them equally in their insides. A man of sense carefully avoids any particular character in his dress; he is accurately clean for his own sake, but all the rest is for other people's. He dresses as well, and in the same manner, as the people of sense and fashion of the place where he is. If he dresses better, as he thinks, that is, more than they, he is a fop;

if he dresses worse, he is unpardonably negligent: but of the two, I would rather have a young fellow too much than too little dressed; the excess on that side will wear off with a little age and reflection; but if he is negligent at twenty, he will be a sloven at forty, and stink at fifty years old. Dress yourselves fine where others are fine, and plain where others are plain; but take care always that your clothes are well made, and fit you, for otherwise they will give you a very awkward air. When you are once well dressed for the day, think no more of it afterwards; and, without any stiffness for fear of discomposing that dress, let all your motions be as easy and natural as if you had no clothes on at all. So much for dress, which I maintain to be a thing of consequence in the polite world. (December 30, 1748)

Flattery. Not to seem to perceive the little weaknesses, and the idle but innocent affectations of the company, but even to flatter them in a certain manner, is not only very allowable, but, in truth, a sort of polite duty. They will be pleased with you, if you do; and will certainly not be reformed by you if you do not. . . . [G]et always into the highest company, and address yourself particularly to the highest in it. The search after the unattainable philosopher's stone has occasioned a thousand useful discoveries, which otherwise would never have been made. (October 29, 1748)

I recommended to you in my last an innocent piece of art—that of flattering people behind their backs, in presence of those who, to make their own court, much more than for your sake, will not fail to repeat, and even amplify, the praise to the party concerned. This is, of all flattery, the most pleasing, and consequently the most effectual. (May 22, 1749)

Poise. The principal of these things is the mastery of one's temper, and that coolness of mind, and serenity of countenance, which hinder us from discovering, by words, actions, or even looks, those passions or sentiments by which we are inwardly moved or agitated, and the discovery of which gives cooler and abler people such infinite advantages over us, not only in great business, but in all the most common occurrences of life. A man who does not possess himself enough to hear disagreeable things without visible marks of anger and change of countenance, or agreeable ones without sudden bursts of joy and expansion of countenance, is at the mercy of every artful knave or pert coxcomb. The former will provoke or please you by design, to catch unguarded words or looks, by which he will easily decipher the secrets of your heart, of which you should keep the key yourself, and trust it with no man living. The latter will, by his absurdity, and without intending it, produce the same discoveries, of which other people will avail themselves. (May 22, 1749)

Introspection. In order to judge of the inside of others, study your own; for men in general are very much alike; and though one has one prevailing passion, and another has another, yet their operations are much the same; and whatever engages or disgusts, pleases or offends you in others, will, *mutatis mutandis*, engage, disgust, please, or offend others in you. Observe, with the utmost attention, all the operations of your own mind, the nature of your own passions, and the various motives that determine your will; and you may, in a great degree, know all mankind. (May 22, 1749)

Cruel wit. The temptation of saying a smart and witty thing, or *bon mot*, and the malicious applause with which it is commonly received, has made people who can say them, and, still oftener, people who think they can, but cannot, but yet try, more enemies, and implacable ones too, than any one other thing that I know of. . . . It is a decided folly, to lose a friend for a jest; but, in my mind, it is not a much less degree of folly, to make an enemy of an indifferent and neutral person for the sake of a *bon mot*. (May 22, 1749)

Women. As the female part of the world has some influence, and often too much, over the male, your conduct, with regard to women (I mean women of fashion, for I cannot suppose you capable of conversing with any others), deserves some share in your reflections. They are a numerous and loquacious body; their hatred would be more prejudicial than their friendship can be advantageous to you. A general complaisance, and attention to that sex, is therefore established by custom, and certainly necessary. But where you would particularly please any one whose situation, interest, or connections can be of use to you, you must show particular preference. The least attentions please, the greatest charm them. The innocent, but pleasing flattery of their persons, however gross, is greedily swallowed, and kindly digested; but a seeming regard for their understandings, a seeming desire of, and deference for, their advice, together with a seeming confidence in their moral virtues, turns their heads entirely in your favour. Nothing shocks them so much as the least appearance of that contempt, which they are apt to suspect men of entertaining of their capacities; and you may be very sure of gaining their friendship, if you seem to think it worth gaining. Here dissimulation is very often necessary, and even simulation sometimes allowable; which, as it pleases them, may be useful to you, and is injurious to nobody. (May 22, 1749)

Dignity. There is a certain dignity of manners absolutely necessary, to make even the most valuable character either respected or respectable.

Horse-play, romping, frequent and loud fits of laughter, jokes, waggery, and indiscriminate familiarity, will sink both merit and knowledge into a degree of contempt. They compose at most a merry fellow; and a merry fellow was never yet a respectable man. . . . Whoever is admitted or sought for in company, upon any other account than that of his merit and manners, is never respected there, but only made use of. We will have such-a-one, for he sings prettily; we will invite such-a-one to a ball, for he dances well; we will have such-a-one at supper, for he is always joking and laughing; we will ask another, because he plays deep at all games, or because he can drink a great deal. These are all vilifying distinctions, mortifying preferences, and exclude all ideas of esteem and regard. (August 21, 1749)

Vulgarity. The very accoutrements of a man of fashion are grievous incumbrances to a vulgar man. He is at a loss what to do with his hat, when it is not upon his head; his cane (if unfortunately he wears one) is at perpetual war with every cup of tea or coffee he drinks; destroys them first, and then accompanies them in their fall. His sword is formidable only to his own legs, which would possibly carry him fast enough out of the way of any sword but his own. His clothes fit him so ill, and constrain him so much, that he seems rather their prisoner than their proprietor. He presents himself in company, like a criminal in a court of justice; his very air condemns him; and people of fashion will no more connect themselves with the one, than people of character will with the other. This repulse drives and sinks him into low company; a gulf from whence no man, after a certain age, ever emerged. (September 27, 1749)

Good Breeding. A friend of yours and mine has very justly defined good-breeding to be, *the result of much good-sense, some good-nature, and a little self-denial for the sake of others, and with a view to obtain the same indulgence from them*. Taking this for granted (as I think it cannot be disputed), it is astonishing to me that anybody who has good-sense and good-nature (and I believe you have both) can essentially fail in good-breeding . . . the substance of it is everywhere and eternally the same. Good manners are, to particular societies what good morals are to society in general,—their cement and their security. And as laws are enacted to enforce good morals, or at least to prevent the ill effects of bad ones, so there are certain rules of civility, universally implied and received, to enforce good manners, and punish bad ones. . . . [N]ext to the consciousness of doing a good action, that of doing a civil one is the most pleasing; and the epithet which I should covet the most, next to that of Aristides [*the Just*], would be that of well-bred. . . .

If a man accosts you, and talks to you ever so dully or frivolously, it is worse than rudeness, it is brutality, to show him, by a manifest inattention to what he says, that you think him a fool or a blockhead, and not worth hearing. It is much more so with regard to women, who, of whatever rank they are, are entitled, in consideration of their sex, not only to an attentive, but an officious good-breeding from men. . . . I will conclude with these axioms:—

That the deepest learning, without good-breeding, is unwelcome and tiresome pedantry, and of use nowhere but in a man's own closet—and, consequently, of little or no use at all.

That a man who is not perfectly well-bred, is unfit for good company, and unwelcome in it; will consequently dislike it [and] soon afterwards renounce it; and be reduced to solitude, or (what is worse) low and bad company.

That a man who is not well-bred, is full as unfit for business as for company.

Make then, my dear child, I conjure you, good-breeding the great object of your thoughts and actions, at least, half the day. Observe carefully the behaviour and manners of those who are distinguished by their good-breeding; imitate, nay, endeavour to excel, that you may at least reach them; and be convinced that good-breeding is, to all worldly qualifications, what charity is to all Christian virtues. Observe how it adorns merit, and how often it covets the want of it. May you wear it to adorn, and not to cover you! Adieu! (November 1749)

PROPERTY AND PATRONAGE

England's civilization at the end of the eighteenth century was not stiffly stratified. There was an extraordinary degree of social mobility. There was not yet the Victorian structure of three mutually exclusive and antagonistic classes—high, middle, and low—which began to emerge under the pressures of industrialization and the explosion of trade. "Class" remained latent in the old society, with power unquestionably in the hands of the great landowners and their friends, and with the various vertical "interests" in the trades, industries, and professions lobbying for the accommodations they needed, representing their respective hierarchies from the highest to the humblest. The word "manufacturer," for example, in those times covered both master and worker.

The England of this old society was predominantly rural, but the first Census in 1801 demonstrated that, while just over a third of all families farmed, over 40 percent were in trade, commerce, and manufacturing. Some of these, like Joe Gargery, were self-employed, independent masters, but many more worked in their cottages for a merchant, on his materials and perhaps with his equipment. England of the 1700s was a classless society, defined as one with a unified elite wielding all political, economic, and social power and holding the strings of connection and interdependency, which kept the hierarchical society stable and in balance. The two principles of control were property and patronage.

One's place in society was wholly determined by the kind and quantity of his property. Land alone granted the gentry their status. "Gentility is nothing but ancient riches," said Sir John Holles in the time of Elizabeth I (quoted in HP 37). Below the landed aristocracy, respect and subservience, power over others, and reciprocal deferment were direct functions of relative wealth, down to the cottager and the blacksmith. And they valued it, for it assured them their status and their stability. Only the outcasts—the vagrants, the beggars, the outlaws—were excluded from the hierarchy of prestige. When Joe Gargery calls Pip "Sir" on his visit to London, he is honoring himself and his place in the scheme of things, even as he recognizes Pip's new place in society. That is the point of his great speech about life being a series of "partings" welded together. As Samuel Johnson put it, Joe is "polished by art, and classed by subordination," and he is comfortable only that way.

The House of Lords was made up almost entirely of great landowners. The House of Commons between 1734 and 1832 was three-quarters landowners and their near-relations. The rest were rich businessmen and professional men, usually with a tie to the land. Landowners dominated the Cabinet and the government at all levels, either directly or through that other principle, patronage.

Patronage was the great principle in the administration of interests flowing from property. Government offices, sinecures (posts yielding income for no work), pensions, contracts, agencies, bishoprics, excise posts, and other petty administrative offices were filled with an eye to maintaining political power. But governmental patronage was only the political aspect of a wide-ranging system of recruitment that operated everywhere: church livings; county, borough, and parish offices; merchants' and lawyers' clerks; estate agents; chaplains and secretaries; tutors and governesses—even tenants and domestics—all were peopled by a private patronage system. "At all levels, patronage, the system of personal *selection from amongst one's kinsmen and connections*, was the instrument by which property influenced recruitment to those positions in society which were not determined by property alone" (HP 45; emphasis added).

The power of patronage was exercised for one's "friends," that is, in descending order of connection, one's nearest relations; the members of a wider family or household; one's tenants and villagers; one's political helpers, associates, and supporters; and, finally, "almost anyone amongst one's acquaintances in whom one recognized special merit or services to oneself" (HP 48). In the old society, ambition, if it could not be realized through inheritance, marriage, or great business success, depended on the friendship of those already rich and powerful. The effect was a mesh of continuing loyalties between patrons and patronized. This web of interrelationships permeated society. Less formal and inescapable than feudal requirements, it was more personal and comprehensive than the capitalistic, cash-based interactions of the time ahead.

MAKING A "GENTLEMAN"

The personal, face-to-face relationships engendered by the patronage system were an attribute of a society dispersed in relatively small units: the villages and small towns where everyone knew everyone else. It goes without saying that the more prestigious the patron, the better the standing of the person patronized. As long as Miss Havisham was believed to be Pip's patron, his status in his own and the Gargerys' eyes, not to mention the Pumblechooks and Trabbs of his world, was enviable and admired.

Miss Havisham, he thought, was making him a gentleman. He fitted the description of a meritorious local villager deemed worthy of promotion and ultimately of marital connection with the Havisham "interest." But what were his qualifications for that advancement? In the beginning, property sufficient to give him a reasonable income without effort on his part would have been enough. The Elizabethan, Sir Thomas Smith, stated, "Who can live idly and without manual labour, and will beare the port, charge and countenaunce of a gentleman, hee . . . shal be taken for a gentleman" (quoted in HP 38). This ancient maxim was known to Dickens's criminals and convicts. "I worked hard that you should be above work," says Magwitch to Pip (39). In Dickens's novel *Little Dorrit* the nefarious Rigaud, first discovered in a Marseilles

"Pip and His Supposed Patron" by George Alfred Williams, from *Ten Boys from Dickens* (1901) by Kate Dickinson Sweetser.

prison, prides himself on requiring his cellmate to serve him: "Cavelletto, you know me for a gentleman? . . . Have I ever done anything here? Ever touched the broom, or spread the mats, or rolled them up, or found the draughts, or collected the dominoes, or put my hand to any kind of work? . . . No! You knew from the first moment when you saw me here, that I was a gentleman!" (1).

For centuries, the landed classes had struggled with monarchs and with feudal restrictions that limited their ability to deal with their tenants and dispose of their land as they wished. They had gained the victory and achieved vindication for their concept of absolute, unfettered ownership of their estates. The landowner's right to enjoy his estate, rather than his function, if any, as investor or businessman, was reflected in the preeminent status of the leisured gentleman. He was distinguished from the rest of society, not so much by the size of his income as by the fact that he did not have to work for it. Society envied, admired, and sought to emulate him. "*For the leisured gentleman was the ideal at which the whole society aimed, and by which it measured its happiness and ambitions*" (HP 55; emphasis added).

Leisure, of course, did not mean simple idleness. It meant freedom to pursue all interests, tastes, and pleasures consistent with gentlemanly honor, unhampered by any demeaning need to earn the wherewithal to pay for them. The aristocracy found recreation in the pleasures of the table and the hunt, the social round, gambling, and travel—but also in science, agricultural improvement, architecture, philosophy, history, musicology, and literature. The "one overriding pursuit of landed gentlemen was government . . . the right, privilege and responsibility of the landed gentlemen who, besides being the only nation-wide class in that otherwise classless society, were in the most literal sense the ruling class" (HP 56).

The crux and the logic of Magwitch's enterprise on behalf of Pip was the remarkable, indeed unique (Holland was the only other case) English openness to "new men," who could become part of the landed aristocracy if they had the one necessary qualification: the purchase-price of an estate. For two hundred years and more before the Reformation, merchants were making their way into the upper sphere, as were able husbandmen with the diligence and acumen to assemble great tracts of land. Once arrived, these families often spun off marriageable progeny, who made propitious connections and broadened the outreach of the new elements on the scene. Daniel Defoe, an acute observer of society as well as creator of Robinson Crusoe and Moll Flanders, saw that a history in trade was no disqualification for this advancement: "after a generation or two, the tradesmen's children, or at least their grandchildren, come to be as good gentlemen, statesmen, parliamentmen, privy counsellors, judges, bishops and noblemen as those of the highest birth and most ancient families" (DF 376).

Magwitch's impatience and precipitation frustrated completion of his plans for Pip, and Jaggers never reveals the full extent of his fortune and his intentions, so we do not know whether Pip was intended to acquire land of his own. Could he be a gentleman without it? The literature beginning to be written at the time clearly suggests so. Indeed, as the century rolled on, a subtle democratization of attitude made even leisure no longer necessary, as the following from Harold Perkin shows:

> the gentlemen included, besides the nobility and gentry, the clergyman, physician and barrister, but not always the Dissenting minister, the apothecary, the attorney, or the schoolmaster; the overseas merchant but not the inland trader; the amateur author, painter, musician but rarely the professional. But wherever the shifting line was drawn, above and below it stretched long scales of social discrimination. If "gentleman" described anyone who might be found dining at a landed gentleman's table, the respect due to a duke was as far removed from that to a curate, as the curate's was from the cottager's. And between duke and curate, as between curate and cottager, there was an unbroken continuum through layer after contiguous layer of status. (HP 24)

(As to this last point, notice the quotation from Trollope's *The Duke's Children* in the following section.)

THE "GENTLEMAN" IN LITERATURE

What is a gentleman to Charles Dickens? He hardly ever asks the question. Decidedly of lower middle class origin himself, he rose through his genius on a ladder all his own, and to the end of his days honoured an aristocracy of talent but not the one of "blood." With the exception of the Dedlocks in *Bleak House* and some Barnacle connections in *Little Dorrit*, there is hardly a nobleman to be found in Dickens, and he has little to say about aristocrats, either individually or as a class.

They are at most a foil to pushy *nouveaux riches* like those he pillories with sadistic skill in *Our Mutual Friend*. Mr. Twemlow, first cousin to Lord Snigsworth, and impeccably a gentleman, though impoverished, is exploited by these people, but he discomfits them at last. In the course of doing so, he gives us as close an approximation of Dickens's idea of a gentleman as we get anywhere in his works.

FROM CHARLES DICKENS, *OUR MUTUAL FRIEND*
(London: Chapman & Hall, 1865)

"The question before the Committee is, whether a young man of very fair family, good appearance, and some talent, makes a fool or a wise man of himself in marrying a female waterman, turned factory girl."

"Hardly so, I think," the stubborn Mortimer strikes in. "I take the question to be, whether such a man as you describe, Lady Tippins, does right or wrong in marrying a brave woman (I say nothing of her beauty) who has saved his life, with a wonderful energy and address; whom he knows to be virtuous, and possessed of remarkable qualities; whom he has long admired, and who is deeply attached to him."

"But excuse me," says Podsnap, with his temper and his shirt-collar about equally rumpled; "was this young woman ever a female waterman?"

"Never. But she sometimes rowed in a boat with her father, I believe."

General sensation against the young woman. Brewer shakes his head. Boots shakes his head. Buffer shakes his head.

"And now, Mr Lightwood, was she ever," pursues Podsnap, with his indignation rising high into those hair-brushes of his, "a factory girl?"

"Never. But she had some employment in a paper mill, I believe." General sensation repeated. Brewer says, "Oh dear!" Boots says, "Oh dear!" Buffer says, "Oh dear!" All in a rumbling tone of protest.

"Then all *I* have to say is," returns Podsnap, putting the thing away with his right arm, "that my gorge rises against such a marriage—that it offends and disgusts me—that it makes me sick—and that I desire to know no more about it." . . .

"Hear, hear, hear!" cries Lady Tippins. "Your opinion of this *mésalliance*, honourable colleague of the honourable member who has just sat down?"

Mrs Podsnap is of opinion that in these matters "there should be an equality of station and fortune, and that a man accustomed to Society should look out for a woman accustomed to Society and capable of bearing her part in it with—an ease and elegance of carriage—that," Mrs Podsnap stops there. . . .

Lady Tippins fancies she has collected the suffrages of the whole Committee . . . when looking round the table through her eye-glass, she perceives Mr Twemlow with his hand to his forehead.

Good gracious! My Twemlow forgotten! My dearest! My own! What is his vote?

Twemlow has the air of being ill at ease, as he takes his hand from his forehead and replies. "I am disposed to think," says he, "that this is a question of the feelings of a gentleman."

"A gentleman can have no feelings who contracts such a marriage," flushes Podsnap.

"Pardon me, sir," says Twemlow, rather less mildly than usual, "I don't agree with you. If this gentleman's feelings of gratitude, of respect, of admiration, and affection, induced him (as I presume they did) to marry this lady—"

"This lady!" echoes Podsnap.

"Sir," returns Twemlow with his wristbands bristling a little, "*you* repeat the word; *I* repeat the word. This lady. What else would you call her, if the gentleman were present?"

This being something in the nature of a poser for Podsnap, he merely waves it away with a speechless wave.

"I say," resumes Twemlow, "if such feelings on the part of this gentleman induced this gentleman to marry this lady, I think he is the greater gentleman for the action, and makes her the greater lady. I beg to say that when I use the word gentleman, I use it in the sense in which the degree may be attained by any man. The feelings of a gentleman I hold sacred, and I confess I am not comfortable when they are made the subject of sport or general discussion."

"I should like to know," sneers Podsnap, "whether your noble relation would be of your opinion."

"Mr Podsnap," retorts Twemlow, "permit me. He might be, or he might not be. I cannot say. But I could not allow even him to dictate to me on a point of great delicacy, on which I feel very strongly."

Somehow, a canopy of wet blanket seems to descend upon the company, and Lady Tippins was never known to turn so very greedy, or so very cross. (iv 17)

Evidently, a "gentle" man for Dickens himself is exactly that: a kind, considerate, courteous individual, sensitive to the feelings of others, respectful of people in all walks of life, and admiring of talent and achievement wherever it shows itself.

While Dickens essentially passes the question by, another great novelist did give extensive space to the question, "What is a gentleman?" What Chesterfield was to the concept of "gentleman" in the eighteenth century, Anthony Trollope (1815–1882) was to that of the nineteenth (and Laski, below, in the twentieth). It is likely that no other writer in English, whether fiction or nonfiction, ever puzzled so much over the matter as Trollope. His discussions can be organized under six headings: ancestry, occupation, merit, education, manners, and conduct. Many of his forty-seven novels contain matter relevant to the issue. Here, we can cite only a few. (Others are listed in the Suggested Readings and Works Cited, at the end of this chapter.) What jumps out as we look at these remarks is that by the second half of the century, landowning and absolute leisure both seem to have dwindled to meaninglessness or disappeared as a consideration altogether.

Ancestry

In judging the position which a man should hold in the world, Sir Peregrine [Orme] was very resolute in ignoring all claims made by wealth alone. Even property in land could not in his eyes create a gentleman. A gentleman, according to his ideas, should at any rate have great-grandfathers capable of being traced in the world's history; and the greater the number of such, and the more easily traceable they might be on the world's surface, the more unquestionable would be the status of the claimant in question. (*Orley Farm* [1862] 3)

[Samuel] Johnson [1709–84] says that any other derivation of this difficult word than that which causes it to signify "a man of ancestry" is whimsical. There are many, who in defining the term for their own use will adhere to Johnson's dictum—but they adhere to it with certain unexpressed allowances for possible exceptions. The chances are very much in favour of the well-born man, but exceptions may exist. (*The Prime Minister* [1876] 1)

Occupation

[Miss Marrable] always addressed an attorney by letter as Mister, raising up her eyebrows when appealed to on the matter, and explaining that an attorney is not an esquire. She had an idea that the son of a gentleman, if he intended to maintain his rank as a gentleman, should earn his income as a clergyman, or as a barrister, or as a soldier, or as a sailor. Those were the professions intended for gentlemen. She would not absolutely say that a physician was not a gentleman, or even a surgeon; but she would never allow the physic the same absolute privileges which, in her eyes, belonged to Law and the Church. There might also possibly be a doubt about the Civil Service and Civil Engineering; but she had no doubt whatever that when a man touched trade or commerce in any way he was doing that which was not the work of a gentleman. He might be very respectable, and it might be very necessary that he should do it; but brewers, bankers and merchants were not gentlemen, and the world, according to Miss Marrable's theory, was going astray, because people were forgetting their landmarks. (*The Vicar of Bull-hampton* [1870] 9)

"He is a gentleman, papa."
"So is my private secretary [said the Duke of Omnium]. There is not a clerk in one of our public offices who does not consider himself to be a gentleman. The curate of the parish is a gentleman, and the medical man who comes here from Bradstock. The word is too vague to carry with it any meaning that ought to be serviceable to you in thinking of such a matter [as your marriage]." (*The Duke's Children* [1880] 8)

Merit

What makes a gentleman? What makes a gentlewoman? What is the inner reality, the spiritualized quintessence of that privilege in the world which men call rank, which forces the thousands and hundreds of thousands to bow down before the few elect? What gives, or can give it, or should give it?
And [Mary Thorne] answered the question. Absolute, intrinsic,

acknowledged, individual merit must give it to its possessor, let him be whom, and what, and whence he might. So far the spirit of democracy was strong within her. Beyond this it could be had but by inheritance, received as it were second-hand, or twenty-second hand. And so far the spirit of aristocracy was strong within her. (*Doctor Thorne* [1858] 6)

Education

She had once ventured to form a doctrine for herself, to preach to herself a sermon of her own, and to tell herself that this gift of gentle blood and of gentle nurture, of which her father thought so much . . . was after all but a weak, spiritless quality. It could exist without intellect, without heart, and with very moderate culture. It was compatible with many littlenesses and with many vices. As for that love of honest, courageous truth which her father was wont to attribute to it, she regarded his theory as based upon legends, as in earlier years was the theory of the courage, and constancy, and loyalty of the knights of those days. The beau ideal of a man which she then pictured to herself was graced, first with intelligence, then with affection, and lastly with ambition. She knew no reason why such a hero as her fancy created should be born of lords and ladies rather than of working mechanics, should be English rather than Spanish or French. The man could not be her hero without education, without attributes to be attained no doubt more easily by the rich than by the poor; but, with that granted, with those attained, she did not see why she, or why the world, should go back beyond the man's own self. (*The Prime Minister* [1876] 31)

Manners

She had probably never questioned the fact, whether Mr Glascock was a gentleman or not, and now she did not analyse it. It probably never occurred to her, even at the present time, to say to herself that he was certainly that thing, so impossible of definition, and so capable of recognition; but she knew that she had to do with one whose presence was always pleasant to her, whose words and acts towards her extorted her approbation, whose thoughts seemed to her to be always good and manly. (*He Knew He Was Right* [1869] 96)

"They can't but despise me, you know," said the tailor.
"Why should anyone despise you?:"

"No one should—unless I be mean and despicable. But they do—
you may be sure. It is only human nature that they should. We are
made of different fabric—though the stuff was originally the same.
I don't think I should be at my ease with them. I should be half
afraid of their gilt and their gingerbread, and should be ashamed of
myself because I was so. I should not know how to drink wine with
them, and should do a hundred things which would make them
think me a beast." (*Lady Anna* [1874] 47)

Conduct

"It's a hard thing to say what is a gentleman, Mr Neville. I don't
know a much harder thing. Them folk at Castle Quin, now,
wouldn't scruple to say that I'm no gentleman, just because I'm a
Popish priest. I say that Captain O'Hara was no gentleman because—he ill-treated a woman." (*An Eye for an Eye* [1879] 14)

In his fiction, Trollope rather slides around the question of the
definition of a gentleman, throwing up ideas, tossing in ingredients, leaving us at last with the feeling that all we are going to get
from him is something like, "You'll know it when you see it." But
in one of his important nonfiction works, *Australia and New Zealand*, when he talks about the life of goldminers, he comes much
closer to telling us what a "gentleman" in the class-conscious sense
of the term really was in his mind. (Magwitch would not have seen
gentleman goldminers, for active search for gold in Australia began
only after the 1849 discoveries in California, a quarter of a century
or so after he arrived at Botany Bay.)

FROM ANTHONY TROLLOPE, *AUSTRALIA*
(Reprint of Australian portion of *Australia and New Zealand*
[1873]. London: Dawson's of Pall Mall, 1968)

I have spoken of a happy family of miners. . . . They were a rough, civil,
sober, hardworking lot—four or five as I think, who were employing
some four or five others, experienced miners, at £3 a week each. Among
such a company it is impossible to recognise the social rank of each.
There are what we call "gentlemen", and what we call "workmen". But
they dress very much alike, work very much alike, and live very much
alike. The ordinary miner who came perhaps from Cornwall or North-
umberland, and whose father was a miner before him, gets a lift in the

world—as regards manners and habits as well as position. The "gentleman", even though in the matter of gold he be a lucky gentleman, gets a corresponding fall. He loses his gentility, his love of cleanliness, his ease of words, his grace of bearing, his preference for good company, and his social exigencies. There are some who will say that these things lost constitute a gain—and that as long as the man is honest and diligent, earning his bread by high energy and running a chance of making a fortune, he is in every way doing better for himself than by thinking of his tub of cold water, his dress coat and trousers, his last new novel, and his next pretty girl.

I cannot agree with these. Idle gentility doubtless is despicable. Idle, penniless, indebted gentility, gentility that will not work but is not ashamed to borrow, gentility that sports itself at clubs on the generosity of toiling fathers, widowed mothers, and good-natured uncles and aunts, is as low a phase of life as any that can be met. From that the rise to the position of a working miner is very great indeed. But gentility itself—the combination of soft words, soft manners, and soft hands with manly bearing, and high courage, and intellectual pursuits—is a possession in itself so valuable, and if once laid aside so difficult to be regained, that it should never be dropped without a struggle. . . .

And probably the class of miners which as a class does worst is that composed of young gentlemen who go to the diggings, led away, as they fancy, by a spirit of adventure, but more generally, perhaps, by a dislike of homely work at home. An office-stool for six or eight hours a day is disagreeable to them, or the profession of the law requires too constant a strain, or they are sick of attending lectures, or they have neglected the hospitals—and so they go away to the diggings. They soon become as dirty as genuine diggers, but they do not quickly learn anything but the dirt. They strive to work, but they cannot work alongside of experienced miners, and consequently they go to the wall. They are treated with contempt, for all men at the diggings are free and equal. As there is no gentility, such men are not subject to any reproach or ill-usage on that score. The miner does not expect that any airs will be assumed, and takes it for granted that the young man will not sin in that direction. Our "gentleman", therefore, is kindly treated; but, nevertheless, he goes to the wall, and becomes little better than the servant, or mining hodsman, of some miner who knows his work. Perhaps he has a little money, and makes things equal with a partner in this way; but they will not long be equal—for his money will go quicker than his experience will come. On one gold-field I found one young man whom I had known at home, who had been at school with my sons, and had frequented my house. I saw him in front of his little tent, which he occupied in partnership with an experienced working miner, eating a beefsteak out of his frying-pan with his clasp-knife. The occupation was not an alluring one, but it was the one happy moment of his day. He was occupied with his companion on a claim, and his work consisted in trundling a rough windlass, by which dirt was drawn up out of a hole. They had found no gold as yet, and did not seem to expect to find it. He had no friend near him but his mining friend—or mate, as he called him. I could not but think what would happen to him if illness came, or if his mate should find him too far removed from mining capability. He had been softly nurtured, well ed-ucated, and was a handsome fellow to boot; and there he was eating a nauseous lump of beef out of a greasy frying-pan with his pocket-knife, just in front of the contiguous blankets stretched on the ground, which constituted the beds of himself and his companion. It may be that he will strike gold and make a fortune. I hope so with all my heart. But my strong and repeated advice to all young English gentlemen is to resort to any homely mode of earning their bread in preference to that of seeking gold in Australia.

Magwitch says he saw Australian stockowners riding on the roads and hugged to himself the thought he shares with Pip:

"And then, dear boy, it was a recompense to me, look'ee here, to know in secret that I was making a gentleman. The blood horses of them colonists might fling up the dust over me as I was walking; what do I say? I says to myself, "I'm making a better gentleman nor ever *you*'ll be!" When one of 'em says to one another, 'He was a convict, a few years ago, and is a ignorant common fellow now, for all he's lucky,' what do I say? I says to myself, 'If I ain't a gentleman, nor yet ain't got no learning, I'm the owner of such. All on you owns stock and land; which on you owns a brought-up London gentleman?' (39)

Robert Hughes pinpoints the power of this thought: he thinks that Magwitch is gaining a revenge against those haughty colonials in "a black joke against English and colonial class relations. . . . Do gentlemen make convicts? Then a convict will 'make' and 'own' a real gentleman, not a colonial facsimile. He will show the truth about gentility: It can be bought. . . . Under the skin of generosity, there is slavery in reverse" (RH 585).

A MODERN VIEW OF THE ENGLISH GENTLEMAN

A fine twentieth-century literary description of an English gentleman comes from a brilliant socialist thinker, Harold Laski (1893–1950). Born in Manchester, he studied at Oxford and lectured widely in the United States before becoming a faculty member of the London School of Economics in 1920. He chaired the British Labour Party in 1945–46. His political philosophy, a modified Marxism, is reflected in his *Authority in the Modern State* (1919), *A Grammar of Politics* (1953), and *The American Presidency* (1940).

Writing in 1932, in the depths of the great worldwide Depression, Laski is witty, cool, and surprisingly balanced. Reading the essay, we can speculate on the audacity of Magwitch's project and how intoxicating Pip's life might have been if his expectations could have been realized and his ambition matched them. Note that Laski's "gentleman" reverts to the original mode and has no occupation at all.

FROM HAROLD J. LASKI, *"ON THE DANGERS OF BEING A GENTLEMAN"* [1932] *AND OTHER ESSAYS*
(New York: Viking Press, 1940)

THE DANGER OF BEING A GENTLEMAN:
REFLECTIONS ON THE RULING CLASS IN ENGLAND

I

It is the boast of England that the idea of being a gentleman is peculiar to her people, and I think there is solid substance in the boast. As an ideal, it has at least the supreme merit of simplicity. The gentleman is, rather than does; he maintains towards life an attitude of indifferent receptivity. He is interested in nothing in a professional way. He is allowed to cultivate hobbies, even eccentricities, but he must not practise a vocation. He must not concern himself with the sordid business of earning his living; and he must be able to show that, at least back to his grandfather, none of his near relations has ever been engaged in trade. It is desirable that he should have attended one of a limited number of schools, preferably Eton or Harrow; and it is practically essential that he should have been to Oxford or Cambridge. He must know how to ride and shoot and cast a fly. He should have relatives in the army and navy, and at least one connexion in the diplomatic service. It is vital that he should belong to a club, urgent that he be a member of the Conservative Party, and desirable that his ideas should coincide with those of the Morning Post. An ability to endure the Riviera in the winter and to make the round of English country houses from August to November is a valuable, though not an integral, part of his equipment.

These may be termed the foundations upon which the ultimate superstructure is raised. But there are certain emotional and intellectual penumbræ which should not go unemphasized. His favourite authors should be Surtees[1] and Kipling. He should deprecate the moral elasticity of modern fiction. He should feel the fine sanity of Gilbert and Sullivan while he is alien to any profound concern about Beethoven or Mozart. He should know how to arrive late at the opera, and his feeling about the theatre should be that a man wants to be amused there. A visit to Paris should leave him with a sense of pleasant proximity to sin, and he should be quite unable to speak intelligible French or German. He should play most games in some fashion and feel that their cultivation is the secret of national greatness; but he should play none so well that he is thereby distinguished from his fellows and he should be convinced that professionalism ruins the true spirit of sport. Under no circumstances can he be a teetotaller except upon medical grounds.

Certain other qualities are important. He should know nothing of political economy and less about how foreign countries are governed. He should equate bolshevism with original sin. While he should never be a free-thinker, he should not be enthusiastic about religion; to be so is to run the risk of obtrusiveness. He should be properly conscious of the merits of Empire and feel that only the strong hand can maintain our prestige in the East. When he dines out he must be able either not to talk at all or to confine his conversation to that plane which indicates a full knowledge of the right gossip without being an index to a dangerous profundity in any special theme. He must feel that America is passionately materialist; but if he marries an American he must take care to ally himself only with those properly endowed families who are received into the best London houses. He may be good at gardening. He may become a director of a company, provided he is not too well informed about its business. He must find speech difficult, and eloquence impossible. He must feel intensely the moral beauty of good form; and he must recognize that to wear, for instance, a black tie with a tail coat in the evening is proof (unless one is a head waiter) of a debased origin which cannot be outgrown. If, finally, he travels he must return without having suffered the deformation of a broader mind.

There are great qualities in the English gentleman which must not be overlooked. He believes with ardour in playing the game with those of his own status. He has the habit of graceful command. Save to Indians, Socialists, trade-union organizers, and poachers, he is almost uniformly tolerant. He is invariably courageous and, to women of his own class, chivalrous and deferential. He rarely parades his vices and he has a horror of ostentatious virtue. If he forgets to pay his tailor, he is always punctual with gambling debts. He profoundly respects the Royal Family (of whose failings he breathes no word in public), and bishops, and those Ministers of the Crown who belong to his own party. He rarely pushes a claim too far, and he is intellectually too humble to take long-term views. If he grumbles much, at least he can laugh at himself; and no one is so apt to extricate himself skilfully from a dangerous situation. He enjoys the exercise of power; and since he rarely knows how to make money, it is still more rare for him to be corrupted by it. Having, in general, received a classical education, he has, like Shakespeare, as a rule, small Latin and less Greek.

He is the type by whom, with the aid of the lawyer, England has been governed until the last half-dozen years; it is only since the [First World] War that his supremacy has been seriously threatened. For the most significant single fact in English history is that we have had no revolution in the modern time. Our social structure has remained largely unchanged since at least the middle of the eighteenth century; and a people with a genius for deference has preserved almost entirely the allotted privileges of leisure and of station. Your average Englishman still admires the class which does not have to earn its living; he feels safe and respectable in its hands. He may have doubted Lord Rosebery[2] when he published a book; but he admitted his title to the Premiership when he won the Derby. Between a self-made Welshman like Mr Lloyd George[3] and a squire whose mind, like that of Mr Henry Chaplin,[4] is unstained by thought, the Englishman has seldom hesitated to choose the latter type. The working-man rarely respects his master; it is rare for him not to respect the peer who lives by owning. The employer may like the individual worker but, in the mass, he is convinced of his unfitness to govern; free trade apart, therefore, all his natural aspirations tempt him to look upwards to the class which represents past tradition and the glamour of high estate. Since the gentleman has always realized how much his power depends on the prosperity of business, the alliance between them has been mutual; and intermarriage with the most eminent of the business community has always persuaded the latter that the preservation of the gentleman is his own best safeguard. And the gentleman's tenacious hold of power has given him something like an instinctive knowledge of when compromise and concession are desirable. However much he may have opposed the wants of other classes, he has never so far challenged them as to threaten his own security. His genius for compromise and his capacity for absorption have given him control for two hundred years of English destiny.

II

The condition upon which he maintained his supremacy was simple enough. For a century after the Industrial Revolution, England's commercial leadership was unchallenged. The state was largely a negative state, and there were neither grave economic nor grave international problems to solve. The prosperity of the upper and middle classes was solid and ample and, save for the brief moment of the Chartist Movement, the rights of private property were never in serious question. England was in a position to afford government by gentlemen. No one had, in politics at least, to take long views; and the main questions in issue did not seem to require any complicated or technical expertise. Just enough national education to produce the foreman who could read and write; just a high enough level of national health to prevent the recurrence of cholera and typhus; a well-advertised charity to meet the wants of the really deserving unemployed—upon these foundations Englishmen might well feel that their lines were fallen in pleasant places. Political economists proved to demonstration that the more exuberant hopes of the working class were impossible of fulfilment; and the capitalist had the satisfaction of knowing that his abstinence made him the effective author of the prosperity which was the wonder of the world.

In that epoch, indeed, the gentleman imposed himself upon civilization. No one in England seriously challenged his right to leadership; and English domination of foreign markets made his habits the example upon which the leisured class of every other state sought to model itself. All the best people used English materials; and their solidity and workmanship gave them an unquestioned title to preeminence. The gentleman's conquests were unending. He made it the right thing to go to the Riviera, to Switzerland, to Egypt. His picture galleries formed the basis of future American triumphs. He made the world mad on golf and tennis; he invented the week-end; he showed how to polish the rough edges of business enterprise by casting the kindly eye of patronage upon the more expensive fine arts. To the theory that a little learning is a dangerous thing, he invented the reply (which England, at least, accepted) that much learning is ungainly, and in any case drives men mad. He made Wimbledon and St Andrews into international cathedrals; while fashionable women of all countries went to St James's and Ascot as a Mahomet might go to Mecca. Until, at any rate, the outbreak of the War, the gentleman had persuaded the world to believe that he was the final term of human evolution. . . .

There is, in fact, little evidence that before the War Englishmen, at least, questioned the title of the gentleman to lead them. . . . The gentlemen of England had made her what she was; not merely Waterloo was won upon the playing fields of Eton. The traditions they embodied saved England from the materialism of America. They prevented her from seeming, like the new industrial Germany, a nation of *nouveaux riches*. Her tolerance permitted wide dissidence of opinion. Her social experiments showed the amazing adaptability of her ideas. The War proved not only that her gentlemen knew how to die; the solidity of her credit in crisis showed that she had absorbed the best lessons of bourgeois economy. [The] plea that England needed to temper her gentlemanly tradition by a dose of social equality seemed largely falsified, at least to the gentlemen themselves, by the victory of 1918.

NOTES

1. Robert Smith Surtees (1805–64) was in his day a highly successful writer of comic fiction. His Mr Jorrocks, the sporting Cockney grocer, was the center of *Jorrocks's Jaunts and Jollities* (1838), illustrated by Dickens's principal illustrator, 'Phiz' (H. K. Browne) and an inspiration for *The Pickwick Papers*.

2. Archibald Philip Primrose, Fifth Earl of Rosebery (1847–1929), was prime minister in 1894–95. Noted for his racehorse stables, in later years he wrote the lives of several British statesmen.

3. David Lloyd George (1863–1945), Liberal statesman and MP for the Welsh borough of Caernarvon for fifty-five years, was Chancellor of the Exchequer (1905–15). His 'people's budget' was vetoed by the House of Lords, leading to a constitutional crisis and the Lords' loss of veto power. He led England as coalition Prime Minister (1916–22) through World War I. His negotiations with Ireland led to the Irish Free State in 1921 and his political downfall.

4. Henry Chaplin (1840–1923), first Viscount Chaplin, a politician and sportsman, was a lifelong friend of the Prince of Wales and the epitome of the "country gentleman" who adored riding to hounds and horse-racing.

PRODUCER OR PARASITE?

Anthony Trollope's *The American Senator* (1877) permits us to look at the phenomenon of the English gentleman, very much as Laski describes him, from an intelligent American's (that is, Trollope's idea of such) point of view. Senator Elias Gotobed is baffled, charmed, offended, fascinated. He never understands, but he does appreciate. Here are Magwitch's wildest dreams made manifest.

> I have lately become acquainted with a certain young lord . . . who has treated me with great kindness, although I have taken it into my head to oppose him as to a matter in which he is much interested. I ventured to enquire of him as to the pursuits of his life. He is a lord, and therefore a legislator, but he made no scruple to tell me that he never went near the Chamber in which it is his privilege to have a seat. But his party does not lose his support. Though he never goes near the place, he can vote, and is enabled to trust his vote to some other more ambitious lord who does go there. . . . Then he told me what he did do. All the winter he hunts and shoots, going about to other rich men's houses when there is no longer sufficient for him to shoot left on his own estate. That lasts him from the 1st of September to the end of March, and occupies all his time. August he spends in Scotland, also shooting other animals. During the other months he fishes, and plays cricket and tennis, and attends races, and goes about to parties in London. His evenings he spends at a card table when he can get friends to play with him. It is the employment of his life to fit in his amusements so that he may not have a dull day. Wherever he goes he carries his wine with him and his valet and his grooms—and if he thinks there is anything to fear, his cook also. He very rarely opens a book. He is more ignorant than a boy of fifteen with us, and yet he manages to have something to say about everything. When his ignorance has been made as clear as the sun at noonday, he is no whit ashamed. One would say that such a life would break the heart of any man, but, upon my word, I doubt whether I ever came across a human being so self-satisfied as this young lord. (*The American Senator* [1877] 29)

In 1814, early in the Industrial Revolution, Patrick Colquhoun applied his attention to the question whether the idle "gentleman" earns his keep in *A Treatise on the Wealth, Power and Resources of the British Empire*:

> Contemplating, therefore, the gradations of society . . . it becomes a matter of interesting enquiry, *by what proportion* of the community at large those different classes are maintained. Assuming . . . that it is by the annual labour of the people employed in agriculture, mines, minerals, manufactures, shipping, commerce, fisheries, and inland trade, assisted by capital, machinery, and skill, that the means of subsistence are obtained; it can be demonstrated that all other classes of the community, although many of them partake largely in the new property annually produced, have no share whatever in its production, and, whatever they may do to diminish, do nothing to increase the national wealth. Many of them indeed labour with great zeal and ability in the affairs of the state and in its judicial and revenue departments, while others are laboriously occupied in offensive and defensive war. . . . But like menial servants their labour adds to the value of nothing, since not like the agriculturist, the manufacturer, and the trader, they work upon no material that possesses a reproductive quality, and yet their consumption of the labour of others generally exceeds that allotted to many of the labourers themselves. . . . [Nonetheless] all who labour in any useful pursuit contribute to the general comfort and happiness of every well governed community. It is only those who pass their lives in vice and idleness . . . who are real nuisances in society—who live upon the land and labour of the people, without fulfilling any useful station in the body politic, or making the smallest return or compensation to society for what they consume. (See PH 5)

The periodical *Crisis* on May 17, 1834, published Colquhoun's tables analyzing English demographics, based upon census reports for the year 1812. Note how the categories are characterized (the italicized comments on the third line of each section). This table is a mine of surprising and valuable information (see PH 6–8).

Pip was to be a member of the group characterized as "Gentlemen and ladies living on incomes in the funds, etc." Their average annual income was £100, and there were 280,000 of them—1.6 percent of a population of over seventeen million. The total of 1,860,535 members of the Fifth Class, "the most wealthy and least useful," was just under 11 percent of the population. This group received over 23 percent of the wealth created annually.

FROM PATRICK COLQUHOUN, "TABLES ON ENGLISH DEMOGRAPHICS"
(*Crisis*, May 17, 1834)

FIRST CLASS THE LABOURING POPULATION *The Producers of All Wealth*	Individual Income £	Aggregate Population NUMBERS	Aggregate Amount £
Agricultural and mining labourers	11	3,154,142	33,396,795
Aquatic labourers and seamen	11	400,000	8,100,000
Mechanical and manufacturing labourers	11	4,343,389	49,054,752
Umbrella, parasol makers, embroiderers, chair coverers, lace workers, etc.	12	150,000	3,800,000
Artists, sculptors, etc.	56	25,000	1,400,000
Pauper labourers	5	774,200	3,871,000
Pensioners receiving for labour	2	46,000 8,892,731	420,000 99,742,547

SECOND CLASS DISTRIBUTORS, SUPERINTENDENTS, AND MANUFACTURERS *Necessary, but too numerous*			
Farmers	22	1,540,000	33,600,000
Capitalists in manufacturing and mechanical operations	134	264,000	35,376,000
Ditto in clothing, etc.	36	218,750	7,875,000
Ditto in building and engineering	60	43,500	2,610,000
Ship builders and ship owners	124	46,750	5,652,000
Merchants, wholesale dealers, brokers, and bankers	149	190,000	28,177,600
Shopkeepers and retail dealers	40	700,000	28,000,000

SECOND CLASS DISTRIBUTORS, SUPERINTENDENTS, AND MANUFACTURERS	Individual Income	Aggregate Population	Aggregate Amount
Necessary, but too numerous (cont.)	£	NUMBERS	£
Innkeepers and publicans	14	437,500	8,750,000
Clerks and shopmen	14	262,500	6,750,000
Hawkers and pedlars	11	5,600	63,000
Physicians, surgeons, etc.	60	96,000	5,400,000
		3,814,600	162,253,600

THIRD CLASS
GOVERNMENT
Much too numerous and expensive

	Individual Income	Aggregate Population	Aggregate Amount
Thc Royal Family	1,670	300	501,000
Persons in higher and lesser civil offices	77	114,500	8,830,000
Judges, barristers, attorneys' clerks, etc.	80	95,000	7,600,000
Army and navy officers	96	65,000	6,295,000
Common soldiers, militia, seamen and marines	9-1/2	770,000	17,004,680
Lunatics, and keepers of lunatic asylums	48	4,700	195,000
Half-pay and pensions	24-1/2	60,500	1,486,600
Persons included in the above, receiving incomes from funds and church	——	——	5,211,063
Prisoners for debt	6	17,500	105,000
Vagrants, prostitutes, rogues, gipsies, vagabonds, in and out of prison	12	308,741	3,704,892
Paupers	7-3/4	774,200	6,000,000
		2,210,441	56,933,235

FOURTH CLASS INSTRUCTION AND AMUSEMENT *Indispensable and eminently useful*	Individual Income £	Aggregate Population NUMBERS	Aggregate Amount £
Clergymen, working	40	87,500	3,500,000
Dissenting ministers	25	20,000	500,000
Universities and chief schools	150	3,496	524,400
Lesser schools	34	210,000	7,140,000
Theatres, concerts, and musicians	50	3,500	175,000
		324,496	11,839,400
FIFTH CLASS *The most wealthy and least useful*			
Nobility and bishops	396	13,620	5,400,480
Dignified clergymen	120	9,000	1,080,000
Baronets, knights, and esquires	205	122,915	25,022,110
Greater and lesser landholders and freeholders	28	1,435,000	40,250,000
Gentlemen and ladies living on incomes in the funds, etc.	100	280,000	28,000,000
		1,860,535	99,752,590
Total amount of wealth created annually in Great Britain and Ireland			£430,521,372
Amount received by the productive classes			£99,742,547
Amount received by the non-producers			£330,778,825
Total number of the productive classes			8,892,731
Total number of the non-producers			8,210,072
The whole population in 1812			17,102,803

If we can go by the commentators we have quoted, Magwitch's simplistic idea of making Pip a gentleman by providing funds so that he would not have to work for a living was perfectly realistic. His enterprise would have succeeded on those terms, given Pip's opportunities for and ability to profit from his education with the Pockets, father and son. The openness of society in England would have permitted Pip to be a gentleman (the tailor Trabb's instant recognition of him as such would have been typical) if he had stayed the course. Had he done so, he might have sought Estella's hand without the trammels of any obligation to Miss Havisham. He lacked ancestry, of course, and would not have pleased Trollope's Sir Peregrine Orme. But he was capable of acquiring the manner, his innate moral standards were excellent, he was kind-hearted and considerate, and there was nothing wrong with his conduct. What he lacked, it appears, was the proper opportunistic spirit. But perhaps his fatal flaw was that he was, after all, a snob: he could not stand being the creature of (patronized by) a former convict, no matter how reformed, no matter how successful. If he could have been gentrified by Miss Havisham, wealthy albeit reclusive figure of great respect in his community, that would have been fine. That was the patronage that everyone understood and no one but perhaps Trabb's boy would have resented. And even Trabb's boy would have understood.

QUESTIONS AND TOPICS FOR DISCUSSION

1. Consider the comments in this chapter on French influence in English vocabulary. As an exercise, consult an unabridged dictionary for the etymologies of words associated with food and meals, including utensils used. Do your discoveries support or undermine our thesis?

2. Consider the status and condition of the laboring classes in England as described in this chapter. Where do the Gargerys fit? What do you think their status was? Write an essay analyzing their property, their food, their friends, and other elements you can think of.

3. Make a list of all the characters in the novel, and arrange them as you think they would rank in society. What changes of status occur in the novel? Joe Gargery describes Mr. Wopsle, for instance, as having had "a fall." What does he mean by that?

4. Samuel Johnson said the social gradations in the "old society" created "no jealousy, since they are held to be accidental." What made Pip so discontented then? Do you think Miss Havisham did him any favor by bringing him into her world?

5. Do Lord Chesterfield's words on vulgarity remind you of a scene in *Great Expectations?* Look up the word "vulgar" in a good dictionary and think about its meaning.

6. Write an essay setting Pip against the standards Lord Chesterfield sets forth in the passages quoted in this chapter.

7. At least since 1800, many Englishmen have regarded a seat in the House of Commons as the highest achievement and honor obtainable. Would the high regard felt for the leisured gentleman, from whose ranks members of Parliament (M.P.s) were originally recruited, tend to explain this? Discuss.

8. In Dickens's *Little Dorrit*, the foppish adventurer Rigaud, of questionable ethics and no visible means of support, sets great store by his aristocratic appearance and manners, and he demands to be regarded and treated as a gentleman. In the story, he is acquitted of a murder charge and later attempts extortion. His plans are foiled when he is killed in the collapse of a building. Would he have been classified as a gentleman?

9. Reflect on the final observations on Pip's strengths and flaws. Do you agree or disagree? Discuss these points in an essay.

10. Apply the concept of irony, discussed in Chapter 1, to Magwitch's Australian achievements and his ultimate failure to gain his goal, arguably a selfless one, of giving his benefactor a better life. Compare him with Miss Havisham as a proper "patron" for Pip.

11. In giving Molly's baby to Miss Havisham, Jaggers "made a lady." Compare this with Magwitch's efforts to "make a gentleman."

SUGGESTED READINGS AND WORKS CITED

Amussen, Susan Dwyer. *An Ordered Society: Gender and Class in Early Modern England*. Oxford: Basil Blackwell, 1988.

Cannadine, David. *The Rise and Fall of Class in Britain*. New York: Columbia University Press, 1998.

Chesterfield, Philip Dormer Stanhope, Earl of. *The Letters of Philip Dormer Stanhope, Earl of Chesterfield, with the Characters*. John Bradshaw, ed. New York: Scribner, 1892.

———. *Letters to His Son: On the Fine Art of Becoming a Man of the World and a Gentleman*. Oliver H. G. Leigh, intro. Washington, DC: M. W. Dunne, 1901.

———. *Letters of Lord Chesterfield to His Son*. Robert K. Root, intro. New York: E. P. Dutton, 1929.

Defoe, Daniel. *The Complete English Tradesman*. London: N.p., 1726.

Dickens, Charles. *Barnaby Rudge*. London: Bentley, 1841.

———. *Little Dorrit*. London: Bradbury & Evans, 1857.

———. *Our Mutual Friend*. London: Chapman & Hall, 1865.

Gilmour, Robin. *The Idea of the Gentleman in the Victorian Novel*. London: Allen & Unwin, 1981.

Hammond, J. L., and B. Hammond. *The Village Labourer*, 1760–1832. London: N.p., 1913.

Harrison, J. F. C. *The Common People of Great Britain: A History from the Norman Conquest to the Present*. Bloomington: Indiana University Press, 1985.

Hill, Christopher. *Reformation to Industrial Revolution: The Making of Modern English Society, 1530–1780*. New York: Pantheon Books, 1968.

Himmelfarb, Gertrude. *The Idea of Poverty: England in the Early Industrial Age*. New York: Knopf, 1984.

Hollis, Patricia, ed. *Class and Conflict in Nineteenth Century England 1815–1850*. London: Routledge & Kegan Paul, 1973.

Hughes, Robert. *The Fatal Shore: The Epic of Australia's Founding*. New York: Vintage Books, a Div. of Random House, 1988.

Johnson, Samuel. *A Dictionary of the English Language*. London: N.p., 1755.

Joyce, Patrick. *Visions of the People: Industrial England and the Question of Class, 1848–1914*. Cambridge: Cambridge University Press, 1991.

————. *Democratic Subjects: The Self and the Social in Nineteenth-Century England*. Cambridge: Cambridge University Press, 1994.

Laski, Harold J. *"On the Dangers of Being a Gentleman" and Other Essays*. New York: Viking Press, 1940.

Neale, R. S., ed. *History and Class: Essential Readings in Theory and Interpretation*. Oxford: Basil Blackwell, 1983.

Perkin, Harold. *The Origins of Modern English Society 1780–1880*. London: Routledge & Kegan Paul, 1969.

Reed, Michael. *The Georgian Triumph, 1700–1830*. London: Routledge & Kegan Paul, 1983.

Reid, Ivan. *Social Class Differences in Britain*. London: Grant McIntyre, 1981.

Thompson, Edward P. *The Making of the English Working Class*. London: Penguin Books, Pelican Edition, 1968.

Trollope, Anthony. *Doctor Thorne*. London: Chapman & Hall, 1858.

————. *Orley Farm*. London: Chapman & Hall, 1862.

————. *He Knew He Was Right*. London: Strahan, 1869.

————. *The Vicar of Bullhampton*. London: Bradbury & Evans, 1870.

————. *Australia*. 2 vols. paperback. Gloucester: Alan Sutton Publishing, 1987 (abstracting the Australian sections from *Australia and New Zealand*. London: Chapman & Hall, 1873).

————. *Lady Anna*. London: Chapman & Hall, 1874.

————. *The Prime Minister*. London: Chapman & Hall, 1876.

————. *The American Senator*. London: Chapman & Hall, 1877.

————. *An Eye for an Eye*. London: Chapman & Hall, 1879.

————. *The Duke's Children*. London: Chapman & Hall, 1880.

Refer also to:

Rachel Ray. London: Chapman & Hall, 1863 (Chapter 6).

Miss Mackenzie. London: Chapman & Hall, 1865 (Chapter 5).

The Last Chronicle of Barset. London: Smith, Elder & Co., 1867 (Chapter 42).

Ralph the Heir. London: Hurst & Blackett, 1871 (Chapters 16, 41).

3

Estella and Biddy: The Dilemma of Victorian Women

> The husband and the wife are one, and the husband is that one.
>
> —William Blackstone, quoted in
> Leonore Davidoff, ed., *Worlds Between: Historical
> Perspectives on Gender and Class*, 18

> By the law of England, the wife surrenders herself entirely to the will and pleasure of her husband; however sentiment and affection may regard the bond of marriage, evidently in the eye of the law, it is rather a feudal than a spiritual relationship. The husband may imprison his wife in his house, may strike her so long as he inflicts no severe bodily injury, leave her, and live in adultery with another, yet return, seize on her inheritance, and use it for himself and paramour.
>
> —E. P. Hood, quoted in B. Dennis and D. Skilton, eds.,
> *Reform and Intellectual Debate in Victorian England*, 133

ESTELLA: HER ONLY CHOICE A BAD ONE

A significant subtext in *Great Expectations* is the status of women in England in early Victorian times. Estella, as a "lady," has, as choices for life, essentially marriage or nothing. Having reached the proper age in the early 1830s, she is sent to embark on her campaign, and she develops it later in the time-honored fashion of girls in search of a husband.

> "Where are you going to, at Richmond?" I asked Estella.
> "I am going to live," said she, "at a great expense, with a lady there, who has the power—or says she has—of taking me about, and introducing me, and showing people to me and showing me to people." (33)

Her decision follows.

> "Your own act, Estella, to fling yourself away upon a brute?"
> "On whom should I fling myself away?" she retorted, with a smile. "Should I fling myself away upon the man who would the soonest feel (if people do feel such things) that I took nothing to him? There! It is done. I shall do well enough, and so will my husband. As to leading me into what you call this fatal step, Miss Havisham would have had me wait, and not marry yet; but I am tired of the life I have led, which has very few charms for me, and I am willing enough to change it." (44)

Miss Havisham dies, leaving most of her estate in trust (this is how we interpret Joe Gargery's report that "she had settled the most of it, which I meantersay tied it up") for Estella (57). Eleven years pass, and in the chosen ending of the novel:

> I had heard of her as leading a most unhappy life, and as being separated from her husband, who had used her with great cruelty, and who had become quite renowned as a compound of pride, avarice, brutality, and meanness. And I had heard of the death of her husband, from an accident consequent on his ill-treatment of a horse. . . .
> "The ground belongs to me. It is the only possession I have not relinquished. Everything else has gone from me, little by little, but I have kept this. It was the subject of the only determined resistance I made in all the wretched years. . . ." (59)

In the cancelled ending, we read: "I had heard of the death of her husband . . . and of her being married again to a Shropshire doctor, who, against his interest, had once very manfully interposed, on an occasion when he was in professional attendance on Mr Drummle, and had witnessed some outrageous treatment of her. . . ."

So we see brutality and suffering prominently in her marriage, and difficulty over her property. We sense as well that she was driven to her choice in part by inertia and in part by anger at her lot. She lacked any real chance for life except through marriage to *someone*, and she hated her existence, going about on display, waiting for that someone to tip his hat and take her in charge, so she threw herself at the worst, lacking, thanks to her upbringing, any way to value herself. Dickens's *Dombey and Son* (1847), spells out the degradation of a protracted life in the "marriage market" through the memorable character Edith Granger.

THE "LADY" IN LITERATURE

In his *An Eye for an Eye* (1879), Anthony Trollope depicts the quandary of a "gentle" girl isolated by circumstances in Ireland and her inability to make choices a "common" girl could have made. We might call it the "gentility trap."

> Had her child not carried the weight of good blood, had some small grocer or country farmer been her father, she might have come down to the neighbouring town of Ennistimon, and found a fitting mate there. Would it not have been better so? From that weight of good blood—or gift, if it please us to call it—what advantage would ever come to her girl? It cannot really be that all those who swarm in the world below the bar of gentlehood are less blessed, or intended to be less blessed, than the few who float in the higher air. . . . Does anyone believe that the countess has a greater share of happiness than the grocer's wife, or is less subject to the miseries which flesh inherits? But such matters cannot be changed by the will. This woman could not bid her daughter go and meet the butcher's son on equal terms, or seek her friends among the milliners of the neighbouring town. The burden had been imposed and must be borne, even though it isolated them from all the world. (5)

Trollope badly damaged his reputation and for a long time the success of his writing career when he wrote *Lady Anna*, published in 1874. The story tells of the determination of a young woman, only lately restored by litigation to her hereditary title, to marry Daniel Thwaite, a young tailor she had known and fallen in love with during a youth of privation and neglect. She does in fact marry this able, devoted man. Despite clear hints that he will be taken up and patronized—be made a gentleman—if he chooses to remain in England, Trollope's public never forgave him.

Trollope makes clear, as only a fictionist can do, the power of childhood associations and connections—the power of environment—which, once instilled and absorbed, determines taste, mode of life, and an individual's capacity for contentment and, perhaps, happiness. Gentility is accidental, indeed irrelevant.

FROM ANTHONY TROLLOPE, *LADY ANNA*
(London: Chapman & Hall, 1874)

"When your ladyship [said Thwaite senior] was good enough to point out to me my boy's improper manner of speech to Lady Anna, I knew how it must be. You were quite right, my lady. There can be no becoming friendship between the future Lady Lovel and a journeyman tailor. I was wrong from the beginning. . . .

"There can be no holding ground of friendship between such as you and such as we. Lords and ladies, earls and countesses, are our enemies, and we are theirs. We may make their robes and take their money, and deal with them as the Jew dealt with the Christians in the play; but we cannot eat with them or drink with them.

"Tailors should consort with tailors," he said, "and lords and ladies should consort together." (8)

• • •

The sweet, perfumed graces of the young nobleman had touched her senses but for a moment. Had she been false-minded she had not courage to be false. But in truth she was not false-minded. It was to her, as that sunny moment passed across her, as to some hard-toiling youth who, while roaming listlessly among the houses of the wealthy, hears, as he lingers on the pavement of a summer night, the melodies which float upon the air from the open balconies above him. A vague sense of un-known sweetness comes upon him, mingled with an irritating feeling of envy that some favoured son of Fortune should be able to stand over the shoulders of that singing siren, while he can only listen with intrusive ears from the street below. And so he lingers and is envious, and for a moment curses his fate—not knowing how weary may be the youth who stands, how false the girl who sings. But he does not dream that his life is to be altered for him, because he has chanced to hear the daughter of a duchess warble through a window.

. . . She was as her bringing up had made her, and it was too late now to effect a change. Ah yes—it was indeed too late. It was all very well that the lawyers should look upon her as an instrument, as a piece of goods that might now, from the accident of her ascertained birth, be made of great service to the Lovel family. Let her be the lord's wife, and everything would be right for everybody. It had been very easy to say that! But she had a heart of her own—a heart to be touched, and won, and given away—and lost. The man who had been so good to them had sought for his reward, and had got it, and could not now be defrauded.

Had she been dishonest she would not have dared to defraud him; had she dared, she would not have been so dishonest. . . . (11)

• • •

"The marriage would be too incongruous," said Mr Hardy.

"Quite horrible," said the Serjeant.

"It distresses one to think of it," said Mr Goffe.

"It would be much better that she should not be Lady Anna at all, if she is to do that," said Mr Mainsail.

"Very much better," said Mr Flick. . . .

"Gentlemen, you have no romance among you," said Sir William. "Have not generosity and valour always prevailed over wealth and rank with ladies in story?"

"I do not remember any valorous tailors who have succeeded with ladies of high degree," said Mr Hardy.

"Did not the lady of the Strachy marry the yeoman of the wardrobe?" asked the Solicitor-General.

"I don't know that we care much about romance here," said the Serjeant. "The marriage would be so abominable, that it is not to be thought of." (30)

• • •

"Neither I nor my children have a drop of noble blood in our veins. It is not that. But God Almighty has chosen that there should be different ranks to carry out His purposes, and we have His word to tell us that we should all do our duties in that state of life to which it has pleased Him to call us." The excellent lady [Mrs. Bluestone] was somewhat among the clouds in her theology, and apt to mingle the different sources of religious instruction from which she was wont to draw lessons for her own and her children's guidance; but she meant to say that the proper state of life for an earl's daughter could not include an attachment to a tailor. . . . (32)

• • •

The inhabitants of the Yoxham rectory—who were well born, ladies and gentlemen without a stain, who were hitherto free from all base intermarriages, and had nothing among their male cousins below soldiers and sailors, parsons and lawyers, who had successfully opposed an intended marriage between a cousin in the third degree and an attorney because the alliance was below the level of the Lovels, were peculiarly averse to any intermingling of ranks. They were descended from ancient earls, and their chief was an earl of the present day. There was but one titled young lady now among them—and she had only just won her right to be so considered. There was but one Lady Anna—and she was going to marry a tailor! "Duty is duty," said Aunt Julia as she hurried away. She meant her nephew to understand that duty commanded her to shut her heart against any cousin who could marry a tailor. (46)

Estella's life and her fate were far more typical of her times than Miss Havisham's queer upbringing might lead us to expect. The social and legal context of such lives was the subject of two seminal essays, seventy years apart. We turn now to the first, written by a woman. After a summary of some relevant events during subsequent decades, we will look at the second, by a man.

MARY WOLLSTONECRAFT: AN EIGHTEENTH-CENTURY ADVOCATE OF WOMEN'S RIGHTS

Mary Wollstonecraft (1759–97), daughter of a drunken wastrel father and sister of two feckless brothers and two helpless sisters, wrote her *Vindication of the Rights of Woman* in 1792, near the end of a controversial life during which she earned a living and helped support her family for years as a governess before going to Paris, where she lived with a man who fathered her child but never married her. When he dropped her, she tried suicide twice, then married William Godwin and promptly died in childbirth, bearing a daughter Mary, who married Percy Bysshe Shelley and wrote *Frankenstein, the Modern Prometheus*.

Wollstonecraft was a pioneer in the battle for individual rights and for equality between the sexes, as was her husband. The thrust of her thought was that women were educated and socialized to be ornamental, to be admired for their uselessness, their appearance—facial beauty, bodies, dress, fashionableness—and nothing more. They are essentially children. The consequence is that half of the human race makes no contribution to its advancement in knowledge, wealth, or power. Writing when she did, Wollstonecraft did not address the franchise: that was decades away even for most men. Nearly one hundred years after the *Vindication*, her words' vindication began in earnest.

The following extracts are from a chapter captioned "Observations on the State of Degradation to which Woman is Reduced by Various Causes." Side-headings have been added.

FROM MARY WOLLSTONECRAFT, *A VINDICATION OF THE RIGHTS OF WOMAN* (1792)
(Published with John Stuart Mill, *The Subjection of Women*; New York: E. P. Dutton & Co., 1929)

Corruption of Idleness. I shall not go back to the remote annals of antiquity to trace the history of woman; it is sufficient to allow that she has always been either a slave or a despot, and to remark that each of these situations equally retards the progress of reason. The grand source of female folly and vice has ever appeared to me to arise from narrowness of mind; and the very constitution of civil governments has put almost insuperable obstacles in the way to prevent the cultivation of the female understanding; yet virtue can be built on no other foundation. The same obstacles are thrown in the way of the rich, and the same consequences ensue.

Necessity has been proverbially termed the mother of invention; the aphorism may be extended to virtue. It is an acquirement, and an acquirement to which pleasure must be sacrificed; and who sacrifices pleasure when it is within the grasp, whose mind has not been opened and strengthened by adversity, or the pursuit of knowledge goaded on by necessity? Happy is it when people have the cares of life to struggle with, for these struggles prevent their becoming a prey to enervating vices, merely from idleness. But if from their birth men and women be placed in a torrid zone, with the meridian sun of pleasure darting directly upon them, how can they sufficiently brace their minds to discharge the duties of life, or even to relish the affections that carry them out of themselves?

Pleasure is the business of woman's life, according to the present modification of society; and while it continues to be so, little can be expected from such weak beings. Inheriting in a lineal descent from the first fair defect in nature—the sovereignty of beauty—they have, to maintain their power, resigned the natural rights which the exercise of reason might have procured them, and chosen rather to be short-lived queens than labour to obtain the sober pleasures that arise from equality. Exalted by their inferiority (this sounds like a contradiction), they constantly demand homage as women, though experience should teach them that the men who pride themselves upon paying this arbitrary insolent respect to the sex, with the most scrupulous exactness, are most inclined to tyrannise over, and despise the very weakness they cherish.

• • •

The Pedestal. Ah! why do women . . . condescend to receive a degree of attention and respect from strangers different from that reciprocation of civility which the dictates of humanity and the politeness of civilisation authorise between man and man? And why do they not discover, when "in the noon of beauty's power," that they are treated like queens only to be deluded by hollow respect, till they are led to resign, or not assume, their natural prerogatives? Confined, then, in cages like the feathered race, they have nothing to do but to plume themselves, and stalk with mock majesty from perch to perch. It is true they are provided with food and raiment, for which they neither toil nor spin; but health, liberty, and virtue are given in exchange. But where, amongst mankind, has been found sufficient strength of mind to enable a being to resign these adventitious prerogatives—one who, rising with the calm dignity of reason above opinion, dared to be proud of the privileges inherent in man? And it is vain to expect it whilst hereditary power chokes the affections, and nips reason in the bud.

The passions of men have thus placed women on thrones, and till mankind become more reasonable, it is to be feared that women will avail themselves of the power which they attain with the least exertion, and which is the most indisputable. . . .

I lament that women are systematically degraded by receiving the trivial attentions which men think it manly to pay to the sex, when in fact, they are insultingly supporting their own superiority. It is not condescension to bow to an inferior. So ludicrous, in fact, do these ceremonies appear to me that I scarcely am able to govern my muscles when I see a man start with eager and serious solicitude to lift a handkerchief or shut a door, when the *lady* could have done it herself, had she only moved a pace or two. . . .

Women, commonly called ladies, are not to be contradicted in company, are not allowed to exert any manual strength; and from them the negative virtues only are expected, when any virtues are expected—patience, docility, good humour, and flexibility—virtues incompatible with any vigorous exertion of intellect.

• • •

Marriage. In the middle rank of life . . . men, in their youth, are prepared for professions, and marriage is not considered as the grand feature in their lives; whilst women, on the contrary, have no other scheme to sharpen their faculties. It is not business, extensive plans, or any of the excursive flights of ambition, that engross their attention; no, their thoughts are not employed in rearing such noble structures. To rise in the world, and have the liberty of running from pleasure to pleasure, they must marry advantageously, and to this object their time is sacrificed, and their persons often legally prostituted. A man when he enters any profession has his eye steadily fixed on some future advantage (and the mind gains great strength by having all its efforts directed to one point), and, full of his business, pleasure is considered as mere relaxation; whilst women seek for pleasure as the main purpose of existence. In fact, from the education, which they receive from society, the love of pleasure may be said to govern them all.

• • •

Superficiality. The same love of pleasure, fostered by the whole tendency of their education, gives a trifling turn to the conduct of women in most circumstances; for instance, they are ever anxious about secondary things; and on the watch for adventures instead of being occupied by duties.

A man, when he undertakes a journey, has, in general, the end in view; a woman thinks more of the incidental occurrences, the strange things that may possibly occur on the road; the impression that she may make on her fellow-travellers; and, above all, she is anxiously intent on the care of the finery that she carries with her, which is more than ever a part of herself, when going to figure on a new scene; when, to use an apt French turn of expression, she is going to produce a sensation. Can dignity of mind exist with such trivial cares?

In short, women, in general, as well as the rich of both sexes, have acquired all the follies and vices of civilisation, and missed the useful fruit. . . . Their senses are inflamed, and their understandings neglected, consequently they become the prey of their senses, delicately termed sensibility, and are blown about by every momentary gust of feeling. Civilised women are, therefore, so weakened by false refinement, that, respecting morals, their condition is much below what it would be were they left in a state nearer to nature. Ever restless and anxious, their over-exercised sensibility not only renders them uncomfortable themselves, but troublesome, to use a soft phrase, to others. All their thoughts turn on things calculated to excite emotion and feeling, when they should reason, their conduct is unstable, and their opinions are wavering—not the wavering produced by deliberation or progressive views, but by contradictory emotions.

• • •

Childishness. And will moralists pretend to assert that this is the condition in which one-half of the human race should be encouraged to remain with listless inactivity and stupid acquiescence? Kind instructors! what were we created for! To remain, it may be said, innocent; they mean in a state of childhood. We might as well never have been born, unless it were necessary that we should be created to enable man to acquire the noble privilege of reason, the power of discerning good from evil, whilst we lie down in the dust from whence we were taken, never to rise again. . . .

Fragile in every sense of the word, they are obliged to look up to man for every comfort. In the most trifling danger they cling to their support, with parasitical tenacity, piteously demanding succour; and their *natural* protector extends his arm, or lifts up his voice, to guard the lovely trembler—from what? Perhaps the frown of an old cow, or the jump of a mouse; a rat would be a serious danger. In the name of reason, and even common sense, what can save such beings from contempt; even though they be soft and fair.

These fears, when not affected, may produce some pretty attitudes; but they show a degree of imbecility which degrades a rational creature in a way women are not aware of—for love and esteem are very distinct things.

I am fully persuaded that we should hear of none of these infantine airs, if girls were allowed to take sufficient exercise, and not confined in close rooms till their muscles are relaxed, and their powers of digestion destroyed. To carry the remark still further, if fear in girls, instead of being cherished, perhaps, created, were treated in the same manner as cowardice in boys, we should quickly see women with more dignified aspects. It is true, they could not then with equal propriety be termed the sweeter flowers that smile in the walk of man; but they would be more respectable members of society, and discharge the important duties of life by the light of their own reason. "Educate women like men," says Rousseau, "and the more they resemble our sex the less power will they have over us." This is the very point I aim at. I do not wish them to have power over men; but over themselves.

. . .

Sensibility, not Reason. Ignorance is a frail base for virtue! Yet, that it is the condition for which woman was organised, has been insisted upon by the writers who have most vehemently argued in favour of the superiority of man; a superiority not in degree, but offence; though, to soften the argument, they have laboured to prove, with chivalrous generosity, that the sexes ought not to be compared; man was made to reason, woman to feel: and that together, flesh and spirit, they make the most perfect whole, by blending happily reason and sensibility into one character.

And what is sensibility? "Quickness of sensation, quickness of perception, delicacy." Thus is it defined by Dr. Johnson; and the definition gives me no other idea than that of the most exquisitely polished instinct. I discern not a trace of the image of God in either sensation or matter. Refined seventy times seven they are still material; intellect dwells not there; nor will fire ever make lead gold!

. . .

A Wife. With respect to women, when they receive a careful education, they are either made fine ladies, brimful of sensibility, and teeming with capricious fancies, or mere notable women. The latter are often friendly, honest creatures, and have a shrewd kind of good sense, joined with worldly prudence, that often render them more useful members of society than the fine sentimental lady, though they possess neither greatness of mind nor taste. The intellectual world is shut against them. Take them out of their family or neighbourhood, and they stand still; the mind finding no employment, for literature affords a fund of amusement which they have never sought to relish, but frequently to despise. The sentiments and taste of more cultivated minds appear ridiculous, even in those whom chance and family connections have led them to love; but in mere acquaintance they think it all affectation.

A man of sense can only love such a woman on account of her sex, and respect her because she is a trusty servant. He lets her, to preserve his own peace, scold the servants, and go to church in clothes made of the very best materials. A man of her own size of understanding would probably not agree so well with her, for he might wish to encroach on her prerogative, and manage some domestic concerns himself; yet women, whose minds are not enlarged by cultivation, or the natural selfishness of sensibility by reflection, are very unfit to manage a family, for, by an undue stretch of power, they are always tyrannising to support a superiority that only rests on the arbitrary distinction of fortune. The evil is sometimes more serious, and domestics are deprived of innocent indulgences, and made to work beyond their strength, in order to enable the notable woman to keep a better table, and outshine her neighbours in finery and parade. If she attend to her children, it is in general to dress them in a costly manner; and whether this attention arise from vanity or fondness, it is equally pernicious.

Besides, how many women of this description pass their days, or at least their evenings, discontentedly. Their husbands acknowledge that they are good managers and chaste wives, but leave home to seek for more agreeable—may I be allowed to use a significant French word—*piquant* society; and the patient drudge, who fulfils her task like a blind horse in a mill, is defrauded of her just reward, for the wages due to her are the caresses of her husband; and women who have so few resources in themselves, do not very patiently bear this privation of a natural right. . . .

• • •

Occupation. Women have seldom sufficient employment to silence their feelings; a round of little cares, or vain pursuits frittering away all strength of mind and organs, they become naturally only objects of sense. In short, the whole tenor of female education (the education of society) tends to render the best disposed romantic and inconstant; and the remainder vain and mean. . . .

[There is] an opinion that young girls ought to dedicate great part of their time to needlework; yet, this employment contracts their faculties more than any other that could have been chosen for them, by confining their thoughts to their persons. Men order their clothes to be made, and have done with the subject; women make their own clothes, necessary or ornamental, and are continually talking about them; and their thoughts follow their hands. It is not indeed the making of necessaries that weakens the mind; but the frippery of dress. For when a woman in the lower rank of life makes her husband's and children's clothes, she does her duty, this is her part of the family business; but when women work only to dress better than they could otherwise afford, it is worse than sheer loss of time. To render the poor virtuous they must be employed, and women in the middle rank of life, did they not ape the fashions of the nobility, without catching their ease, might employ them, whilst they themselves managed their families, instructed their children, and exercised their own minds. Gardening, experimental philosophy, and literature, would afford them subjects to think of and matter for conversation, that in some degree would exercise their understandings. . . .

The thoughts of women ever hover round their persons, and is it surprising that their persons are reckoned most valuable? Yet some degree of liberty of mind is necessary even to form the person; and this may be one reason why some gentle wives have so few attractions beside that of sex. Add to this, sedentary employments render the majority of women sickly—and false notions of female excellence make them proud of this delicacy, though it be another fetter, that by calling the attention continually to the body, cramps the activity of the mind.

THE FEMINIST MOVEMENT IN THE NINETEENTH CENTURY

For most of the nineteenth century, married women had no property they could control. A single woman or a widow (the *feme sole*) had the same property rights as a man, except the right to vote, but a married woman had no independent existence. She was "merged" in her husband. The legal ramifications, in terms of carrying on a business, making contracts, filing lawsuits, injuring third parties, giving evidence, making a will, and so forth are complex and cannot be covered in detail here. But we must note that not only the property but the person of the wife was subject to the husband. This could sometimes have had results helpful to a wife: if she committed a crime, short of murder or treason, in her husband's presence, she was assumed to have been coerced to the action by him. Not until 1925 was this assumption abolished.

The husband was expected to be the breadwinner. So perhaps it was understandable that he control and even own what had originally been his wife's property to help him in that task. But the wife could not make him support her. He could do whatever he wished with her money, even taking and supporting a mistress, and she had essentially no redress. Even if a husband bound himself in writing to maintain her, in a separation for example, she had no standing to enforce the obligation in law. "By depriving married women of property the law deprived them of legal existence, of the rights and responsibilities of other citizens, and thus of self-respect" (LH 35).

As to the children, the common law gave the husband all rights, the wife none. He could take the children against her will, and that was that. The law saw her as having no means by which to support them, since she had no control over her assets, so it gave her no standing to gain their custody.

These hardships for women were especially felt among the working classes, where the wife's contribution to the household economy was often essential, and often enough the sole means of support for her family. The development of a second body of law, "Equity," aided women in the upper classes, who had the wherewithal to incur legal expense and property sufficient to warrant creating trusts (and compensating trustees) and other devices to give her some protection and recourse in case of need. But Equity was far from establishing married women on a par with their husbands in dealing with their own affairs.

Reform, however, was in the air as the century progressed, and Victorians had consciences. Certain prominent women took the lead, the first being Mrs. Caroline Norton, whose husband had taken away her children. In 1837 she published a pamphlet called *The Natural Claim of a Mother to the Custody of Her Children as Affected by the Common Law Right of the Father*. Sympathetic members of Parliament took up her cause, notably Dickens's close friend Thomas Noon Talfourd.

In 1839 the first law to give mothers some relief, the Infant Custody Bill, said that a mother deprived of her children under the age of seven could sue for their custody. If they were older, she could get an order permitting her to visit them. In 1873 the law raised the custodial age to sixteen. Further laws in 1886 and 1925 helped mothers, but only in 1973 did the Guardianship of Minors Act grant mothers the same rights as fathers.

Mrs. Norton, whose husband was a textbook tyrant, battled for reform of the divorce laws also, publishing a pamphlet in 1854 called *English Laws for Women in the Nineteenth Century*. She told how she had "learned the English law piecemeal by suffering under it" (LH 56). Her eloquence and persistence did lead to major reforms in the divorce law in 1857.

Other women took up the struggle. One was Barbara Leigh Smith, now considered to be the founder of the feminist movement because in 1855 she formed the first committee of women in England organized to discuss and agitate for women's rights. It began a countrywide campaign to reform the law on married women's property, holding public meetings and encouraging writing letters to report flagrant abuses, such as:

- A young woman had worked and saved a considerable sum. Courted by a man who posed as a successful doctor, she married him, only to find he was a former footman. He took and squandered her savings.

- A young lady of fortune whose parents were dead married a poor but apparently respectable man who had risen in his master's business. He agreed to a settlement of several hundred pounds for his wife, taking the rest of her property to invest. He eloped with his master's wife and his own wife's fortune.

- A poor woman, deserted by her husband, got help from friends to set up as a laundress and was able to save a goodly sum to retire on. Her husband learned of it, went to the bank where it was deposited and demanded and got the money. She was left penniless.

- Another deserted woman set up a school to support herself. Her husband, having failed in Australia, returned and seized all her assets.

- The brutal husband of a battered wife was convicted of assault on her. Her father died, leaving her considerable property, but, because the husband was its legal owner and was a convicted felon, all of it was forfeit to the crown.

- A woman whose husband had failed in business set up her own millinery establishment and succeeded. She supported her husband. When he died, his will left her property to his illegitimate children. She was left with nothing.

These examples were assembled by the committee's most eloquent spokeswoman, Caroline Frances Cornwallis. The *Westminster Review* published two articles by her which ignited nationwide debate: "The Property of Married Women" in 1856, and "Capabilities and Disabilities of Women" in 1857.

The committee circulated petitions to be submitted to Parliament and quickly gained 26,000 signatures, including those of Elizabeth Barrett Browning, Jane Welsh (Mrs. Thomas) Carlyle, and the well-known writers Harriet Martineau and Elizabeth Gaskell. This is the petition submitted:

PETITION FOR REFORM OF
THE MARRIED WOMEN'S PROPERTY LAW
PRESENTED TO PARLIAMENT
14 MARCH 1856
(In Lee Holcombe, *Wives and Property: Reform of the Married Women's Property Law in Nineteenth Century England*. Toronto: University of Toronto Press, 1983)

To the Honourable the House of Peers [and House of Commons] in Parliament assembled. The Petition of the undersigned Women of Great Britain, Married and Single, Humbly Sheweth—That the manifold evils occasioned by the present law, by which the property and earnings of the wife are thrown into the absolute power of the husband, become daily more apparent. That the sufferings thereupon ensuing, extend over all classes of society. That it might once have been deemed for the middle and upper ranks, a comparatively theoretical question, but is so no longer, since married women of education are entering on every side the fields of literature and art, in order to increase the family income by such exertions.

That it is usual when a daughter marries in these ranks, to make, if possible, some distinct pecuniary provision for her and her children, and to secure the money thus set aside by a cumbrous machinery of trustee-ship, proving that few parents are willing entirely to entrust the welfare of their offspring to the irresponsible power of the husband, to the chances of his character, his wisdom, and his success in a profession.

That another device for the protection of women who can afford to appeal, exists in the action of the Courts of Equity, which attempt, within certain limits, to redress the deficiences of the law; but that trustees may prove dishonest or unwise in the management of the funds entrusted to their care, and Courts of Equity may fail in adjusting differences which concern the most intimate and delicate relation of life;—that legal de-vices, patched upon a law which is radically unjust, can only work clum-sily, and that here, as in many other departments of justice, a clearance of the ground is the chief thing necessary. That since this is a truth, which has gradually come to be recognized in regard to protective restrictions upon trade, to titles of property in land, and to the legal machinery for conveying such property from one owner to another, &c, we would hope that, before long, it will also come to be recognized in matrimonial leg-islation.

That it is proved by well known cases of hardship suffered by women of station, and also by professional women earning large incomes by pursuit of the arts, how real is the injury inflicted.

That if these laws often bear heavily upon women protected by the forethought of their relatives, the social training of their husbands, and the refined customs of the rank to which they belong, how much more unequivocal is the injury sustained by women in the lower classes, for whom no such provision can be made by their parents, who possess no means of appeal to expensive legal protection, and in regard to whom the education of the husband and the habits of his associates offer no moral guarantee for tender consideration of a wife.

That whereas it is customary, in manufacturing districts, to employ women largely in the processes of trade, and as women are also engaged as sempstresses, laundresses, charwomen, and in other multifarious oc-cupations which cannot here be enumerated, the question must be rec-ognized by all as of practical importance.

That newspapers constantly detail instances of marital oppression, "wife-beating" being a new compound noun lately introduced into the English language, and a crime against which English gentlemen have lately enacted stringent regulations.

But that for the robbery by a man of his wife's hard [earned] earnings there is no redress,—against the selfishness of a drunken father, who wrings from a mother her children's daily bread, there is no appeal. She may work from morning till night, to see the produce of her labour wrested from her, and wasted in a gin-palace; and such cases are within the knowledge of every one.

That the law, in depriving the mother of all pecuniary resources, deprives her of the power of giving schooling to her children, and in other ways providing for their moral and physical welfare; it obliges her in short, to leave them to the temptations of the street, so fruitful in juvenile crime.

That there are certain portions of the law of husband and wife which bear unjustly on the husband, as for instance, that of making him responsible for his wife's debts contracted before marriage, even although he may have no fortune with her. Her power also, after marriage, of contracting debts in the name of her husband, for which he is responsible, is too unlimited, and often produces much injustice.

That in rendering the husband responsible for the entire maintenance of his family, the law expresses the necessity of an age, when the man was the only money-getting agent; but that since the custom of the country has greatly changed in this respect the position of the female sex, the law of maintenance no longer meets the whole case. That since modern civilisation, in indefinitely extending the sphere of occupation for women, has in some measure broken down their pecuniary dependence upon men, it is time that legal protection be thrown over the produce of their labour, and that in entering the state of marriage, they no longer pass from freedom into the condition of a slave, all of whose earnings belong to his master and not to himself.

That the laws of various foreign countries are in this respect much more just than our own, and afford precedent for a more liberal legislation than prevails in England;—and your petitioners therefore humbly pray that your Honourable House will take the foregoing allegations into consideration, and apply such remedy as to its wisdom shall seem fit—

And your Petitioners will ever pray.

JOHN STUART MILL AND THE FEMINIST MOVEMENT

Stimulated by the efforts of his countrywomen in the feminist movement, John Stuart Mill (1806–73) published his essay *The Subjection of Women* in 1861, the year the serialization of *Great Expectations* was completed. Reading it today, we find it almost unbelievable that barely more than a century ago women still had the degraded status and crippling disabilities, both in body and in property, which he describes. (Whether these matters have been altogether cleared up since is beyond the province of this book.) Mill fought hard in Parliament for reform, and his efforts, combined with those of many others of both sexes, were eventually crowned with some success.

Mill's first chapter is primarily historical and analytical. The second depicts the naked facts of women's status under the marriage contract in his (and Dickens's) time. The third, extracted below in the section on Biddy, discusses women's admissibility to the various professions and occupations. Finally the fourth, which is omitted, asks, "Would man be at all better off if women were free?"

In nearly every case, only portions of numbered paragraphs are included. Some numbers have been omitted altogether. Italics emphasize language of particular importance and penetration, or of special relevance to the plight of Estella. Sometimes additional paragraphing has been provided.

FROM JOHN STUART MILL, *THE SUBJECTION OF WOMEN* (1861)
(Buffalo, NY: Prometheus Books, 1986)

CHAPTER I

1. The object of this Essay is to explain, as clearly as I am able . . . [t]hat the principle which regulates the existing social relations between the two sexes—the legal subordination of one sex to the other—is wrong in itself, and now one of the chief hindrances to human improvement; and that it ought to be replaced by a principle of perfect equality, admitting no power or privilege on the one side, nor disability on the other.

• • •

5. [T]he opinion in favour of the present system, which entirely subordinates the weaker sex to the stronger, rests upon theory only; for there

never has been trial made of any other. . . . [And] the adoption of this system of inequality never was the result of deliberation, or forethought, or any social ideas, or any notion whatever of what conduced to the benefit of humanity or the good order of society. *It arose simply from the fact that from the very earliest twilight of human society, every woman (owing to the value attached to her by men, combined with her inferiority in muscular strength) was found in a state of bondage to some man.*

In early times, the great majority of the male sex were slaves, as well as the whole of the female. . . . [T]he slavery of the male sex has, in all the countries of Christian Europe at least . . . been at length abolished, and that of the female sex has been gradually changed into a milder form of dependence . . . the primitive state of slavery lasting on, through successive mitigations and modifications occasioned by the same causes which have softened the general manners, and brought all human relations more under the control of justice and the influence of humanity. *It has not lost the taint of its brutal origin.*

6. It was inevitable that this one case of a social relation grounded on force would survive through generations of institutions grounded on equal justice, an almost solitary exception to the general character of their laws and customs; but which, so long as it does not proclaim its own origin, and as discussion has not brought out its true character, is not felt to jar with modern civilization, any more than domestic slavery among the Greeks jarred with their notion of themselves as a free people.

• • •

8. Less than forty years ago, Englishmen might still by law hold human beings in bondage as saleable property: within the present century they might kidnap them and carry them off, and work them literally to death. This absolutely extreme case of the law of force . . . was the law of civilized and Christian England within the memory of persons now living: and in one half of Anglo-Saxon America, three or four years ago, not only did slavery exist, but the slave trade, and the breeding of slaves expressly for it, was a general practice between slave states. . . .

So extreme an instance makes it almost superfluous to refer to any other: but consider the long duration of absolute monarchy. In England at present it is the almost universal conviction that military despotism is a case of the law of force, having no other origin or justification. Yet in all the great nations of Europe except England it either still exists, or has only just ceased to exist, and has even now a strong party favourable to it in all ranks of the people, especially among persons of station and consequence. . . .

How different are these cases from that of the power of men over women. . . . Whatever gratification of pride there is in the possession of power, and whatever personal interest in its exercise, is in this case not confined to a limited class, but common to the whole male sex. . . . *[I]t comes home to the person and hearth of every male head of a family*, and of every one who looks forward to being so. The clodhopper exercises, or is to exercise, his share of the power equally with the highest nobleman. And the case is that in which the desire of power is the strongest: *for every one who desires power, desires it most over those who are nearest to him, with whom his life is passed, with whom he has most concerns in common, and in whom any independence of his authority is oftenest likely to interfere with his individual preferences.* . . .

In the case of women, each individual of the subject-class is in a chronic state of bribery and intimidation combined. . . . If ever any system of privilege and enforced subjection had its yoke tightly riveted on the necks of those who are kept down by it, this has.

9. The smallest acquaintance with human life in the Middle Ages shows how supremely natural the dominion of the feudal nobility over men of low condition appeared to the nobility themselves, and how unnatural the conception seemed, of a person of the inferior class claiming equality with them, or exercising authority over them. It hardly seemed less so to the class held in subjection. So true is it that unnatural generally means only uncustomary, and that everything which is usual appears natural. *The subjection of women to men being a universal custom, any departure from it quite naturally appears unnatural.* . . .

10. But, it will be said, the rule of men over women differs from all these others in not being a rule of force: it is accepted voluntarily; women make no complaint, and are consenting parties to it. In the first place, a great number of women do not accept it. Ever since there have been women able to make their sentiments known by their writings (the only mode of publicity which society permits to them), an increasing number of them have recorded protests against their present social condition: and recently many thousands of them, headed by the most eminent women known to the public, have petitioned Parliament for their admission to the parliamentary suffrage. The claim of women to be educated as solidly, and in the same branches of knowledge, as men, is urged with growing intensity, and with a great prospect of success; while the demand for their admission into professions and occupations hitherto closed against them becomes every year more urgent.

It is a political law of nature that those who are under any power of ancient origin never begin by complaining of the power itself, but only of its oppressive exercise. There is never any want of women who complain of ill usage by their husbands. There would be infinitely more, if complaint were not the greatest of all provocatives to a repetition and increase of the ill usage. . . . In no other case (except that of a child) is the person who has been proved judicially to have suffered an injury replaced under the physical power of the culprit who inflicted it. Accordingly wives, *even in the most extreme and protracted cases of bodily ill usage*, hardly ever dare avail themselves of the laws made for their protection. . . .

11. *Men do not want solely the obedience of women, they want their sentiments*. All men, except the most brutish, desire to have, in the woman most nearly connected with them, not a forced slave but a willing one; not a slave merely, but a favourite. . . . The masters of women wanted more than simple obedience, and they turned the whole force of education to effect their purpose. All women are brought up from the very earliest years in the belief that their ideal of character is the very opposite to that of men; not self-will, and government by self-control, but submission, and yielding to the control of others. All the moralities tell them that it is the duty of women, and all the current sentimentalities that it is their nature, to live for others; to make complete abnegation of themselves, and to have no life but in their affections.

And by their affections are meant the only ones they are allowed to have—those to the men with whom they are connected, or to the children who constitute an additional and indefeasible tie between them and a man. When we put together three things—first, the natural attraction between opposite sexes; secondly, the wife's entire dependence on the husband, every privilege or pleasure she has being either his gift, or depending entirely on his will; and lastly, that the principal object of human pursuit, consideration, and all objects of social ambition, can in general be sought or obtained by her only through him—*it would be a miracle if the object of being attractive to men had not become the polar star of feminine education and formation of character*. And, this great means of influence over the minds of women having been acquired, an instinct of selfishness made men avail themselves of it to the utmost as a means of holding women in subjection, by representing to them meekness, submissiveness, and resignation of all individual will into the hands of a man, as an essential part of sexual attractiveness.

• • •

13. [H]uman beings are no longer born to their place in life, and chained down by an inexorable bond to the place they are born to, but are free to employ their faculties, and such favourable chances as offer, to achieve the lot which may appear to them most desirable. . . . The modern conviction, the fruit of a thousand years of experience, is, that things in which the individual is the person directly interested never go right but as they are left to his own discretion; and that any regulation

of them by authority, except to protect the rights of others, is sure to be mischievous. . . . Nobody thinks it necessary to make a law that only a strong-armed man shall be a blacksmith. Freedom and competition suffice to make blacksmiths strong-armed men, because the weak-armed can earn more by engaging in occupations for which they are more fit.

14. [I]f the principle is true, we ought to act as if we believed it, and not to ordain that to be born a girl instead of a boy, any more than to be born black instead of white, or a commoner instead of a nobleman, shall decide the person's position through all life—shall interdict people from all the more elevated social positions, and from all, except a few, respectable occupations. . . . If only once in a dozen years the conditions of eligibility exclude a fit person, there is a real loss, while the exclusion of thousands of unfit persons is no gain. . . . In all things of any difficulty and importance, those who can do them well are fewer than the need, even with the most unrestricted latitude of choice: and any limitation of the field of selection deprives society of some chances of being served by the competent, without ever saving it from the incompetent.

15. The disabilities . . . to which women are subject from the mere fact of their birth, are the solitary examples of the kind in modern legislation. In no instance except this, which comprehends half the human race, are the higher social functions closed against anyone by a fatality of birth which no exertions, and no change of circumstances, can overcome; for even religious disabilities . . . do not close any career to the disqualified person in case of conversion.

16. *The social subordination of women thus stands out an isolated fact in modern social institutions; a solitary breach of what has become their fundamental law*; a single relic of an old world of thought and practice exploded in everything else.

· · ·

18. It may be asserted, without scruple, that no other class of dependents have had their character so entirely distorted from its natural proportions by their relations with their masters; for, if conquered and slave races have been, in some respects, more forcibly repressed, whatever in them has not been crushed down by an iron heel has generally been let alone, and if left with any liberty of development, it has developed itself according to its own laws; but *in the case of women, a hot-house and stove cultivation has always been carried on of some of the capabilities of their nature, for the benefit and pleasure of their masters*. Then, because certain products of the general vital force sprout luxuriantly and reach a great development in this heated atmosphere and under this active nurture and watering, while other shoots from the same root, which are left outside in the wintry air, with ice purposely heaped all

round them, have a stunted growth, and some are burnt off with fire and disappear; men . . . indolently believe that the tree grows of itself in the way they have made it grow, and that it would die if one half of it were not kept in a vapour bath and the other half in the snow.

• • •

20. The profoundest knowledge of the laws of the formation of character is indispensable to entitle anyone to affirm even that there is any difference, much more what the difference is, between the two sexes considered as moral and rational beings; and since no one, as yet, has that knowledge (for there is hardly any subject which, in proportion to its importance, has been so little studied), no one is thus far entitled to any positive opinion on the subject.

21. . . . The most favourable case which a man can generally have for studying the character of a woman is that of his own wife: for the opportunities are greater, and the cases of complete sympathy not so unspeakably rare. And, in fact, this is the source from which any knowledge worth having on the subject has, I believe, generally come. But most men have not had the opportunity of studying in this way more than a single case: accordingly one can, to an almost laughable degree, infer what a man's wife is like, from his opinions about women in general. . . . Even with true affection . . . thorough knowledge of one another hardly ever exists but between persons who, besides being intimates, are equals.

CHAPTER II

1. It will be well to commence the detailed discussion of the subject by the particular branch of it to which the course of our observations has led us: the conditions which the laws of this and all other countries annex to the marriage contract. *Marriage being the destination appointed by society for women, the prospect they are brought up to, and the object which it is intended should be sought by all of them*, except those who are too little attractive to be chosen by any man as his companion; one might have supposed that everything would have been done to make this condition as eligible to them as possible, *that they might have no cause to regret being denied the option of any other*. Society, however, both in this and, at first, in all other cases, has preferred to attain its object by foul rather than fair means: but this is the only case in which it has substantially persisted in them even to the present day. . . .

After marriage, the man had anciently (but this was anterior to Christianity) the power of life and death over his wife. *She could invoke no law against him; he was her sole tribunal and law.* For a long time he could repudiate her, but she had no corresponding power in regard to him. By the old laws of England, the husband was called the *lord* of the wife; he was literally regarded as her sovereign, inasmuch that the murder of a man by his wife was called treason (*petty* as distinguished from *high* treason), and was more cruelly avenged than was usually the case with high treason, for the penalty was burning to death. Because these various enormities have fallen into disuse (for most of them were never formally abolished, or not until they had long ceased to be practised) men suppose that all is now as it should be in regard to the marriage contract; and we are continually told that civilization and Christianity have restored to the woman her just rights.

Meanwhile, the wife is the actual bond-servant of her husband: no less so, as far as legal obligation goes, than slaves commonly so called. She vows a lifelong obedience to him at the altar, and is held to it all through her life by law. Casuists may say that the obligation of obedience stops short of participation in crime, but it certainly extends to everything else. *She can do no act whatever but by his permission, at least tacit. She can acquire no property but for him; the instant it becomes hers, even if by inheritance, it becomes* ipso facto *his.* In this respect the wife's position under the common law of England is worse than that of slaves in the laws of many countries. . . .

By means of settlements the rich usually contrive to withdraw the whole or part of the inherited property of the wife from the absolute control of the husband: but they do not succeed in keeping it under her own control; the utmost they can do only prevents the husband from squandering it, at the same time debarring the rightful owner from its use. The property itself is out of the reach of both; and as to the income derived from it, the form of settlement most favourable to the wife (that called "to her separate use") only precludes the husband from receiving it instead of her: it must pass through her hands, but if he takes it from her by personal violence as soon as she receives it, he can neither be punished nor compelled to restitution. This is the amount of the protection which, under the laws of this country, the most powerful nobleman can give to his own daughter as respects her husband.

In the immense majority of cases there is no settlement: and the absorption of all rights, all property, as well as all freedom of action, is complete. The two are called "one person in law," for the purpose of inferring that whatever is hers is his, but the parallel inference is never drawn that whatever is his is hers; the maxim is not applied against the man, except to make him responsible to third parties for her acts, as a master is for the acts of his slaves or of his cattle.

I am far from pretending that wives are in general no better treated than slaves; but *no slave is a slave to the same lengths, and in so full a sense of the word, as a wife is.* Hardly any slave, except one immediately attached to the master's person, is a slave at all hours and all minutes;

in general he has, like a soldier, his fixed task, and when it is done, or when he is off duty, he disposes, within certain limits, of his own time, and has a family life into which the master rarely intrudes. "Uncle Tom" under his first master had his own life in his "cabin," almost as much as any man whose work takes him away from home is able to have in his own family. But it cannot be so with the wife.

Above all, a female slave has (in Christian countries) an admitted right, and is considered under a moral obligation, to refuse to her master the last familiarity. Not so the wife: however brutal a tyrant she may unfortunately be chained to—though she may know that he hates her, though it may be his daily pleasure to torture her, and though she may feel it impossible not to loathe him—he can claim from her and enforce the lowest degradation of a human being, that of being made the instrument of an animal function contrary to her inclinations. . . .

This is her legal state. And from this state she has no means of withdrawing herself. If she leaves her husband, she can take nothing with her, neither her children nor anything which is rightfully her own. If he chooses, he can compel her to return, by law, or by physical force; or he may content himself with seizing for his own use anything which she may earn, or which may be given to her by her relations.

It is only legal separation by a decree of a court of justice, which entitles her to live apart, without being forced back into the custody of an exasperated jailer—or which empowers her to apply any earnings to her own use, without fear that a man whom perhaps she has not seen for twenty years will pounce upon her some day and carry all off. This legal separation, until lately, the courts of justice would only give at an expense which made it inaccessible to anyone out of the higher ranks. Even now it is only given in cases of desertion, or of the extreme of cruelty; and yet complaints are made every day that it is granted too easily.

. . . in some slave codes the slave could, under certain circumstances of ill usage, legally compel the master to sell him. But no amount of ill usage, without adultery superadded, will in England free a wife from her tormentor.

2. I have no desire to exaggerate, nor does the case stand in any need of exaggeration. I have described the wife's legal position, not her actual treatment. The laws of most countries are far worse than the people who execute them, and many of them are only able to remain laws by being seldom or never carried into effect. If married life were all that it might be expected to be, looking to the laws alone, society would be a hell upon earth. . . .

Because this is true; because men in general do not inflict, nor women suffer, all the misery which could be inflicted and suffered if the full power of tyranny with which the man is legally invested were acted on;

the defenders of the existing form of the institution think that all its iniquity is justified, and that any complaint is merely quarrelling with the evil which is the price paid for every great good. But the mitigations in practice, which are compatible with maintaining in full legal force this or any other kind of tyranny, instead of being any apology for despotism, only serve to prove what power human nature possesses of reacting against the vilest institutions, and with what vitality the seeds of good as well as those of evil in human character diffuse and propagate themselves. . . .

3. [L]aws and institutions require to be adapted, not to good men, but to bad. Marriage is not an institution designed for a select few. Men are not required, as a preliminary to the marriage ceremony, to prove by testimonials that they are fit to be trusted with the exercise of absolute power . . . there are all grades of goodness and wickedness in men, down to those whom no ties will bind, and on whom society has no action but through its *ultima ratio*, the penalties of the law. In every grade of this descending scale are men to whom are committed all the legal powers of a husband. The vilest malefactor has some wretched woman tied to him, against whom he can commit any atrocity except killing her, and, if tolerably cautious, can do that without much danger of the legal penalty. And how many thousands are there among the lowest classes in every country, who, without being in a legal sense malefactors in any other respect, because in every other quarter their aggressions meet with resistance, indulge the utmost habitual excesses of bodily violence towards the unhappy wife, who alone, at least of grown persons, can neither repel nor escape from their brutality; and towards whom the excess of dependence inspires . . . a notion that *the law has delivered her to them as their thing*, to be used at their pleasure. . . .

4. When we consider how vast is the number of men, in any great country, who are little higher than brutes . . . the breadth and depth of human misery caused in this shape alone by the abuse of the institution [of marriage] swells to something appalling. Yet these are only the extreme cases. They are the lowest abysses, but there is a sad succession of depth after depth before reaching them. . . .

Even the commonest men reserve the violent, the sulky, the undisguisedly selfish side of their character for those who have no power to withstand it. . . . If the family in its best forms is . . . a school of sympathy, tenderness, and loving forgetfulness of self, it is still oftener, as respects its chief, a school of wilfulness, overbearingness, unbounded selfish indulgence, and a double-dyed and idealized selfishness.

• • •

12. The morality of the first ages rested on the obligation to submit to power; that of the ages next following, on the right of the weak to the forbearance and protection of the strong. How much longer is one form of society and life to content itself with the morality made for another? We have had the morality of submission, and the morality of chivalry and generosity; the time is now come for the morality of justice. . . .

MILL'S LOGIC; OR, FRANCHISE FOR FEMALES.

"PRAY CLEAR THE WAY, THERE, FOR THESE—A—PERSONS."

An 1867 cartoon from *Punch*.

THE REFORM OF MARRIED WOMEN'S PROPERTY LEGISLATION

Success in the struggle for married women had been delayed by another reform: that of the Divorce Law, which passed in 1857. The effort to achieve this exhausted many of those working for the property rights of women who were in and remained in a marriage. The rock had to be pushed up the hill again and again, but at last on August 18, 1882, the great goal was reached. The act is far too long and complex for full quotation here. The landmark first two clauses will be enough both to indicate the scope of the change and highlight the state of things which made such a bill necessary in the first place.

FROM MARRIED WOMEN'S PROPERTY ACT, 1882
(45 & 46 Vict., c. 75, 18 August 1882; in Lee Holcombe, *Wives and Property: Reform of the Married Women's Property Law in Nineteenth Century England*. Toronto: University of Toronto Press, 1983)

1. (1) A married woman shall, in accordance with the provisions of this Act, be capable of acquiring, holding, and disposing by will or otherwise, of any real or personal property as her separate property, in the same manner as if she were a feme sole, without the intervention of any trustee.

(2) A married woman shall be capable of entering into and rendering herself liable in respect of and to the extent of her separate property on any contract, and of suing and being sued, either in contract or in tort, or otherwise, in all respects as if she were a feme sole, and her husband need not be joined with her as plaintiff or defendant, or be made party to any action or other legal proceeding brought by or taken against her; and any damages or costs recovered by her in any proceeding brought by or taken against her; and any damages or costs recovered by her in any such action or proceeding shall be her separate property; and any damages or costs recovered against her in any such action or proceeding shall be payable out of her separate property, and not otherwise.

(3) Every contract entered into by a married woman shall be deemed to be a contract entered into by her with respect to and to bind her separate property, unless the contrary be shown.

(4) Every contract entered into by a married woman with respect to and to bind her separate property shall bind not only the separate property which she is possessed of or entitled to at the date of the contract, but also all separate property which she may thereafter acquire.

(5) Every married woman carrying on a trade separately from her husband shall, in respect of her separate property, be subject to the bankruptcy laws in the same way as if she were a feme sole.

2. Every woman who marries after the commencement of this Act [January 1, 1883] shall be entitled to have and to hold as her separate property, and to dispose of in manner aforesaid, all real and personal property which shall belong to her at the time of marriage, or shall be acquired by or devolve upon her after marriage, including any wages, earnings, money, and property gained or acquired by her in any employment, trade, or occupation, in which she is engaged, or which she carries on separately from her husband, or by the exercise of any literary, artistic, or scientific skill.

MATRIMONY IN DICKENS

Having seen through Mill's eyes the horrific implications of Estella's status as the wife of a beast, as Pip had good reason to suspect Drummle was, we cannot wonder at his agony on learning of her plan to marry. It was not just that the woman he loved was lost to him: she would be lost, under the law, to the physical appetites and sadistic whims of a man he considered almost subhuman. Dickens does not stress this aspect at all: not until the end of the book do we learn, and then only in distant retrospect, that in truth Estella was physically mistreated. But to understand what he had in mind, we can turn to an earlier tale: his *Martin Chuzzlewit*, where a flirtatious, rather heartless Mercy Pecksniff makes the egregious mistake of marrying the domineering, wholly heartless Jonas Chuzzlewit to spite her sister, and discovers too late what she has done.

FROM CHARLES DICKENS, *MARTIN CHUZZLEWIT*
(London: Chapman & Hall, 1844)

It was the merry one herself. But sadly, strangely altered! So careworn and dejected, so faltering and full of fear; so fallen, humbled, broken; that to have seen her quiet in her coffin would have been a less surprise.

She set the light upon a bracket in the hall, and laid her hand upon her heart; upon her eyes; upon her burning head. Then she came on towards the door with such a wild and hurried step that Mr Bailey lost his self-possession. . . .

In the midst of her astonishment as she recognised him in his altered dress, so much of her old smile came back to her face that Bailey was glad. But next moment he was sorry again, for he saw tears standing in her poor dim eyes. . . .

The ill-favoured brute, with dress awry, and sodden face, and rumpled hair, sat blinking and drooping, and rolling his idiotic eyes about, until, becoming conscious by degrees, he recognised his wife, and shook his fist at her. . . .

"Look at her!" cried Jonas, pushing her off with his extended arm. "Look here! Look at her! Here's a bargain for a man!"

"Dear Jonas!"

"Dear Devil!" he replied, with a fierce gesture. "You're a pretty clog to be tied to a man for life, you mewling, white-faced cat! Get out of my sight!"

"I know you don't mean it, Jonas. You wouldn't say it if you were sober". . . .

"I wouldn't say it if I was sober!" retorted Jonas. "You know better. Have I never said it when I was sober?"

"Often, indeed!" she answered through her tears.

"Hark ye!" cried Jonas, stamping his foot upon the ground. "You made me bear your pretty humours once, and ecod I'll make you bear mine now. I always promised myself I would. I married you that I might. I'll know who's master, and who's slave!"

"Heaven knows I am obedient!" said the sobbing girl. "Much more so than I ever thought to be!"

Jonas laughed in his drunken exultation. "What! you're finding it out, are you! Patience, and you will in time! Griffins have claws, my girl. There's not a pretty slight you ever put upon me, nor a pretty trick you ever played me, nor a pretty insolence you ever showed me, that I won't pay back a hundred-fold. What else did I marry you for? *You*, too!" he said, with coarse contempt. . . .

"I hate you. I hate myself, for having been fool enough to strap a pack upon my back for the pleasure of treading on it whenever I choose. Why, things have opened to me, now, so that I might marry almost where I liked. But I wouldn't; I'd keep single. I ought to be single, among the friends *I* know. Instead of that, here I am tied like a log to you. Pah! Why do you show your pale face when I come home? Am I never to forget you?" . . .

There was another interval of silence; and the boy was stealing away, when he heard her footstep on the floor, and stopped. She went up to him, as it seemed, and spoke lovingly: saying that she would defer to him in everything, and would consult his wishes and obey them, and they might be very happy if he would be gentle with her. He answered with an imprecation, and—

Not a blow? Yes. Stern truth against the base-souled villain: with a blow.

No angry cries; no loud reproaches. Even her weeping and her sobs were stifled by her clinging round him. She only said, repeating it in agony of heart, How could he, could he, could he! And lost utterance in tears.

Oh woman, God beloved in old Jerusalem! The best among us need deal lightly with thy faults, if only for the punishment thy nature will endure, in bearing heavy evidence against us on the Day of Judgement! (28)

If we had any doubt that Dickens knew the facts Mill describes, this pathetic scene should eliminate it.

But in Dickens, all in marriage is not so black. We cannot leave the subject without referring to his most famous comment on the relations of the sexes under the law. In *Oliver Twist* (1837), Mr. Bumble, the famous bully, calls upon Mrs. Corney and considers her property.

> Mr Bumble's conduct on being left to himself, was rather inexplicable. He opened the closet, counted the teaspoons, weighed the sugar-tongs, closely inspected a silver milk-pot to ascertain that it was of the genuine metal, and, having satisfied his curiosity on these points, put on his cocked hat corner-wise, and danced with much gravity four distinct times round the table. Having gone through this very extraordinary performance, he took off the cocked hat again, and, spreading himself before the fire with his back towards it, seemed to be mentally engaged in taking an exact inventory of the furniture. (13)

> Having listened at the keyhole . . . Mr Bumble, beginning at the bottom, proceeded to make himself acquainted with the contents of the three long drawers: which, being filled with various garments of good fashion and texture, carefully preserved between two layers of old newspapers, speckled with dried lavender: seemed to yield him exceeding satisfaction. Arriving, in course of time, at the right-hand corner drawer (in which was the key), and beholding therein a small padlocked box, which, being shaken, gave forth a pleasant sound, as of the chinking of coin, Mr Bumble returned with a stately walk to the fireplace; and, resuming his old attitude, said, with a grave and determined air, "I'll do it! . . ."
>
> "The board allow you coals, don't they, Mrs Corney?" inquired the beadle, affectionately pressing her hand.
>
> "And candles," replied Mrs Corney, slightly returning the pressure.
>
> "Coals, candles, and house-rent free," said Mr Bumble. "Oh, Mrs Corney, what a Angel you are!" (27)

Later, Mr Bumble begins to think he may have been precipitate. The balance of power in his marriage is seen to derive, not from its legal context, but from the personalities, particularly the courage and aggressiveness, of the protagonists.

"Are you going to sit snoring there, all day?" inquired Mrs Bumble.

"I am going to sit here, as long as I think proper, ma'am," rejoined Mr Bumble; "and although I was *not* snoring, I shall snore, gape, sneeze, laugh, or cry, as the humour strikes me; such being my prerogative."

"*Your* prerogative!" sneered Mrs Bumble, with ineffable contempt.

"I said the word, ma'am," said Mr Bumble. "The prerogative of a man is to command."

"And what's the prerogative of a woman, in the name of Goodness?" cried the relict of Mr Corney deceased.

"To obey, ma'am," thundered Mr Bumble. "Your late unfortunate husband should have taught it you; and then, perhaps, he might have been alive now. I wish he was, poor man!" (37)

Mrs. Bumble weeps briefly, but, seeing this to be inefficacious, tries physical assault and achieves resounding success. Mr. Bumble is surprised and quickly beaten into submission, from which he never recovers. Mrs. Bumble's ascendancy thereafter is complete and gives rise to that famous comment about the sexes and the Law.

"It was all Mrs Bumble. She *would* do it," urged Mr Bumble; first looking round to ascertain that his partner had left the room.

"That is no excuse," replied Mr Brownlow. "You were present on the occasion . . . and indeed are the more guilty of the two, in the eye of the law; *for the law supposes that your wife acts under your direction*."

"*If the law supposes that*," said Mr Bumble, squeezing his hat emphatically in both hands, "*the law is a ass—a idiot. If that's the eye of the law, the law is a bachelor*; and the worst I wish the law is, that his eye may be opened by experience—by experience." (51; emphasis added)

Anthony Trollope, the astute observer of the woman's dilemma, gives it a benign, if slightly cynical, tinge, in his *Is He Popenjoy?* (1878):

[The dean] had told her how to behave to her husband. Men, he had assured her, were to be won by such comforts as he described. A wife should provide that a man's dinner was such as he liked to eat, his bed such as he liked to lie on, his clothes arranged as he liked to wear them, and the household hours fixed to suit his convenience. She should learn and indulge his habits, should suit herself to him in external things of life, and could thus win from him a liking and a reverence which would wear better than the feeling generally called love, and would at last give the woman her proper influence. The dean had meant to teach his child how she was to rule her husband, but of course had been too wise to speak of dominion. (28)

BIDDY: ABILITY LACKING OUTLET

Biddy typifies the constrictions which poverty, femininity, and class status impose. She helps her grandmother keep a rudimentary school and she manages her relative's general shop. Like Pip and Estella, she is an orphan, and she is unkempt and slovenly. In altered circumstances, she blossoms, and it becomes apparent that she is gifted.

> Her shoes came up at the heel, her hair grew bright and neat, her hands were always clean. She was not beautiful—she was common, and could not be like Estella—but she was pleasant and wholesome and sweet-tempered. . . . [S]he had curiously thoughtful and attentive eyes; eyes that were very pretty and very good. . . .
>
> I began to think her rather an extraordinary girl. For, I called to mind now, that she was equally accomplished in the terms of our trade, and the names of our different sorts of work, and our various tools. In short, whatever I knew, Biddy knew. Theoretically, she was already as good a blacksmith as I, or better. . . .
>
> I recalled the hopeless circumstances by which she had been surrounded in the miserable little shop and the miserable little noisy evening school, with that miserable old bundle of incompetence always to be dragged and shouldered. I reflected that even in those untoward times there must have been latent in Biddy what was now developing. (17)

With her abilities, in another era Biddy would have had many occupational choices. She seems never to have considered any possibility but remaining in her role as schoolmistress. If she had, would she have had opportunities? We can be sure there would have been nothing commensurate with her talent.

In the author's *Everyone in Dickens*, (1995), volume III, there are tables of the occupations held by the men and women who appear as characters in Dickens's works. The picture is startling. Among named characters, the males list 489 specific occupations, the females 108, hardly more than one-fifth as many. A total of 414 female characters are mentioned, of whom 151 (36 percent) are in domestic service (including four governesses and sixteen "companions"). There are thirty-one actresses and singers, thirty schoolmistresses and teachers, twenty-nine landladies, twenty-one schoolgirls, nine seamstresses, seven charity workers, six nurses, six prostitutes, and sundry other workers, largely in service professions (milliners, dancing teachers, school assistants, and so on). Out of the total there is one woman in business for herself: the waxworks proprietor in *The Old Curiosity Shop*. In *Little Dorrit* there is a merchant-firm proprietor who inherited the business from her husband. This survey is a telling statistical portrait of a fictional universe congruent with the real one.

THE EXCLUSION OF WOMEN FROM PROFESSIONAL LIFE

Mill devotes a chapter of his great essay *The Subjection of Women* to the reasons why women were so limited in their choices in life. He holds that they were excluded generally from business and the professions so that they would have no alternative but to marry and bear children, and thus subject themselves to the dominance of men.

FROM JOHN STUART MILL, *THE SUBJECTION OF WOMEN* (1861)
(Buffalo, NY: Prometheus Books, 1986)

CHAPTER III

1. On the other point which is involved in the just equality of women, their admissibility to all the functions and occupations hitherto retained as the monopoly of the stronger sex, I should anticipate no difficulty in convincing anyone who has gone with me on the subject of the equality of women in the family. I believe that their disabilities elsewhere are only clung to in order to maintain their subordination in domestic life; because the generality of the male sex cannot yet tolerate the idea of living with an equal. Were it not for that, I think that almost every one . . . would admit the injustice of excluding half the human race from the greater number of lucrative occupations, and from almost all high social functions; ordaining from their birth either that they are not, and cannot by any possibility become, fit for employments which are legally open to the stupidest and basest of the other sex, or else that, however fit they may be, those employments shall be interdicted to them, in order to be preserved for the exclusive benefit of males.

In the last two centuries, when . . . any reason beyond the mere existence of the fact was thought to be required to justify the disabilities of women, people seldom assigned as a reason their inferior mental capacity; which . . . no one really believed in. The reason given in those days was not women's unfitness, but the interest of society, by which was meant the interest of men. . . . In the present day, power holds a smoother language, and, whomsoever it oppresses, always pretends to do so for their own good: accordingly, when anything is forbidden to women, it is thought necessary to say, and desirable to believe, that they are incapable of doing it, and that they depart from their real path of success and happiness when they aspire to it. . . .

Now, the most determined depreciator of women will not venture to deny that, when we add the experience of recent times to that of ages past, women, and not a few merely, but many women, have proved themselves capable of everything, perhaps without a single exception, which is done by men, and of doing it successfully and creditably. . . . Are we so certain of always finding a man made to our hands for any duty or function of social importance which falls vacant, that we lose nothing by putting a ban upon one-half of mankind, and refusing beforehand to make their faculties available, however distinguished they may be? And even if we could do without them, would it be consistent with justice to refuse to them their fair share of honour and distinction, or to deny to them the equal moral right of all human beings to choose their occupation (short of injury to others) according to their own preferences, at their own risk?

Nor is the injustice confined to them: it is shared by those who are in a position to benefit by their services. To ordain that any kind of persons shall not be physicians, or shall not be advocates, or shall not be members of parliament, is to injure not them only, but all who employ physicians or advocates, or elect members of parliament, and who are deprived of the stimulating effect of greater competition on the exertions of the competitors, as well as restricted to a narrower range of individual choice.

QUESTIONS AND TOPICS FOR DISCUSSION

1. We state that Estella in the early 1830s had essentially only two choices: marriage or nothing. If she had had a significant talent or calling in the arts, literature, or some profession, might that have made a difference?

2. Miss Havisham, we assume, is at least a generation older than Estella. Were her choices at Estella's age any different? Was her decision to immure herself altogether eccentric? Might there have been any realistic basis for it?

3. From his own selfish standpoint, did Compeyson do the most intelligent thing by jilting Miss Havisham? What would have happened if he had married her?

4. What parallels do you see between Estella and Lady Anna? What were the pressures on each? Compare the status of Pip and Thwaite: Without the intervention of Magwitch, how would you assess their eligibilities for the marriages they sought?

5. Discuss the "gentility trap." Do you see instances of it anywhere in the world today?

6. Do you recognize Trollope's allusion in *Lady Anna* to the Jew who dealt with Christians? Discuss the appropriateness of the reference.

7. We have noted that the English public did not forgive Trollope for marrying his heroine to a tailor. What if Estella's parentage had been upper-class? Could Dickens have married Pip to her then? Review Chapter 2's extract from *Our Mutual Friend*. Write a scene: a conversation of observers commenting on Estella's marrying "beneath her" as Eugene Wrayburn has done. Make a choice of characters in the novel to be your protagonists.

8. Carefully read the Petition of 1856. Do you see Joe Gargery's childhood experience reflected in it? Cite the paragraph and summarize Joe's story as he tells it to Pip.

9. Study and compare the Wollstonecraft and Mill extracts in this chapter. Which do you think more persuasive? More insightful? Then reread the fictional extracts from *Lady Anna* and *Martin Chuzzlewit*. Look back at the passage from *Our Mutual Friend* in Chapter 2. How does fiction compare with advocacy nonfiction in terms of power to make its point?

10. Dickens and Trollope were impressionable, even vulnerable, men when it came to the attractions of the opposite sex. Yet neither signed a petition, let alone worked, for any reform aimed at ameliorating their "disabilities." On the contrary, when the subject of Women's

Rights comes up in their works, they are both inclined to be snide and to caricature the feminists, belittling their efforts. Discuss why you think that would have been so.

11. We hear everywhere today about "sexual harassment" and the "feminist movement." Has the status of women in the marketplace changed much since Dickens's time? What about their social status in or out of marriage? What is the term "family values" code for?

12. The equal rights amendment, after a good start, failed to achieve the requisite endorsements of the states. Some prominent women opposed it. Did it die because it was not needed, or because we are still not ready for it? Discuss, or initiate a research project.

SUGGESTED READINGS AND WORKS CITED

Beard, Mary. *Woman as Force in History: A Study in Traditions and Realities*. New York: Macmillan, 1946.

Davidoff, Leonore, ed. *Worlds Between: Historical Perspectives on Gender and Class*. Cambridge, UK: Polity Press, 1995.

Dennis, B., and D. Skilton, eds. *Reform and Intellectual Debate in Victorian England*. London: Croom Helm, 1987.

Dicey, A. V. *Lectures on the Relation between Law and Public Opinion in England during the Nineteenth Century*. London: Macmillan, 1920.

Dickens, Charles. *Oliver Twist*. London: Bentley et al., 1837–1840.

———. *Martin Chuzzlewit*. London: Chapman & Hall, 1844.

———. *Dombey and Son*. London: Chapman & Hall, 1847.

Fisher, Helen E. *The First Sex: The Natural Talents of Women and How They Are Changing the World*. New York: Random House, 1999.

Frost, Ginger Suzanne. *Promises Broken: Courtship, Class, and Gender in Victorian England*. Charlottesville: University Press of Virginia, 1995.

Holcombe, Lee. *Wives and Property: Reform of the Married Women's Property Law in Nineteenth Century England*. Toronto: University of Toronto Press, 1983.

Hunt, Pauline. *Gender and Class Consciousness*. London: Macmillan, 1980.

Low, Bobbi S. *Why Sex Matters*. Princeton, NJ: Princeton University Press, 2000.

Mill, John Stuart. *The Subjection of Women* (1861). Buffalo, NY: Prometheus Books, 1986.

Newlin, George. *Everyone in Dickens*. Vol. III. Westport, CT: Greenwood Press, 1995.

Teachman, Debra. *Understanding* Pride and Prejudice. Westport, CT: Greenwood Press, 1997.

Trollope, Anthony. *Lady Anna*. London: Chapman & Hall, 1874.

———. *Is He Popenjoy?* London: Chapman & Hall, 1878.

———. *An Eye for an Eye*. London: Chapman & Hall, 1879.

Vicinus, Martha, ed. *A Widening Sphere: Changing Roles of Victorian Women*. Bloomington: Indiana University Press, 1977.

Wollstonecraft, Mary. *A Vindication of the Rights of Woman* (1792), published with John Stuart Mill, *The Subjection of Women*. New York: E. P. Dutton & Co., 1929.

4

Apprenticeship and the Blacksmith

THE BOUND APPRENTICE IN NINETEENTH-CENTURY ENGLAND

In medieval times, as we learn in our studies of history, most activities involving investment and a degree of education and skill—handicrafts such as shoemaking, goldsmithing, locksmithing, and many more; shopkeeping and merchandising of all sorts—were carried on through the guild system. Guild members earned the right to engage in their specialty by working their way up through apprenticeship. There were virtues in this: stability, a kind of self-policing to maintain standards, and predictability in the sense that if one put in the time and behaved onself one would likely achieve standing among one's peers and an assured livelihood. Drawbacks were inflexibility, resistance to change and improvement, and exclusionary and monopolistic practices. Over the centuries, the system broke down by degrees, but even to this day "ancient and honourable" guilds of various sorts are still visible on ceremonial occasions in England.

The apprentice was bound, often before he had reached his teens, to a particular trade or craft by means of an "indenture" under which he was committed to serve his master for a term of years. The indenture was so-called originally because the sides of

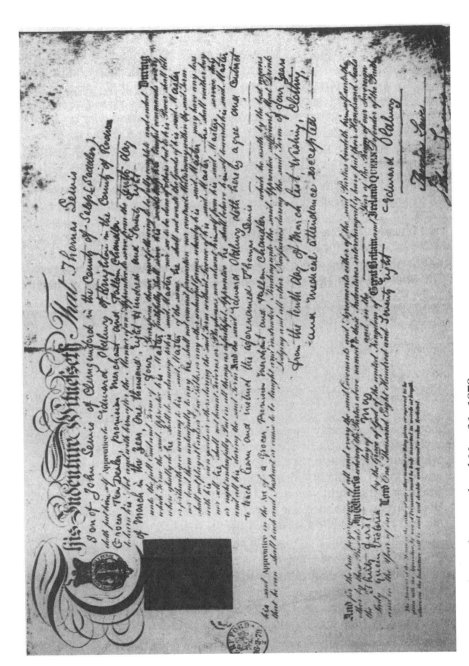

Apprenticeship indenture dated May 31, 1878.

This indenture witnesseth that Thomas Lewis son of John Lewis of Clungunford in the County of Salop (Saddler) doth put himself apprentice to Edward Oldbury of Knighton in the County of Radnor Grocer, Tea Dealer, Provision Merchant and Tallow Chandler to learn his art and with him after the Manner of an Apprentice to serve from the tenth day of March in the year one thousand eight hundred and seventy-eight unto the full End and Term of four years from thence next following to be fully complete and ended During which Term and said Apprentice his Master faithfully shall serve his secrets keep his lawful commands everywhere gladly do he shall do no damage to his said Master nor see to be done of others but to his Power shall tell or forthwith give warning to his said Master of the same he shall not waste the Goods of his said Master nor lend them unlawfully to any he shall not commit fornication nor contract Matrimony within the said Term shall not play at Cards or Dice Tables or any other unlawful Games whereby his said Master may have any loss with his own goods or during the said Term without Licence of his said Master he shall neither buy nor sell he shall not haunt Taverns or Play houses nor absent himself from his said Masters service day or night unlawfully. But in all things as a faithful Apprentice he shall behave himself towards his said Master and all his during the said Term And the said Edward Oldbury doth hereby agree and contract to teach learn and instruct the aforenamed Thomas Lewis his said Apprentice in the Art of a Grocer, Provision Merchant and Tallow Chandler which he useth by the best means that he shall teach and Instruct or cause to be taught and instructed. Finding unto the said Apprentice sufficient Meat Drink Lodging and all other Necessaries during the said term of four years from the tenth day of March last, Washing, Clothing and Medical attendance excepted
And for the true performance of all and every the said Covenants and Agreements either of the said Parties bindeth himself unto the other by these Present In Witness whereof the Parties above named to these Indentures interchangeably have put their Hand and Seals the Thirty first day of May and in the year of the Reign of our Sovereign Lady Queen Victoria by the grace of God of the United Kingdom of Great Britain and Ireland Queen Defender of the Faith and in the Year of our Lord One Thousand Eight Hundred and Seventy Eight

> Edward Oldbury
> Thomas Lewis
> John Lewis

the pages were arbitrarily clipped, or indented, simultaneously, and hence identically, on two copies (the one underneath exactly aligned with the one on top), one for each party, so that the contract could be forever identified in case of dispute. The indenture illustrated in this chapter was executed in 1878, only eight years after Dickens's death. It evidences an apprenticeship to a tallow-chandler and tradesman—not far from Mr. Pumblechook's line.

Servants, particularly those who could not pay their way to America, could come under indenture, bound in effect to work out their passage. During the term of their bond, these indentured servants were not slaves, but they were not far from it. Their obligation was one-sided: to work and stray not until the end of their term. But the apprentices of England had rights and privileges that compensated them materially for their loss of freedom.

The text of the indenture illustrated shows that the obligations of apprentice and master were reciprocal: the apprentice worked and behaved himself; the master taught him his trade and fed and sheltered him. Note the words inserted in the printed form: "washing, clothing and medical attendance excepted." Entering into an arrangement of this sort was an important solemnity—a rite of passage on the road to manhood.

APPRENTICESHIP TO AN HONOURABLE TRADE

Pip from the earliest days of his arrival at the Gargerys' had the modest but honorable expectation of being Joe's apprentice and in due time a blacksmith in his own right. We read that at times he was content with his prospects and worked with a will. But at other times, remembering Estella's critical remarks about the size of his hands and what she called his clumsiness, he hated his life. It certainly meant that he could not be spared to go off to a good school and get the education he craved (just as the young Dickens yearned for a path to develop his mind while he slaved away in the blacking warehouse).

But that the occupation fate had chosen for him required real skill is apparent already in Chapter 5, when Joe's aid is sought (well, commanded) to make some delicate repairs of a locksmithing nature.

> "You see, blacksmith," said the sergeant, who had by this time picked out Joe with his eye, "we have had an accident with these [handcuffs], and I find the lock of one of 'em goes wrong, and the

coupling don't act pretty. As they are wanted for immediate service, will you throw your eye over them?"

Joe threw his eye over them, and pronounced that the job would necessitate the lighting of his forge fire, and would take nearer two hours than one. . . .

Joe had got his coat and waistcoat and cravat off, and his leather apron on, and passed into the forge. One of the soldiers opened its wooden windows, another lighted the fire, another turned to at the bellows, the rest stood round the blaze, which was soon roaring. Then Joe began to hammer and clink, hammer and clink, and we all looked on. (5)

Dickens does not take us very far into the blacksmith profession, but we learn that it goes well beyond horseshoes:

"Here am I, getting on in the first year of my time, and, since the day of my being bound I have never thanked Miss Havisham, or asked after her, or shown that I remember her."

"That's true, Pip; and unless you was to turn her out a set of shoes all four round—which I meantersay as even a set of shoes all four round might not act acceptable as a present in a total wacancy of hoofs—

". . . Or even," said he, "if you was helped to knocking her up a new chain for the front door—or say a gross or two of shark-headed screws for general use—or some light fancy article, such as a toasting-fork when she took her muffins—or a gridiron when she took a sprat or such like. . . ." (15)

Requirements of strength and skill, both in high degree, seem to impress Pip little once he is infatuated with the seemingly un-attainable Estella, pristine and feminine, haughty and always alert to demean:

What I wanted, who can say? How can *I* say, when I never knew? What I dreaded was, that in some unlucky hour I, being at my grim-iest and commonest, should lift up my eyes and see Estella looking in at one of the wooden windows of the forge. I was haunted by the fear that she would, sooner or later, find me out, with a black face and hands, doing the coarsest part of my work, and would exult over me and despise me. Often after dark, when I was pulling the bellows for Joe, and we were singing Old Clem [St. Clement was the patron saint of blacksmithing], and when the thought how we used to sing it at Miss Havisham's would seem to show me Estella's face in the fire, with her pretty hair fluttering in the wind and her

Blacksmith with his apprentice, acting here as striker and holding the heavy hammer, or sledge. The bellows above was controlled by pulling on the hanging handle attached to the lever. From *The Boy's Book of Trades* (1888).

eyes scorning me,—often at such a time I would look towards those panels of black night in the wall which the wooden windows then were, and would fancy that I saw her just drawing her face away, and would believe that she had come at last. (14)

What was he ashamed of? The social standing of blacksmiths was historically not inferior, though it was not an occupation taken up by landed gentry. Measured by such criteria as the amount of premium paid, the social level of parents putting their sons as apprentice in the trade, and the numbers of pauper and charity children taken under indenture, it was highly respectable. A premium of £5 was the most common (it was used in about 30 percent of the indentures recorded in Sussex, Warwickshire, Wiltshire and Surrey), but £10 was frequently paid. Miss Havisham's £25 was strikingly high and should have been a source of pride to Pip, though we get no hint of this, for Mr. Pumblechook manages to seize all the credit for her munificence.

The "farrier" concerned himself solely with horses—shoeing and, in the early days, veterinary medicine—which gave him higher status than the typical blacksmith, who, of course, had a broader gauge practice. Apprenticeship in farriery was deemed a respectable first step during the eighteenth century, and a considerable number of instruction manuals in the field appeared during the years 1730–60.

Both farriers and blacksmiths had shops. They needed fairly commodious premises for the forge and storage of equipment, and it required at least £50, perhaps as much as £100, to set up a proper enterprise. This substantial sum was another indication of the respectable status of blacksmithing.

At the end of the seventeenth century, the farrier's status was high enough so that, for example, in 1675 one John Greswold, a gentleman, of Olton End, Solihull, was prepared to bind his son for seven years to a Walsall farrier, Thomas Morrisey, at a premium of £7. In the early eighteenth century, farriers and blacksmiths were still considered to be among the upper ranks of skilled craftsmen, but later, while their services were just as essential as ever, their status, as measured by premiums charged and the proportion of pauper to financially capable boys apprenticed, declined. By the early nineteenth century, their civilian standing had dropped to the point that farriers' sons were bound to humble trades like

This picture, drawn by one W. Small in 1883, includes well-dressed schoolchildren stopping to watch the blacksmith and his apprentice at their work.

shoemaking and weaving; in the army, however, farriers were regularly accorded rank as noncommissioned officers.

The blacksmith's skills were as necessary in the cities and towns as in the countryside, and by the middle of the nineteenth century, the trade was widely distributed throughout England. Farriers' children not infrequently made careers in veterinary medicine, an emerging college-trained specialty that proportionally diminished the status of plain farriers and blacksmiths in the mid-nineteenth century.

Apprentices to blacksmiths had to do heavy physical work. Young, small, or weak boys need not apply. Most blacksmiths' apprentices began at age fourteen or older, for a seven-year term. There were occupational hazards: the iron gave off sulphurous fumes, which made the apprentice bleary-eyed. It was believed that workers constantly near fire became constipated, and beets were the sovereign country remedy. Pip gives no hint that such things affected him, but he makes it clear that the inevitable soiling of skin and clothing, and the sweaty fatigue of the trade caused him embarrassment. As the illustration suggests, the blacksmith's shop was a natural stop and entertainment for children on the way home from school, though there is nothing in *Great Expectations* to suggest any ogling by passersby.

BLACKSMITHING: INVESTMENT, SKILL, KNOWLEDGE, AND THE RIGHT TEMPERAMENT

Joe Gargery, the gentle giant, was well suited to his trade. He was very strong, as his quick whipping of the redoubtable Orlick demonstrates, and he had a patient, equable temperament well suited to dealing with fractious horses and pugnacious workmen. The tools he had to have, the techniques he had to know, the versatility he had to be able to display, are amply demonstrated by the manuals which were written from time to time on his profession. A recent example will help us understand what was involved.

FROM RONALD WEBBER, *THE VILLAGE BLACKSMITH*
(Newton Abbot: David & Charles, n.d. [after 1969])

THE CRAFT OF THE BLACKSMITH
"A working smith all other trades excels"
—Anonymous: *Ode on Smithery, 1610*

Forging is one of the oldest and best ways of making objects from iron and steel, for metal forged at the correct temperature retains all its strength. When metal is forged it is heated until soft and then hammered into shape before it cools and sets again.

Wrought iron has long been regarded as the traditional material for the blacksmith. . . .

There are two vital qualities in wrought iron—ductility, which means that it can be drawn out when hot, and malleability, which allows it to be hammered to any desired shape. Not all wrought iron is of top quality: an excess of phosphorus and sulphur in the metal can produce what is termed "cold short," a type of iron liable to break when cold; while an excess of silicon, on the other hand, can produce "red short" iron, which is liable to break when hot. . . .

Mild steel . . . is less ductile and malleable than wrought iron but has the advantage of possessing greater tensile strength. It can also be readily forged and welded within a narrower range of temperature, but it cannot be hardened or tempered. When fractured, it shows a granular structure as opposed to the fibrous structure of wrought iron. . . .

For the making of horseshoes the iron usually comes in 18 foot concave bars graded according to their section. For very heavy shoes the bar is plain without fullering for the nails, the nails being individually countersunk below the surface. Plain iron is preferred for heavy work especially for farm horses working on the land, for plain shoes do not collect so much soil.

A forge can mean the blacksmith shop or the smithy itself but more correctly the name should be applied to the hearth or fire. It is rectangular, usually made of brick but sometimes of iron, and on it the blacksmith builds his pit or bed of coal or coke breeze. Over the pit is a cowl or canopy of brick or sheet iron, designed to take away the smoke and fumes; though at times the smoke produced in a blacksmith's shop is far too much to be absorbed in this way.

At the end of the hearth farthest from the fire there is a trough of water for cooling tools, hardening and tempering ironwork and containing the fire. It is sometimes known as the bosh. . . .

Tools for the hearth include a poker, shovel, rake and swab though some blacksmiths dispense with the rake and swab. The shovel is sometimes given the name of slice; it is a long-handled, light, nearly flat shovel for scooping up the fuel and arranging it around and over the fire. For cooling and containing the fire with water a perforated can fastened to a long iron handle may be used, or a bunch of twigs.

The air to keep the fire burning comes from a hand-driven bellows or a mechanical blower usually in a recess behind the hearth. In old village forges there were often two bellows so that the blacksmith and his assistant could each work on one side of the hearth, where they had their own anvil and set of tools. Most bellows have a double action so that a blast of air is produced both on the downward and upward strokes. The cow's horn seen on the end of many a bellows' lever [see illustration, page 116] is to give a good grip and is particularly liked because it keeps clean and is very hard wearing. Bellows are thought to have originated from a goatskin with a small opening, into which was fitted a hollow reed or clay pipe. The early bellows operators used two goatskins and pressed each in turn with their foot. In either hand they held a leather thong attached to the upper surface of the goatskin and by alternately transferring their weight from one skin to the other they operated a rhythmic and effective bellows. Bellows menders toured the country repairing damage.

The experienced blacksmith can obtain a wide range of heats by skilful use of the bellows and the coal or breeze. The names given to these heats are "warm" when the heated iron is just not hot enough to glow in shadow, and "black" when it glows very faintly; and these are followed in order by such self-explanatory named heats as cherry-red, dull-red, blood-red, bright-red, and bright-yellow. Other heats (for welding) have names like snow-ball, full, light, slippery, greasy and sweating. . . .

After a hearth, the most important large item in a blacksmith's shop is the anvil. The first anvils were probably lumps of crude iron ore but over the centuries a definite pattern has evolved.

Today anvils are made of wrought iron or mild steel with a specially hardened surface. . . . A good anvil weighs up to three hundredweight. It needs to be good, for working on a poor one can be compared with jumping in a heap of sand, while working on a good one is like jumping on to a spring-board, the rebound from each blow of the hammer helping toward the next. . . .

The anvil is best placed on a block of wood for this improves its spring. A squared-up trunk of elm is preferable, and the block should be set some three feet at least into the ground, with the grain standing vertical and the height of the anvil arranged to suit the blacksmith. It must also be set at the correct distance and angle from the hearth or the blacksmith will do a great deal of unnecessary work. The face is generally arranged so that it slopes away slightly from the user, for this allows the metal scales to fall away from the object being hammered.

A bench equipped with vices and a drill is a main part of the smithy and on this are kept most of the tools. One of the vices is usually a steel leg vice; this allows the strain and shock at the jaws to be taken by the leg, which is often let into a steel socket on the floor. For lighter work a paralleled-jaw or engineer's vice is often used. . . .

The principal tools are hand and sledge hammers, chisels, drills, punches, and a selection of tongs with variously shaped jaws. . . .

The two main hammers are the straight or cross-peen and the ball-peen. . . . The ball-peen is the blacksmith's general purpose hammer. . . . It is from one and three quarter pounds to three pounds in weight and the balance is carefully tested to suit the individual blacksmith.

The sledge is the heavy hammer used by the striker, who is generally the blacksmith's chief assistant. Its weight can be seven, twelve or twenty pounds and it has a haft of hickory a good yard long. It must be well made to stand up to the heavy work it has to do.

With the ball-peen and the sledge the blacksmith and his assistant work in rhythm, the smaller hammer indicating where and when the sledge must make its massive strokes. The signal for the sledge to stop is a lighter tap of the smaller hammer on the face of the anvil away from the object being hammered.

There are various shafted tools which the smith uses to bring the metal to the shape he requires. Some have chisel-like edges for cutting hot or cold metal, some are used for smoothing or flattening its surface and others have square or round edges for forging inside corners. There are also forming tools, which make rounded grooves in the metal, and swages made in two parts for forging rounded portions. . . .

For measuring and checking his work the smith uses dividers, callipers and a rule made of brass so that it will not rust nor discolour with heat and become unreadable. If he is making a number of articles of the same size he may use a template or pattern to guide him in his forging, or a special gauge with which to check his work quickly.

In the actual forging the blacksmith may use only a hammer or he may employ a combination of tools: it will depend on what he is making and the shape of the metal he is making it from.

All the time he watches the changing colour of the metal: when it is in the fire he must be able to judge not only when it has reached the correct heat for working but also whether or not it is reaching it at the right speed. The changes of colour give him the information he needs. If the metal is kept in the fire too long it begins to burn and form scaly lumps. The spoiled metal then has to be cut off and thrown away, which means a loss of both time and material.

When the metal has reached the correct heat for forging, the smith withdraws it from the fire and, unless it is a long piece which he can handle safely at the cold end, he uses tongs to hold it. Before starting to forge he removes any scale which has formed by knocking it off with his hammer or using a wire brush. . . .

But as the village blacksmith is, or at least was, almost always a farrier— one who shoes horses—as well, he needs additional tools for this purpose. . . .

When a horse is brought in for shoeing it is generally tied to a ring-bolt on the wall of the smithy. Awkward horses are often given a nose-bag to keep them occupied and a young horse being shod for the first time is often accompanied by an older one. The farrier examines the fore feet first so that the horse will not be nervous. He taps the foot to tell the horse which one is needed and then he lays his hand on the fore foot and gently slides the hand down to the hoof. This seems automatically to make the horse raise its foot. A special three-footed iron stand . . . with a smooth polished top is available for the horse to rest its fore foot when being shod.

Shoeing the hind feet is more difficult and more tiring for the farrier. Because he is out of the horse's vision the horse can tend to become restive and as it can send the iron stand flying this is rarely used to rest the hind feet. The foot is taken in the lap of the leather apron as the blacksmith bends beneath the haunches of the horse with his back to the animal.

Clinched ends of shoe-nails are knocked off and the nails pulled out with pincers. The hoof is rasped and picked clean and pared with the knife. The shoe is heated and tried for size and this makes a dense smoke which gives a smithy its characteristic smell. The cold shoe is then nailed on, starting from the front, and the nails are clinched where they protrude. Finally the hoofs are given a dressing of oil and paraffin to make them look good and the horse is ready to go home.

A good blacksmith rarely uses force and seldom raises his voice, though an especially recalcitrant animal can try the patience of the best of them. A soothing voice achieves more than all the shouting. (47–60)

THE BARD OF BLACKSMITHING

It was an American (though many English blacksmiths were sure he was writing about them), Henry Wadsworth Longfellow (1807–82), who in 1841 wrote and published the famous *The Village Blacksmith*. To some today it may seem sentimental, but one suspects that had Pip known it and really taken it in, it might have done him much good, for it depicts a resilient life of self-discipline, self-reliance, and, above all, usefulness. The blacksmith in the real world has no idle dreams.

FROM HENRY WADSWORTH LONGFELLOW,
THE VILLAGE BLACKSMITH (1841)

Under the spreading chestnut-tree
The village smithy stands;
The smith, a mighty man is he,
With large and sinewy hands;
And the muscles of his brawny arms
Are strong as iron bands.

His hair is crisp, and black, and long;
His face is like the tan;
His brow is wet with honest sweat,
He earns whate'er he can,
And looks the whole world in the face,
For he owes not any man.

Week in, week out, from morn till night,
You can hear his bellows blow;
You can hear him swing his heavy sledge,
With measured beat and slow,
Like a sexton ringing the village bell,
When the evening sun is low.

And children coming home from school
Look in at the open door;
They love to see the flaming forge,
And hear the bellows roar,
And catch the burning sparks that fly
Like chaff from a threshing-floor.

This illustration appeared in an early edition of Longfellow's poems. It may depict the original smith who inspired the poem.

He goes on Sunday to the church,
    And sits among his boys;
He hears the parson pray and preach,
    He hears his daughter's voice
    Singing in the village choir,
And it makes his heart rejoice.

It sounds to him like her mother's voice
    Singing in Paradise!
He needs must think of her once more,
    How in the grave she lies;
And with his hard, rough hand he wipes
    A tear out of his eyes.

Toiling,—rejoicing,—sorrowing,
    Onward through life he goes;
Each morning sees some task begin,
    Each evening sees it close;
Something attempted, something done,
    Has earned a night's repose.

Thanks, thanks to thee, my worthy friend,
    For the lesson thou hast taught!
Thus at the flaming forge of life
    Our fortunes must be wrought;
Thus, on its sounding anvil shaped
    Each burning deed and thought.

QUESTIONS AND TOPICS FOR DISCUSSION

1. Charles Dickens probably had little practical knowledge of blacksmithing and, unlike his practice in other cases, seems to have done little research on the subject. Does this make any difference in terms of the plot?

2. The introduction touched on the autobiographical aspect of *Great Expectations*. Why did Dickens choose blacksmithing as the trade for Pip? Was the status of a blacksmith's apprentice likely to be higher or lower than that of a warehouse boy sticking labels on bottles of bootblack?

3. Pip develops strength working at the forge. What occurrences in the story reflect this?

4. It seems never to have occurred to Miss Havisham to arrange for Trabb's boy to come and play with Estella. Does that suggest anything about the relative status of that boy and Pip?

5. Review the symbolism of the forge as relevant to the creation of fiction. How does it work as a symbol for life? What does Longfellow have to say on this? What figure of speech does he use? What other elements in blacksmithing does he touch on this way?

SUGGESTED READINGS AND WORKS CITED

Davies, G. Stella. *North Country Bred: A Working-Class Family Chronicle*. London: Routledge & Kegan Paul, 1963.

Ittmann, Karl. *Work, Gender and Family in Victorian England*. Houndmills, Basingstoke, Hampshire: Macmillan, c1995.

Lane, Joan. *Apprenticeship in England, 1600–1914*. London: UCL Press, 1996.

Lewis, Thomas. *Blue Ribbon Days: A Tale of Victorian Childhood, Apprentice-ship, Love and Marriage in Shropshire*. Shropshire: Shropshire Books (Shropshire County Council), c1992.

Richardson, Milton Thomas, ed. *Practical Blacksmithing*, 4 vols. in 1. Articles published in 1889, 1890, 1891, originally contributed to *"The Blacksmith and Wheelwright."* New York: Weathervane Books, 1978.

Rorabaugh, W. J. *The Craft Apprentice: From Franklin to the Machine Age in America*. New York: Oxford University Press, 1986.

Webber, Ronald. *The Village Blacksmith*. Newton Abbot: David & Charles, n.d., after 1969.

5

Crime and Punishment in *Great Expectations*

COINING: A CAPITAL OFFENSE

In an apparent diversion from the thrust of his plot, Dickens takes us with Pip on an excursion to Newgate Prison, the venerable home for the convicted, those waiting for trial, and the criminal court itself. The trip kills time while Pip awaits Estella's coach, but it also gives a good sense of the professional Wemmick and grounds for suspicion as to the source of his many watch-fobs, seals and other adornments. In his interview with the luckless man in the olive-colored frock-coat who has been condemned to die for making fake coins, he seems sympathetic but does not overlook the chance, sacred to him as we know, to accumulate "portable property."

"I think I shall be out of this on Monday, sir," he said. . . .
"If what I had upon me when taken, had been real . . . I should have asked the favour of your wearing another ring—in acknowledgment of your attentions."
"I'll accept the will for the deed," said Wemmick. "By-the-bye; you were quite a pigeon-fancier." The man looked up at the sky. "I am told you had a remarkable breed of tumblers. *Could* you commission any friend of yours to bring me a pair, if you've no further use for 'em?"

"It shall be done, sir."

"All right," said Wemmick, "they shall be taken care of. Good afternoon, Colonel. Good-bye!" They shook hands again, and as we walked away Wemmick said to me, "A Coiner, a very good workman. The Recorder's report is made to-day, and he is sure to be executed on Monday. Still you see, as far as it goes, a pair of pigeons are portable property, all the same." (32)

As is apparent, this form of counterfeiting was at the time punishable by death. A younger contemporary of Dickens, Percy Fitzgerald, who wrote several studies of old London, tells the true story of a well-known thief-taker (somewhat akin to today's bounty hunters) and his success in catching a coiner. The exploit was well known at the time it occurred and may easily have been in Dickens's mind when he made a coiner Wemmick's "dead plant." The events narrated occurred sometime after 1828 but before 1844. It is stated that this man (and likely Dickens's character) was the last coiner to go to the scaffold. The story offers a fine insight into the methods, and the patience and thoroughness, sometimes found in law-enforcement in the early nineteenth century.

FROM PERCY FITZGERALD, *CHRONICLES OF BOW STREET POLICE-OFFICE*
(London: Chapman & Hall, 1888)

One of the most persevering and successful of these thief-takers was Keys, who is said to have captured the last malefactor that was executed for coining. To the detection of this branch of crime—"smashing," as it was called—he devoted himself. There was a coiner, one James Coleman, who was so shrewd and cautious as to defy all attempts made to secure him. Such was his ingenuity and tact that he evaded justice, during a hot pursuit of the police, for many months. Keys, at that time, was in the Bow Street day patrole; he knew that Coleman was *"making a showful,"* as it was called in the slang, but could not discover where he lived. The plan pursued by the coiner was this: he never entered even the street where he lived if he observed any one about at all strange to the neighbourhood, nor did he take the produce of his labour out himself for sale, but was always followed by a little girl with a basket containing it. He supplied shillings at the rate of four shillings a score, and other spurious moneys in proportion. The little girl left the counterfeits with the *smashers*, and Coleman received the money.

Limbrick, of the Hatton Garden office, who was at the time very zealous in the cause of the Mint, and had earned some fame by apprehending coiners, used every exertion to take this man, but without effect. Either Keys or Limbrick could have brought home to him the connection with the little girl and the basket, but that was not sufficient for the ends the Mint had in view; their object was to get him taken for the capital offence, viz. in the act of coining; and to that end Keys set his ingenuity to work. He hired a man, at an expense of three-and-sixpence per day, to pass through the street where he suspected Coleman lived, morning and after-noon, in the garb of a milkman, carrying a yoke and a pair of pails, having previously been made acquainted with the person of Coleman by Keys.

After the man had done this duty for nearly two months he began to think it useless, but Keys knew that if Coleman did reside in the street, the longer the man with the pails continued his employment the better, because it would lull suspicion to him, if he entertained any, of his being a spy. At length their patience was rewarded by Coleman making his appearance. Looking out about eight o'clock one morning, and seeing no one in the street but the milkman, he ventured from his door to feed his chickens. The supposed milk-dealer hastened to inform Keys of the circumstance, and that officer, in conjunction with others of the patrole, surprised the coiner that night.

"When I got to the top of the stairs," said Keys, "I could hear Jem and his woman, Rhoda Coleman, as she was called, conversing about the coin while working. 'That's a rum 'un, Rhoda,' said Jem. I was about," contin-ued Keys, "to break the door in with my foot; in fact, I had lifted my leg up, and had placed my back against the opposite wall for that purpose, when I heard Coleman say, 'Rhoda, go and get us a quartern of gin.' I waited about two minutes, and she opened the door to go out for the gin. I and my comrades rushed in and secured Coleman with the moulds and work red-hot in his hands. He was surprised, but cool. 'Do yer want me, master?' said he, looking up in my face. 'Of course I do, Jem,' said I; and having handcuffed him, I proceeded to search the place. We took away upwards of twenty pounds' worth of counterfeit coin, as well as all the implements, &c., used in the process of manufacturing it." Coleman was tried, convicted, and executed. The woman was acquitted.

"Rhoda," continued Keys, "removed the body to her lodgings, and kept it for twelve days. I had information three times that if I went I should find Rhoda coining again, and that the moulds, &c., were concealed in the coffin, under the body of poor Jem Coleman. This, I afterwards ascer-tained, was the fact." (118–20)

THE STATE OF THE PRISONS

Charles Dickens had a lifelong interest in prisons and their methods. In his early years, he was relatively "liberal" in his concern for conditions and their effect on the inmates, for whom he had considerable sympathy when he believed their fate was substantially the result of little or no education, overcrowding in the cities, and other social shortfalls. In later life, he became stricter and was particularly contemptuous of some prison reform efforts that he thought soft-headed. Actual prisons appear frequently in his work, and symbolic ones as well.

Toward the end of the eighteenth century, prison overcrowding was becoming a major scandal. The punishment of imprisonment went well beyond simple incarceration and involved high risk of death from disease or even starvation. The Napoleonic wars, with their consequent influx of prisoners of war, and the loss of the American colonies, which had formerly been the repository of many transported felons, made the burden all the more crushing. The next chapter focuses on the condition and purpose of the hulks, the floating prisons; here, we include a firsthand description of the abysmal state of things in English prisons of the time. It led to the audacious creation of a new safety valve: transportation of felons to the antipodes—Australia.

Reading the next extract, we can imagine something of the horrors Magwitch faced, raised as he was (that is, not raised at all) and living as he lived: "In jail and out of jail, in jail and out of jail, in jail and out of jail. There, you've got it" (42). What he endured and survived offers a striking reflection: had he remained in Australia after getting his "ticket of leave" and making a success against all probability, he would have been living proof of the efficacy of the transportation system and a vindication of the government's policy for alleviating the abominations of prison conditions at home.

FROM HENRY WALTER PARKER, *THE RISE, PROGRESS, AND PRESENT STATE OF VAN DIEMAN'S LAND WITH ADVICE TO EMIGRANTS. ALSO, A CHAPTER ON CONVICTS, SHOWING THE EFFICACY OF TRANSPORTATION AS A SECONDARY PUNISHMENT* (London: J. Cross and Simpkin and Marshall, 1833)

The attention of the philanthropist, [John] Howard [1726–90], was first turned to the distress of prisoners by what fell under his own notice as Sheriff of Bedford, in 1773. The circumstance which first excited his attention, was seeing some who, by the verdict of juries, were declared not guilty; some, against whom grand juries ignored the bills, or against whom prosecutors did not appear, after having been confined for months,—dragged back, and again locked up in gaol, until they should pay the fees of the gaoler and of the clerk of assize. In extending his inquiries, he not only found that these abuses existed in other counties, but he became acquainted with other scenes of the most painful character. From the prisons he extended his observation to houses of correction, and found that both the former and the latter were full of the most crying abuses, and the most shocking evils. The gaol fever and the small pox first arrested his attention, as prevailing to the destruction of multitudes, not only of felons, but also of debtors; the horrid state in which prisons were kept, made them the hot-beds of a distemper, deriving its name, as it did its origin, from those retreats of vice, misery and legal revenge, miscalled justice.

In proceeding to present "a general view of the distress in prisons," he says, "there are some prisons that we cannot look into, without perceiving, at the first glance at their inmates, that there is some great error in the management of them. Many who go in healthy, are in a few months changed to emaciated, dejected objects. Some are seen pining under diseases, sick, and in prison, expiring on the floors of loathsome cells, of pestilential fevers, and the confluent smallpox." The cause of this distress was declared by that philanthropist to be, that many prisons were scantily supplied, and some almost totally destitute of the necessaries of life. There were several bridewells [women's prisons], in which prisoners had no allowance of food. In some, the keeper farmed what little was allowed them and where he engaged to supply each prisoner with one or two pennyworth of bread a day, it was sometimes, by the cupidity of the gaoler, reduced one half.

Although the inmates of the bridewells were nominally condemned to hard labour, out of the avails of which it was intended they should be supported, there were few of these establishments in which any work was or could be accomplished. The prisoners had neither tools nor stock of any kind furnished them, and, accordingly, spent their time in sloth and debauchery. Some keepers of these houses who represented to the magistrates the wants of their prisoners, and desired for them necessaries, were silenced with these inconsiderate words, "Let them work or starve." As those gentlemen knew the former was impossible, they, by that thoughtless sentence inevitably doomed the poor creatures to the latter. Many prisons had no supply of water within their walls. The prisoners locked up in cells, were dependent on the mercy of the gaoler, and got no more than the keeper and his servants thought fit to bring them. In one place they were limited to three pints a day; "a scanty provision for drink and cleanliness" [said Howard].

Nor was the supply of air less scanty than that of food and water. As the gaolers had to pay the Window Tax, they often stopped up the windows to escape this imposition. In many goals, and most bridewells, no allowance was made for bedding or straw. When a little was furnished, it remained unchanged for months, till corrupted and worn to dust. When I [said Howard] have complained of this to the keepers, their justification has been, "the county allows no straw; the prisoners have none but at my cost." What the moral condition of the gaols was at this period, may be estimated from the fact that prisoners of all sorts were confined together—debtors and felons, men and women, the novice and the confirmed thief. With all these, many were sentenced to the county gaols for slight misdemeanours, who would have been sent to the bridewell, but that there was no allowance made there for the support of the prisoners.

These few observations inform the reader of the miserable state in which felons and prisoners were maintained in the gaols, and will enable him to appreciate the system, forming a remarkable contrast, followed in Van Dieman's Land. (36–39)

CAPITAL PUNISHMENT IN ENGLAND

When Pip arrives in London and goes to see his guardian, Jaggers, he is struck by how much in demand he is.

I became aware that other people were waiting about for Mr Jaggers, as well as I. . . . "Jaggers would do it if it was to be done." There was a knot of three men and two women standing at a corner, and one of the women was crying on her dirty shawl, and the other comforted her by saying, as she pulled her own shawl over her shoulders, "Jaggers is for him, 'Melia, and what more *could* you have?" There was a red-eyed little Jew . . . of a highly excitable temperament, performing a jig of anxiety under a lamp-post, and accompanying himself, in a kind of frenzy, with the words, "Oh Jaggerth, Jaggerth, Jaggerth! all otherth ith Cag-Maggerth, give me Jaggerth!" These testimonies to the popularity of my guardian made a deep impression on me, and I admired and wondered more than ever. (20)

Why such anxiety? Why such apparent desperation?

"Oh! Amelia, is it?"

"Yes, Mr Jaggers."

"And do you remember," retorted Mr Jaggers, "that but for me you wouldn't be here and couldn't be here?" (20)

In the early nineteenth century there was a great paradox in English jurisprudence. It combined a high degree of attention to the protection of individual rights, with a level of severity of punishment, when the protection was unavailing in the courts, unmatched anywhere else in the world. Getting a good lawyer was quite literally a matter of life and death.

For most of its history, England has been the world's leading executioner of offenders. There is an old story of the shipwrecked Englishman washed ashore in an unknown country. He quickly realised he was home when he saw a gallows near the beach, presumably intended for pirates. "Ah! Thank God! I am in a Christian country!" he cried.

The first recorded execution in England occurred in 695 A.D. The offense was theft. Throughout English history, sins against property constituted the vast majority of offences punished by death. There were eras of enlightenment, however: Alfred the Great revoked the death penalty for many offenses and "for the mercy that Christ taught" substituted restitution for retribution, except for treason. According to legend, he made an exception by hanging forty-four of his own judges in one year for excessive zeal in condemning others to death. King Canute forbade that "Christian men should be condemned to death on any slight cause," and William the Conqueror abolished the death penalty altogether (in his mercy substituting castration for it).

But the general trend was in the opposite direction, increasingly so because of the familiar assumption that crime will be deterred the more pervasive the extreme penalty becomes. In Leicestershire in 1124, forty-four thieves were hanged all in one ceremony.

Hanging was not the only mode: there was beheading (for the gentry), burning, and even boiling. In his *A Child's History of England* Dickens reports that one David of Wales was sentenced to be hanged, drawn, and quartered, and that from that time (about 1300) this became the established mode of punishing traitors: "a punishment wholly without excuse, as being revolting, vile, and cruel, after its object is dead; and which has no sense in it, as its only real degradation (and that nothing can blot out) is to the country that permits on any consideration such abominable barbarity" (16).

Murder was the offense that most often drew the full penalty. In the early fifteenth century, more than one-third of those convicted of homicide were executed in East Anglia, compared with a fifth of those guilty of other crimes of violence and less than one-sixth of those whose offenses were against property (but these offenses were much more numerous than the others: one witnessing a hanging was five times more likely to be watching punishment for theft or housebreaking than for murder or assault).

It was alleged that during the reign of Henry VIII (1509–47), as many as 72,000 people were put to death. Henry was unique among monarchs in permitting Sunday executions. Once he prescribed boiling instead of hanging to punish a cook who had poisoned his master's guests. His daughter Elizabeth may have presided over nearly as much carnage; estimates, possibly exaggerated, are that five hundred people on average died annually during her reign (1558–1603).

By the mid-seventeenth century, the church was intervening. It could extend benefit of clergy to all literate felons (in 1692 to all women, whether they could read or not), and the definition of literacy became looser with time, to the point where one was eligible for sparing if he could recite the first verse of the fifty-first Psalm (the "neck verse"): "*Have mercy upon me, O God, according to thy lovingkindness: according unto the multitude of thy tender mercies blot out my transgressions.*" "Benefit of clergy thus operated as a kind of automatic reprieve for convicted literates. The pen was mightier than the sword" (HP 3).

But by the end of the eighteenth century, English criminal law, known as "The Bloody Code," provided the death penalty more pervasively than Europe had ever before known. It was a Protestant phenomenon: in the two hundred years ending with the death of the last Roman Catholic monarch, Henry VII, only six new capital crimes had been put on the books. In Henry VIII's reign, some offenses were for the first time declared ineligible for benefit of clergy, and after the Glorious Revolution of 1688 this trend greatly accelerated: whereas in 1688 there had been only fifty capital crimes (under the common law before Parliament added more, there had been only five), by the early eighteenth century there were over 220. *All felonies except petty larceny and maiming were capital.* On the continent during this period, executions declined greatly with the spread of the Enlightenment.

England's record was a consequence of the rise of Parliament and the Industrial Revolution. Commercial and landed classes, as they grew more wealthy, became more and more insecure. Fear of violent crime against individuals and their property was widespread by the first half of the eighteenth century, though homicides actually declined. There was good reason for this: law and order seemed structured to protect the criminal, for there was no regular police force. (The gentry disliked the idea of such a force, having been burned badly by the pretensions of the Stuart kings.) The law and the rights of the individual were respected, and personal liberty was far better protected in England than elsewhere in Europe. The result of its judicial safeguards was that when a conviction was in fact obtained, punishment was likely to be draconic.

The Waltham Black Act of 1723, intended as an emergency measure to deal with deer-stealing and other poaching in the royal forests, made more than fifty distinct offenses capital for seven different offender categories. This one law contained more capital penalties than most other countries' entire criminal codes. Intended to be temporary, it stayed in effect for over a century. Virtually no capital punishment law contemplated any alternative. "Hanging was not to be the ultimate deterrent for the most serious crimes but the usual deterrent for almost all crimes" (HP/*HJ* 5). It was imposed for impersonating a pensioner, for associating with gypsies, for forging a birth certificate, or for picking a pocket if the spoil was more than one shilling.

But no child under seven could be hanged (what a mercy!). If he was over fourteen, he could be, and in between, it might depend on whether malice could be shown. In 1748, a boy of ten was sentenced to death for murdering a five-year-old. The Chief Justice postponed the execution while he consulted with other judges on the propriety of hanging so young a subject. Unanimously, they concluded that little William York was "certainly a proper subject for capital punishment and ought to suffer; for it would be a very dangerous consequence to have it thought that children may commit such atrocious crimes with impunity" (HP/*HJ* 7). In 1801, thirteen-year-old Andrew Brenning was condemned for stealing a spoon, but his sentence was commuted to transportation. The only documented nineteenth-century hanging of a child occurred in 1831, when John Bell, age thirteen, was executed for murder, but a fourteen-year-old died in 1833 for stealing, and the same year a nine-year-old was sentenced to death (but later reprieved) for poking a stick through a cracked shop window and making off with two pennyworth of paint. During the nineteenth century, nine-tenths of all executions disposed of subjects not yet twenty-one years of age. Not until 1908 was the death penalty abolished for those under sixteen.

But it is only fair to note that this severity was more theoretical than real. The Bloody Code was a threat far more often than it was an actual death sentence. Between 1749 and 1819, executions punished only twenty-five categories of felony; the other 170 were unrepresented on the gallows. Between 1749 and 1758, more than two-thirds of the convicted died, but less than one-third were executed between 1790 and 1800. By 1810, about one in seven got the rope, and half that number by the mid-1830s. The national hanging rate annually was about seventy, largely for offenses against the person.

The only property offense that regularly was punished with death was forgery. Between 1775 and 1815, between 50 percent and 75 percent of these offenders met the fate of Wemmick's colonel. Forgery was an attack on the new system of paper credit, critical to the emerging commercial nation. Dennis Daly was hanged at Reading in 1803 for forging a cheque for £10, despite widespread protests.

Quaker agitation at the beginning of the nineteenth century began to make a great difference. The Religious Society of Friends was "conscientiously persuaded that under the Christian dispensation the punishment of death ought to be unknown" and that a Christian country was "obliged to be guided in its legislation by the principles of the gospel." Parliament heeded, and in 1820 removed shoplifting and theft from the ambit of capital punishment.

The Waltham Black Act was almost completely repealed in 1823, its one-hundredth anniversary, through the leadership of Sir Robert Peel, the creator of the centralized police force. Peel was cautious: to obtain enactments with the cooperation of the House of Lords, he raised minimums (as for value of goods stolen in a burglary) mandating execution rather than abolishing capital punishment altogether. But others were impatient, and they carried the day. Abolishment for category after category of felony became the norm.

In 1830, the Whigs came to power. Charles Grey, the Prime Minister, and Henry Peter Brougham, the Lord Chancellor, had spoken out against capital punishment while in opposition, but criminal law reform was not a priority for them once they came into office. The private citizen, however, was not to be denied. Juries sometimes neutralized laws they thought too harsh, regardless of the evidence (a phenomenon we see in our own time). Individual members of Parliament agitated for action, and a Royal Commission on Criminal Law was constituted and met between 1833 and 1836. It concluded that many capital statutes could be repealed without danger and with moral benefit.

As a result of the Commission's report, Lord John Russell, the Home Secretary, in 1837 sponsored a bill abolishing hanging for twenty-one of the thirty-seven offenses still subject to it. Liberal member William Ewart offered an amendment abolishing it for everything but murder, but it lost by seventy-three votes to seventy-two, with Russell, Peel and William Ewart Gladstone voting against. Hanging was retained for sixteen offenses but was thereafter applied in peacetime only for murder. By 1841, only seven categories of felony still remained capital crimes, and in 1861 this number was down to four: murder, treason, piracy with violence, and arson in the royal dockyards.

QUESTIONS AND TOPICS FOR DISCUSSION

1. Review Chapter 1 and its discussion of themes in *Great Expectations*. Does it give a clue as to why Dickens inserts the apparent diversion of the plot for a visit to Newgate?

2. How many ways can you think of in which prisons and law enforcement affect the story of *Great Expectations*?

3. How many characters in the novel are convicts or criminals? Name or identify as many as you can.

4. Discuss the point that in other circumstances Magwitch would have been a credit to the penal policies of Britain.

5. What is your opinion of the use of capital punishment? Discuss.

SUGGESTED READINGS AND WORKS CITED

Chesney, Kellow. *The Anti-Society: An Account of the Victorian Underworld*. Boston: Gambit, 1970.

Dickens, Charles. *A Child's History of England*. Oxford Illustrated Dickens. London: Oxford University Press, 1958.

Fitzgerald, Percy. *Chronicles of Bow Street Police-Office*. London: Chapman & Hall, 1888.

Hibbert, Christopher. *The Roots of Evil: A Social History of Crime and Punishment*. London: Weidenfeld & Nicolson, 1963.

Howard, Derek L. *The English Prisons: Their Past and Their Future*. London: Methuen, 1960.

Ignatieff, Michael. *A Just Measure of Pain: The Penitentiary in the Industrial Revolution, 1750–1850*. New York: Pantheon, 1978.

Mandeville, Bernard. *Enquiry into the Causes of the Frequent Executions at Tyburn, and a Proposal for some Regulations Concerning Felons in Prison and the Good Effects to Be Expected from Them. To Which Is Added a Discourse on Transportation, and a Method to Render that Punishment More Effectual*. London: J. Roberts, 1725.

Mitchel, John. *Jail Journal: or, Five Years in British Prisons*. Glasgow: n.p., 1876.

Parker, Henry Walter. *The Rise, Progress, and Present State of Van Dieman's Land with Advice to Emigrants. Also, a Chapter on Convicts, Showing the Efficacy of Transportation as a Secondary Punishment*. London: J. Cross and Simpkin, and Marshall, 1833.

Potter, Henry. *Hanging in Judgment: Religion and the Death Penalty in England from the Bloody Code to Abolition*. London: SCM Press Ltd., 1993.

Radzinowicz, Leon. *A History of English Criminal Law and Its Administration from 1750*, 3 vols. New York: Macmillan, 1948.

Tobias, J. J. *Crime and Industrial Society in the 19th Century*. London: Batsford, 1967.

6

The Hulks and Penal Transportation

THE HULKS

The sight of the hulks at Portsmouth, Deptford or Woolwich was deservedly famous. They lay anchored in files on the gray heaving water, bow to stern, a rookery of sea-isolated crime. As the longboat bearing its prisoners drew near, the bulbous oak walls of these pensioned-off warships rose sheer out of the sea, patched and queered with excrescences, deckhouses, platforms, lean-tos sticking at all angles from the original hull. They had the look of slum tenements, with lines of bedding strung out to air between the stumps of the masts, and the gunports barred with iron lattices. They wallowed to the slap of the waves, and dark fleeces of weed streamed in the current from the rotting water lines. Some were French warships captured in battle, but most were obsolete first-raters that had once borne a hundred guns for England; now all that remained of their pride was a battered figurehead and the rusty chains, each link half the size of a man, that held them to their last anchorage. They were like floating Piranesi ruins, cramped and wet inside, dark and vile-smelling. (RH 138)

When the American Revolution cut off the outlet for transported felons (see "Botany Bay" below), Parliament passed the Hulks Act

"H.M.S. *York*, as a hulk at Portsmouth, 1818," by E. W. Cooke, R.A.

(1776), to take advantage of the many old troop transports and fighting ships rotting at anchor but still afloat and habitable. Convicts intended for transportation were to be placed in these ships and kept there pending a decision on where to send them.

Though the hulks of *Great Expectations* were prison ships inhabited by convicted felons, some had earlier been used to house prisoners of war. A contemporaneous description of the conditions of life aboard comes from an unlucky Frenchman who was taken in 1806 and spent nine years immured in one of these floating prisons. M. Louis Garneray, a painter, had taken to a seafaring life. His ship, the *Belle Poule*, one of a squadron that was to cruise on the west coast of Africa, was captured by the English sloop *Ramillies*. Garneray was wounded and made prisoner. His story begins then, and it will be apparent that some aspects of his life were probably not enjoyed by Magwitch and Compeyson: there were likely no practicing dancing-masters among their colleagues. On the other hand, the methods used in attempting escape are instructive; our convicts would have made use of one or more of them.

FROM ARTHUR GRIFFITHS, *THE HISTORY AND ROMANCE OF*
CRIME FROM THE EARLIEST TIMES TO THE PRESENT DAY
(London: The Grolier Society, n.d. [prior to 1915])

Vol. 8: Non-Criminal Prisons

I thought I was dead to the past, but my blood boils with indignation
when I recall the unheard-of sufferings that I endured in those tombs of
the living. The lot of a solitary prisoner awakens compassion, but at least
he is not tortured by witnessing the woes of a herd of poor wretches,
brutalised and exasperated by privations and misery. Far from exagger-
ating I would even wish to abate something of the truth in my account
of the terrible miseries of the English hulks.

It took six weeks to reach Portsmouth Roads, and on the morning after
our arrival, I was transferred with some others to the hulk *Proteus*. For
the benefit of those who do not know what a hulk is, I may explain that
it is an old dismasted vessel, a two or three decker, which is moored fast
so as to be almost as immovable as a stone building.

I passed between rows of soldiers on to the deck, and was brutally
thrust into the midst of the wretched, hideous mortals that peopled the
hulk. . . . Imagine a crowd of corpses leaving their graves for a moment—
hollow eyes, wan, cadaverous complexions, bent backs, beards neglected,
emaciated bodies, scarcely covered with yellow rags, almost in shreds,
and you will then have some notion of the scene that I saw. . . .

The forecastle and the space between it and the quarter-deck were the
only parts where the prisoners were allowed to take air and exercise, and
not always even there. This space was about 44 feet long by 38 wide.
This narrow space was called by the prisoners "the park." Fore and aft
were the English; at one end the lieutenant in command; the officers,
their servants and a few soldiers at the other. The part allotted to the
prisoners was strongly boarded over, and the planks were thickly studded
with broad-headed nails, making them almost as impenetrable as a wall
of iron; and at intervals were loopholes, which, in case of an outbreak,
would enable the garrison to fire upon us without exposing themselves.

The prisoners' berths were on the lower gun-deck and the orlop-deck,
each of which was about 130 feet long by 40 wide. In this space were
lodged nearly seven hundred men. The little light which could have
reached us through the portholes was obscured by gratings two inches
thick, which were inspected daily by our jailers. All round the vessel ran
a gallery with open floor, so that, had anyone attempted to hide underneath, he would have been immediately seen by the sentinels, who were
always on duty in this gallery. Our guard consisted of about forty or fifty
soldiers; about twenty sailors and a few boys were also on board. Senti-

nels were placed all over the vessel and on the quarter-deck were always eight or ten men ready to take arms at the least noise. . . .

At six o'clock in the evening, during summer, and two in winter, the English went round striking the sides of the hulk and the gratings over the portholes, to see that all was right; later, soldiers armed with loaded and bayoneted muskets came into our part of the hulk, and made us go on deck that we might be counted. After this, the hatches and portholes were closed, in winter at least, for in summer the portholes were left open or we should have been all dead in the morning. As it was the air was so poisoned by the close shutting up together of so many persons, that the English, after opening the hatches in the morning, rushed away from them immediately.

The furniture of the hulk was very simple; it consisted of a long bench placed against the walls, and four others in the middle. Each prisoner was given, on coming on board, a hammock, a thin blanket, and a flock mattress. The seven hundred hammocks were arranged in two rows, one above the other. There was no distinction of rank among us, but those of the prisoners who could afford it, had made a sort of frame, which they themselves fitted with mattresses; they were thus a little more comfortable, but the poisonous air and vermin were the lot of all alike.

It was, however, in our provisions that the hatred of the English showed itself most clearly. Each prisoner's ration consisted of a pound and a quarter of brown bread, and seven ounces of cow-beef; for soup at noon we were allowed three ounces of barley and an ounce of onion for every four men. One day in the week, instead of meat and soup, we had a pound of red herring and a pound of potatoes; and on another, a pound of dried cod, with the same quantity of potatoes. These quantities would have been sufficient, but the contractors always cheated; there were also deductions made from a prisoner's allowance for any attempted escape, and for other alleged misconduct; and we had made a rule that each should contribute his share towards these diminutions.

There were also other reductions made voluntarily by ourselves to pay for a newspaper clandestinely introduced, and to supply money to those who had escaped. The provisions were cooked by some of our number. We breakfasted on dry bread; at noon we had our soup with bread in it, and the meat was reserved for supper. The herrings were so detestable that we generally sold them back again to the contractors at a low price; they came round to us the next week; and in this way some of them did duty faithfully for more than ten years! With the money realised by their sale, we bought a little butter or cheese.

. . . Water was brought to us by little boats, from which we ourselves had to raise it; those who were too weak, too old or too dignified to share in this task, paid a halfpenny to their substitutes. We had also to take each his part in cleaning our decks and "the park." Crimes and disorders, the reader may suppose, would be frequent enough in such an assembly of men, exasperated by suffering and misfortune. . . .

This was the community to which I was now introduced. When I went to take the post assigned to me, there seemed to me to hang about the long chamber a thick cloud, bearing in it the germs of epidemics. I had been in my life in a slaver with 250 slaves packed in the hold, I knew how poisonous was the atmosphere there, and thought that nothing could be worse—I now learnt my mistake. The horrible den in which I found myself was dimly lighted by the portholes covered with gratings; as my eyes became accustomed to the dim light, I saw around the pale corpse-like, ragged wretches I have described.

Except a few who, stretched on the boards at full length, wan and dull-eyed, seemed at the point of death, all in this hideous den were busily engaged. Some, armed with planes, were carpentering; others were at work in bone, making ornaments and chessmen; others were making really beautiful models of ships; some were making straw hats, and others knitted night caps; there were also among them tailors, shocmakcrs and one man who manufactured, Heaven knows from what, tobacco; nor must I omit the professors of fencing, the baton, and, above all, dancing-masters, whose lessons were charged at the rate of a halfpenny for an hour's instruction. . . .

It may be supposed that there was no lack of attempts to escape from this life. . . . The first of these attempts after my arrival was made in the following manner. I have stated that water was brought over to us by little boats; these boats carried back empty the barrels they had previously left. Accordingly, the night before the arrival of the waterboat, one of our number hid himself in an empty barrel. I and another were in the secret, and it happened to be our turn to assist in raising and lowering the casks. We had raised all the full barrels, and the order was given to lower the empty ones. I could hear my heart beat, when, after having lowered all but the row which would remain at the top, my companion and I moved towards a barrel marked with a notch, to show us that it was there our friend lay hidden. It descended safely and the boat, after a while, pushed off. The man who had invented this desperate means of escaping intended to remain till the following night in his barrel, and then, when all was quiet, to get somehow to shore. Wild as the undertaking seemed, it succeeded, nevertheless; but some time afterwards when, from not hearing of his capture, we concluded that he had made good his escape, and were about to repeat the attempt, we observed, to our bitter disappointment, that the English carefully inspected the barrels before lowering them.

Various other methods were put in practice; and it was not seldom that, in the dead of night, we were awakened by the firing of a musket, followed perhaps by a cry, whereby we learnt that some attempt had been discovered. The water would be immediately illuminated and boats would put off from the other hulks to aid in the chase if necessary, and presently soldiers would invade our den, and wake up those who still slept with blows of the fist or the butt-ends of their muskets. Then, for two hours, perhaps, we would have to turn out on deck, while we were counted several times over; and when we at last regained our hammocks, the rest of the night would pass in questions and suppositions as to who had escaped, and whether he had got safely off.

For an intended escape was made known only to those who were to share in it, and a few friends who could be relied on. Men driven desperate by hunger would, for the sake of a little relief, turn traitors, and inform against their companions in wretchedness. So many escapes were effected, that at last, in order to reduce their number, the English Government decreed that the flight of a prisoner should be punished by the death of two others, who were to be hanged in his place, in case he should not be retaken. . . .

After long and patient labour, assisted by a companion, I had managed to cut through the side of the hulk, but we were seen as we ventured forth by some of the sentinels who laid rough hands upon us and wounded us severely. Again, with a companion I got overboard, but was recaptured when within an inch of drowning, the sad fate which overtook my friend. [Once more, with two others, he contrived to seize a boat and get out to sea, but when actually within sight of the French coast, they were overtaken by an English corvette and secured.] I was utterly broken down. The ill-treatment we had so long suffered grew worse. . . . One day my patience was exhausted, and I knocked down a sailor who had grossly insulted me; others rushed up, and a fight ensued; the captain came up; and bruised and bleeding I was thrust into the blackhole. Five days had I been here when earlier in the morning than usual came the man who generally brought me the morsel of horrible bread which was to last till the following day: "You may come out," he said kindly; "you are free." I rushed on deck to get fresh air, where, to my surprise, I found my comrades crying, laughing, dancing, shouting. The peace had been signed and we were free! (179–94)

BOTANY BAY: PENAL TRANSPORTATION TO THE ANTIPODES

In 1597, under the reign of Queen Elizabeth, there was adopted "An Acte for Punyshment of Rogues, Vagabonds and Sturdy Beggars." It decreed that such "shall . . . be banished out of this Realm . . . and shall be conveyed to such parts beyond the seas as shall be . . . assigned by the Privy Council." The act provided that if someone so banished returned to England without permission, he would be hanged. In the seventeenth century, the act was used to provide labor to the plantations of the Virginia Company. Transportation as a mode of punishment (and as a way to deal with prison overcrowding) accelerated in the eighteenth century after a law passed in 1717 provided for seven years' transportation for minor offenders, in lieu of flogging and branding, and fourteen years for prisoners whose capital sentences were commuted. Over the next sixty years, 40,000 men and women were sent to the Caribbean and America under the statute, providing useful labor to the colonists and forestalling an explosion in the prisons.

The American Revolution stopped this outlet, and the hulks in the Thames and southern coastal ports became a stopgap, which was quickly overwhelmed by an influx of about a thousand prisoners a year. Disease was endemic, and the shore populations were terrified of the contagion of typhus, cholera, and other plagues. Desperate for a solution, the authorities "chose the least imaginable spot on earth, which had been visited only once by white men. It was Australia, their new, vast, lonely possession, a useless continent at the rim of the world. . . . From there, the convicts would never return" (RH 42).

The first convict ships made landfall in what is now Sydney Harbour, New South Wales, on January 26, 1788. The fleet of eleven vessels carrying over one thousand people, including 548 male and 188 female convicts, was commanded by the remarkable and redoubtable Captain Arthur Phillip in his flagship *Sirius*. Exactly eighty years later, in January 1868, the thirty-seventh and last convict ship landed 279 prisoners at Fremantle in Western Australia. Some 160,000 prisoners (25,000 women) had been landed in Australia by then. "This was the largest forced exile of citizens at the behest of a European government in pre-modern history. Nothing in earlier penology compares with it" (RH 2).

Dickens is not explicit in telling us when Magwitch would have arrived in Australia, but we can infer that it was during the first quarter of the nineteenth century. The crime for which he was sent out, he tells Pip, was "putting stolen notes in circulation—and there were other charges behind" (42). Crimes against property were standard among transportees. Those represented in the very first vessel to go out were:

Minor theft	431
"Privy theft," including breaking and entering	93
Highway robbery	71
Stealing cattle or sheep	44
Robbery with violence	31
Grand larceny	9
Fencing (receiving stolen goods)	8
Swindling, impersonation	7
Forgery of documents, banknotes, etc.	4
Other	<u>35</u>
	733 (RH 72)

In terms of age, Magwitch was probably in a small minority. Parliament wanted to emphasize youth for its colony, and prisoner distribution in the first vessel was predominantly under the age of thirty-five (122 men out of 140; 110 women out of 122).

Van Diemen's (commonly misspelled Van Dieman by the English) Land, now known as Tasmania, is a large island off the southeastern coast of Australia. It was named for the Dutch Governor-General of the East Indies by Dutch navigator Abel Jansen Tasman, who discovered it on December 1, 1642. It was not visited again until March 11, 1673, when Captain Fureneaux of the *Adventure* in Captain Cook's expedition made contact. It was a prime early destination for transported convicts.

We can draw upon the testimony of three sources as to the circumstances and conditions affecting transported prisoners in Australia. In chronological order, they grow less and less sanguine and more and more critical, even devastating, in their descriptions of the sufferings the prisoners endured. Henry Walter Parker wrote in 1833 in the midst of the active functioning of the transportation system, for which he was an obvious apologist. He may not have been as fully informed as later students were, and he may have had political reasons to be cautious in his characterizations of the conduct of the authorities, but his descriptions of the housekeeping details are likely to have closely approximated what Magwitch would have experienced. He describes the "ticket of leave" system, under which Magwitch obtained freedom and a chance to do something for himself. Anthony Trollope reported forty years later, basing his frank, compassionate, and critical observations on first-hand recollections of people he interviewed in Australia. Robert Hughes's powerfully written *The Fatal Shore* (1986) is hard to read without weeping. We must content ourselves with brief allusions to Hughes's testimony, but the others can with profit be extracted at length. Strangely, Hughes seems not to have consulted Parker at all, for there is no mention of his work in *The Fatal Shore*'s voluminous bibliography.

FROM HENRY WALTER PARKER, *THE RISE, PROGRESS, AND PRESENT STATE OF VAN DIEMAN'S LAND WITH ADVICE TO EMIGRANTS. ALSO, A CHAPTER ON CONVICTS, SHOWING THE EFFICACY OF TRANSPORTATION AS A SECONDARY PUNISHMENT* (London: J. Cross and Simpkin and Marshall, 1833)

CONVICTS

Chap. IV

In England it is generally thought that the presence of convicts must be highly injurious to the colonies; but let those who so think weigh the advantages and disadvantages. . . . Those who do not give themselves the trouble to weigh, consider, and investigate, will hear with satisfaction that Government has resolved, in future, to send only the least wicked offenders to Van Dieman's Land; the colonists, however, will receive the information with different feelings: they know the benefits derived from convict labour—they know the expense of free labour—and they also know that the freeman is often more insolent, more idle, and more dissolute than the convict. . . .

The new arrangement is that the convicts shall be formed into three classes, according to the measure of their crimes. The first class, which is to consist of the most hardened offenders, is to be sent to the penal settlement at Norfolk Island, where they are to be subjected for the remainder of their lives to labour; the second class, consisting of persons convicted of less heavy offences, and of whom there are some hopes of reformation entertained [this would have been Magwitch's classification], is to be sent to Van Dieman's Land, or New South Wales, there to be kept to labour in chains upon the high roads, and upon public works; and the third class, consisting of prisoners convicted of minor offences, is to be sent to the colonies for distribution among the settlers. . . .

It has been said and written, that it is no punishment to a convict to be transported. In former days there might have been some truth in the observation, if I may judge from the thieves' old song, which has encouraged many an incipient rogue to pursue his wicked courses until he has been sentenced to transportation. The reader will judge of the whole of the song from the first lines

> "Let us haste away
> To Botany Bay,
> Where there is plenty
> And nothing to pay."

But the song is never now heard: and why? Because the system of punishment is changed, and that joyous life which it anticipates is never experienced by the convicts. Transportation is now a severe punishment. . . .

Hitherto, the convict on arriving in the settlement has been placed in a situation, in which he is enabled immediately to commence self-reformation (and in this condition will the third class still stand). If, however, they committed any offence, they were immediately punished by being placed a grade lower in the scale than new convicts: they therefore felt that they had something to lose and much to gain, and that very feeling induced them to behave well. The unhappy beings who will form the first class will not possess this incitement, and I fear results will shew very little reformation. . . .

The expense of sending a male convict to Van Dieman's Land is now about £21., and of a female about £22. The ships taken up for the service, however, are generally very old and very unfit for long voyages . . . some gentlemen in one of the Government departments, exert a very improper influence for friends, ship-owners, tendering their vessels for the service. . . . If better ships were taken up, and coarser but equally wholesome provisions were supplied on the voyage, without increasing the expense of transport, more humanity would be displayed. . . .

The transport is scarcely anchored in the harbour, at Hobart Town, ere the convict feels his degraded situation. The principal Superintendant, and the Muster-Master, immediately commence taking an account, both of his person and of every circumstance that can be collected from himself, or is recorded of his former life or character. He is placed in a gauge to measure his height; his complexion, hair, features, and so forth, are carefully noted down; his body is examined to discover any particular marks that may serve to identify him in case he should ever attempt to abscond. . . .

On landing, they are marched up from the beach to the large gaol, called the Prisoners' Barracks. There, attended by the chief Police Magistrate, the principal Superintendant of Convicts, the Superintendant of the Prisoners' Barracks, and other officers, as well as by the Surgeon-Superintendant and Master of the ship to deliver up their charge, the Lieutenant-Governor inspects and scrutinises them, one by one, while the principal Superintendant points out the destination of each, as recommended by the Board of Assignment, in the service of the several settlers who had applied for men in rotation. His Excellency inquires as to the conduct of each prisoner while on board the vessel, and ascertains whether any one among them has just cause of complaint against the Surgeon or Master. He then addresses them all—reminds them of the miserable situation to which they have reduced themselves by transgressing the laws of their country; exhorts them to take warning by the past, and to commence a new life in the new country; points out to them that the way to wipe away the stain which disgraces them, is to pursue a line of good conduct; patiently to submit to, and comply with the laws and regulations to which they are now subjected; to be respectful and obedient to their employers. . . .

In the course of his address his Excellency usually takes occasion to hold out to them that great incentive to good conduct, *the ticket of leave*, or the permission, under certain government regulations, to labour for their own advantage, which has hitherto been granted, at the end of four years, to prisoners transported for seven, who have observed a uniform course of good conduct till that time; at the end of six years, to those transported for fourteen; and at the end of eight years, to those transported for life; while in some *special cases of remarkably* good conduct, it is granted before those several periods. It is never conferred in any instance, however, until the whole conduct of the prisoner has undergone the most minute scrutiny, nor unless his former employers, the Colonial Secretary, the Police Magistrate of the district in which he resided in the service of the settler, and the principal Superintendant, as well as the Lieutenant-Governor, sanction or recommend it. . . .

The settler to whom he is assigned, then receives him from the hands of the principal Superintendant, and from that moment his course of discipline commences. As his new master conducts him to his house, he gives him an outline of what he is to expect—he convinces him that it is only by a close adherence to his duty—by the faithful and honest discharge of the labour allotted to him, that he can escape sinking into a condition far worse than any he has witnessed in England. As he goes along the road, he perhaps remarks a gang of offenders who have fallen to that state. Every thing, indeed, he sees and hears is calculated to make the strongest impressions on him. The convict learns more practical instruction in one day, than he did probably all his former life, during all the opportunities he might have had; for he is most sensibly convinced that his own interest is at stake, and he listens with great eagerness to all that is told him. He is speedily set to work, and he as soon finds that the only way to escape censure or renewed punishment, is at once to resign himself to his condition, hard as it may be, and to strain every nerve by the full performance of his task to give his employer satisfaction.

He is watched and admonished at every step; he cannot commit the least inaccuracy, but it is remarked and corrected, while at the same time, he has the satisfaction of knowing that if he does right, if he uses his best endeavours to do well in his new occupation, his conduct is observed and appreciated. His duty is for the most part very laborious, and he is liable to be called upon even in the middle of the night upon any necessary or urgent occasion. If he is set to break up new land or to grub up the roots of trees, especially if he be unused to manual exertion, no labour perhaps in any country can be more severe; and it is moreover of that nature, of that stimulating kind, that the persons engaged in it are drawn on as it were to increased exertion, from the desire they feel to accomplish their work. The duty of a stock keeper, who would obtain his master's approbation, is also very severe in this mountainous and thickly wooded country. . . .

On the 31st October 1832, the total number of male convicts in Van Dieman's Land, amounted to eleven thousand and forty; of these one hundred and eight-two were at the penal settlement of Macquarie Harbour; two hundred and forty were at the penal settlement of Port Arthur; forty-six were confined in gaols, and five hundred and forty-three were employed in chain gangs in the colony: making a total of nine hundred and twenty-one, actually undergoing an additional severity of punishment which the colonial regulations assign to offenders who have subjected themselves, by renewed crimes, to a second sentence of condemnation after their arrival in the colony: so that not one out of eleven (Doctor Ross reckons one in twenty) again subjects himself to a second punishment—a proof that the moral condition of the convict is much improved.

The following account of the distribution of the convicts will shew how they were and are generally employed:—

Assigned to settlers	6,396
Tickets of leave	1,160
Constables and Field Police	155
Artificers on Loan to Settlers	267
Employed in the Public Works	1,645
Sentence of Transportation Expired	24
Free and Conditional Pardons	12
Invalids	52
Sick in Hospital	49
Died	5
Missing*	60
At Macquarie Harbour	182
At Port Arthur	240
Confined in Gaols	46
Employed in Chain Gangs	543
Absconded*	204
Total	11,040

*The two items absconded and missing, include those whose fate, from the first era of the settlement, has not been ascertained on complete evidence, though it is pretty well known most of them are dead.

The great number of suicides known to be committed in fits of despair, forms an instructive though melancholy proof of the extreme severity of the present system adopted in the colony. It shows that the feelings of the unfortunate beings are returning to a sort of morbid sensibility, that they see their errors, but have not strength of mind sufficient to bear up against the disgrace of the punishment to which they have subjected themselves. . . .

[The prisoners] require constant watching and attention. If they know not how to work with the axe, the pick, the saw, and the shovel, or to drive a team, they must learn, notwithstanding the inconvenience which their blunders and ignorance may cause. Their career in England is usually one continued scene of debauchery and depravity, and the time necessarily occupied in the voyage is often worse than uselessly employed in telling stories of crime and wickedness, in which the narrator has been the most prominent actor. Nothing is more common than for the prisoners on their arrival, knowing the demand for farming men, and the chance otherwise of their remaining in the public works, which they very naturally conclude is a harder lot than service under the settlers; nothing is more common, than, as they term it, "to hail themselves" for farming men, whether they are so or not; and no sooner do they come to the disappointed settler than a regular course of instruction must commence.

A gentleman not long since received a prisoner as a ploughman. "Well, my man," said his new master, "can you plough?" "No, Sir, I don't know what it is." "What! and you are sent to me as a regular ploughman?" "Yes, sir, they *called* me that, and you know I must not contradict them."—"But what were you bred to?" asked his master. "I be come from Coventry, sir; and I've been all my life a ribbon-weaving, till the day afore I was taken, when I was a-driving a cart." There was no alternative but to try the man with a cart, which he contrived to break in pieces the first day. The next time he only broke the pole, and the third experiment sufficed to fix the carriage, with its load, a yard deep in a slough. The patience of his master being exhausted, he directed the man to cut down some trees, as being a more harmless employment; but he was sadly mistaken. The fellow contrived, by dint of real exertion, to cut through a stupendous gum-tree, the lofty branches of which sheltered the barn from the westerly winds and the afternoon's sun; and just a week before harvest, when the corn was about to be housed, he let the huge tree fall directly across the building, which it levelled to the ground. A farmer in England, on such an occasion, would scratch his head, lament his misfortune, and get rid of his servant; not so with the Van Dieman's Land settler—he repines not, but sets the convict to repair the mischief which he has caused. The effect is, that he ultimately acquires habits fitting him for his new mode of life, and he becomes a useful member of the community.

It falls however to the lot of a settler, sometimes to have sent him a convict stubborn and indolent, and, as is generally the case, ignorant of agricultural operations. Then it is that the patience of the settler is tried, and then it is that he is apt to lament the scarcity of free labour. A man will put up with much, without repining, from a servant who is willing, but he is sorely galled when he finds that to ignorance are added indolence and obstinacy. In the year 1830 there was an instance of this at Jericho. A convict named Andrew Hulton, was set to grub up trees, which he obstinately refused to perform, on the plea that being bred up a weaver, he could not handle an axe, pick, or shovel. To avoid work he decamped, but was speedily apprehended, and on his way to the magistrate he seized an opportunity to cut off his left hand at the wrist, which he accomplished with an axe at two strokes!

It is not to be concealed that the system pursued in the colony has no effect upon some few prisoners who will persist in committing crimes until they are sent to a penal settlement, where they are subjected to labour of the most severe kind. The following case is an instance, but I should say it proceeded more from weakness and infirmity of intellect than innate crime.

James Williams, a lad brought up and employed in the neighbourhood of Hereford, as a farmer's labourer, till the age of nineteen, was, after running the usual preparatory gauntlet of lesser punishments at home, convicted of picking pockets and sentenced to transportation for seven years. He landed at Hobart Town in December 1823, and had been but a very short time in the colony when he was arrested on a charge of grand larceny, of which he was found guilty on the 2nd November 1824, and again sentenced to seven years' transportation. As a matter of course, he was then placed to endure a season of purgation in the lowest gang employed in the public works. He evidently felt his situation of the most galling kind; for, besides the misery of wearing heavy chains and undergoing close confinement, especially at night, deprived of all means of indulgence, the daily labour exacted from him, operating upon the indolent habits he had acquired during a long series of gaol imprisonments, both here and in England, proved in the highest degree irksome.

The orders of his overseer, always submitted to with reluctance, were by degrees answered with insolence, and at last with direct disobedience. For this repeated misconduct he was taken before a magistrate and severely reprimanded, agreeably to the general practice in the colony of trying the mildest means first, and afterwards gradually increasing in severity according to the repetition and enormity of the offence. Only a few weeks elapsed before he absented himself from his gang altogether, and when apprehended, as the next step, he received twenty-five lashes, and was sent back to his duty to the chain-gang. In less than a week he again stubbornly refused to work, and a similar punishment of twenty-five lashes was a second time inflicted. This refractory conduct continued until, in a few more months, he subjected himself to a punishment of fifty lashes, and to receive no other food for fourteen days than bread and water; having, in addition to his oft-repeated refusal to work, threatened to knock his overseer down with a hammer.

Two months had not elapsed after this, before he absconded into the woods, and on apprehension received one hundred lashes, and was condemned to work in irons. True to the text he had chosen for his fate, he was caught plundering a gang of convicts in nearly the same miserable plight as himself, while at work on the roads near the Jordan River, of the whole of their provisions. In such a case as his, what could the law superadd to the measure of the hardships it had already condemned him to endure? However, one hundred more lashes suggested themselves to the justices, and these he received.

His next offence was stealing some tobacco from the pocket of a fellow-prisoner, for which he received fifty more lashes. His back must by this time have been tolerably seared and callous. On the 27th August 1829, while in the prisoners' barracks, he was found with two clothes lines, and a quantity of sugar, evidently stolen, for which he was imprisoned and kept at as hard labour as could be exacted from him for six months, and deprived of any chance, whatever his future conduct might be, of ever being assigned to a settler, except in the remote part of the interior. He successively received twenty-five lashes for outrageous conduct, and fighting in the presence of the gang; he worked ten days on the tread wheel for being drunk and disorderly; he received a third sentence of seven years (his former ones being unexpired) for stealing a hat, of which he was convicted at the Quarter Sessions; in November, 1831, he was again tried and convicted capitally for being illegally at large while under sentence of transportation; in seven months, being committed for a similar offence, he was handed over to the Chief Police Magistrate by the Attorney-General for summary punishment; he contrived to secrete himself on board a vessel in the harbour, bound to New Zealand, in order to escape from the colony, where he was discovered and placed in what to any less expert man would have proved inextricable confinement, but in a few days after, he was detected in a second attempt in another vessel about to sail from the colony, and he is now sentenced to undergo a term of condemnation for three years, at the penal settlement at Macquarie Harbour.

At Macquarie Harbour, one of the penal settlements, the convicts' punishment is rendered as severe as almost any circumstances on earth may be supposed to admit. Shut up at night within a wretched hovel, on a rock in the ocean, where the only symptom of comfort is that which security presents; as soon as the prisoners are called from rest in the morning, they are fed with a dish of porridge, composed of flour and water, with a little salt. They then embark in boats and row several miles to the wood-cutting stations, where they continue to work until their return at night, when they are supplied with the only substantial meal they receive in the twenty-four hours. Their labour consists in cutting up the trees growing near the coast, into heavy logs, which they carry on their shoulders, or slide to the water's edge, and form into rafts. During the greater part of this duty the convict has to work up to his middle in water, and even in the woods from the moist and swampy nature of the country, his employment is of the most disagreeable and harassing kind. . . .

No situation is more worthy of pity than that of a person coming out of prison after a term of merited punishment. The mistrust inspired by a knowledge of his late situation, is directly opposed to his procuring employment. Often without a refuge, and without bread even for the day, there is presented to him no other mode of existing, than at the price of a new crime, or of subjecting himself to an act of mendicity or of vagrancy.

In Van Dieman's Land the convict, if he behaves well is sure of gaining a ticket of leave, and the means (for labour is dear) of obtaining an honest existence are before him. From the moment he sets foot on shore the seed of reformation is sown, and that it frequently takes root and becomes a goodly tree, is shewn by the result that only one convict in eleven sins again. . . .

The average annual expense of maintaining each prisoner in the Millbank Penitentiary is about £30, and those who have been confined within its walls, on regaining liberty, seldom walk in the path of virtue, or become useful members of society. How different at Van Dieman's Land— the actual cost of maintaining a prisoner does not amount to half £30 per annum, whilst the value of his labour is double the cost of his maintenance, and the punishment works reformation. (36–64)

FROM ANTHONY TROLLOPE, *AUSTRALIA* (1873)
(reprint from *Australia and New Zealand*. London: Dawson's of
Pall Mall, 1968)

In the old days, Moreton Bay—as the district was called in which Brisbane, the present capital of Queensland, is situated—was a penal settlement dependent on the Government of New South Wales. It was so named by Captain Cook in 1770. Though it kept its name, it seems to have attracted no notice till 1823–24 and '25. A penal settlement for doubly dyed ruffians was then founded at Moreton Bay, where Brisbane now stands, and many of the public works, and not a little of the cultivation of the lands round Brisbane, are due to the forced labour of these unfortunates. When the great question was being mooted within the would-be new colony, its whole population did not exceed 15,000 souls. Among the pastoral aspirants—squatters as my readers must learn to call them—the want of labour was the one great difficulty of these days. The squatter, alone, was not afraid of the convict. The freeman, whose lot it would be to work alongside of him should he come, and the shopkeepers, and the small nascent agriculturists, did not wish for him. It was therefore decided that the colony should never take convicts, and it has never taken them. What became of those who had been sent thither up to that date, it is hard to say. (I, 2)

• • •

From this time, 1804, down to the year 1856, when responsible government began, the history of Van Diemen's Land is simply the history of a convict establishment. How to manage convicts, how to get work out of them with the least possible chance of escape, how to catch them when they did escape, how to give them liberty when they made no attempt to escape, how to punish them, and how not to punish them, how to make them understand that they were simply beasts of burden reduced to that degree by their own vileness, and how to make them understand at the same time that if under the most difficult circumstances for the exercise of virtue they would cease to be vicious, they might cease also to be beasts of burden—these were the tasks which were imposed, not only upon the governors and their satellites, not only on all officers military and civilian, not only on the army of gaolers, warders, and such like, which was necessary, but also on every free settler and on every free man in the island. For no one who had cast in his lot with Van Diemen's Land could be free from the taint of the establishment, or unconnected with the advantages which it certainly bestowed.

A double set of horrors is told of the convict establishment of Van Diemen's Land—of horrors arising from the cruelty of the tyrant gaolers to their prison slaves, and of horrors created by these slaves when they escaped and became bushrangers. It must be borne in mind that almost every squatter was a gaoler, and that almost every servant was a slave. . . . no doubt the work to be done was very nasty work, and there was of necessity much of roughness on both sides. It must be understood that these prisoners in Van Diemen's Land were not to be kept as prisoners are kept in our country gaols and penitentiaries at home. They were to be out at work wherever the present need of work might be. Nor were they to be watched when at work by regular wardens as many of us have seen to be done with gangs of prisoners at Portland, Portsmouth, and elsewhere at home—so watched that immediate escape, though not perhaps impossible, is very difficult. A portion of the convicts sent to Van Diemen's Land were no doubt locked up from the first, a portion were employed on government works and were probably kept under close though not continued surveillance;—but the majority both of men and women were sent out as servants to the free settlers, who were responsible, if not directly for the safe custody of those entrusted to them, at least for immediate report should any escape. The first preliminaries of escape were easy. A man could run into the bush, and be quit at any rate of the labour of the hour. If he were shepherding sheep, or building fences, or felling timber, during the greater part of the day, no eye unless that of a brother convict was upon him. He could go, and the chances of the world were open to him. . . .

Of course the escapes were numerous, and of course the punishments were severe. And it was not only that the men would escape, but also that when punctual to hours and punctual in receipt of their rations, they would not earn their rations by work. They would not work after such a fashion as to please their masters;—and, as a necessity, the masters had a redress for such occasions. A convict who would only eat rations and never earn them—and who could not be dismissed as can an ordinary idle servant—required some treatment more or less severe. The master himself was not allowed to inflict corporal punishment—but the neighbouring magistrate was entrusted with that power. The magistrate could, on hearing sufficient evidence of wilful idleness or other delinquency, inflict a certain number of lashes. The thing became so common, of such everyday occurrence, that very light evidence was soon found to be sufficient. The neighbouring settler or squatter was probably the friend of the magistrate, who was a squatter himself; and what better—indeed what other evidence could the magistrate have than his friend's word? The practice became very simple at last. If the man would not work, or worked amiss, or was held to have sinned in any way against his master's discipline, he was sent to the magistrate to be flogged. He himself would be the bearer of some short note. "Dear Sir—Please give the bearer three dozen, and return him." The man as a rule would take the note—and the three dozen, and would return. A bold spirit would perhaps run away. Then he would be tracked and dogged and starved, till he either came back or was brought back—and the last state of that man would be worse than the first.

Of course there were horrors. The men who did escape, and some who did not, committed fresh crimes and underwent fresh trials—with very small chance of verdicts in their favour. And of all crimes murder and attempts to murder seem to have been most in excess. Men were hung for murder and attempts to murder and for various other crimes. The hangings were frequent and gave rise to sharp expostulations. There is a story in the island that the gaol chaplain at Hobart Town once remonstrated—not against hanging in general or the number that were hung—but as to the inconvenient celerity with which the ceremony was performed. Thirteen men, he said, could be comfortably hung at once, but no more. The crowding had been too great, and he trusted that for the future the accommodation afforded by the gaol might not be too far stretched. The hangman was a great and well-paid official. There were flagellators also, generally convicts themselves, promoted to the honourable employment of flogging their brethren at the different stations. There is still, I am told, an old pensioned hangman living under protection in the island. The flagellators have disappeared, some having gone to Victoria as miners, some having died in their bed—a reasonable proportion having been murdered. It may be understood that the flagellators would not be popular. . . .

Though one hears much of flogging in Van Diemen's Land, one hears still more of the excellence of the service rendered by convicts. Ladies especially are never weary of telling how good and how faithful were the females allotted to them and to their mothers. Indeed it is from the ladies of the colony that one hears the loudest regrets in regard to the good things that have now been lost for ever. And though the ladies are the loudest, men also tell of the convicts by whose labour they were enriched in the old days.

Again, on the other hand, the inquirer is constantly startled by the respectability of career and eminent success of many a pardoned convict. Men who came out nominally for life were free and earning large incomes within comparatively few years. Unless a man was reconvicted he was sure to be made free, having at first a ticket of leave, which enabled him to work within a certain district on his own behalf, and then a conditional pardon, which allowed him to go anywhere except to England. In the records of Tasmania, which we have at home, we are told of the cruelty and sufferings inflicted and endured on both sides, of the cruelty of masters and of all that their slaves endured, of the blood thirsty malignity of bushrangers, and of the evils which they perpetrated on the community. Horrors are always so popular that of course such tales are told the loudest. Enduring good conduct with good results creates no sensational enjoyment, and therefore we hear little or nothing of masters and mistresses so satisfied with the docility of convicts as to find them superior to free servants, or of men who have been sent from England as abject, nameless wretches, who have risen, after a period of penal service, to opulence, respectability, and almost to honour.

When the establishment was first set on foot in Van Diemen's Land, not only were convicts sent out to certain of the settlers as labourers without hire, but the settlers who took them had with each convict a grant of land—so many acres for each convict taken. The owner of the slave was then bound to feed and clothe the man, but was not required to pay him any wages. That the convicts were sufficiently fed and clad by their employers I have never heard denied. Indeed food was so cheap— or at least meat was so—that no deficiency in this respect was probable. Nor, as far as I can learn, were the men overworked. No doubt the amount of labour performed by them daily was less than that ordinarily given by free labourers. But absolute submission was required from them—that absolute touch-your-hat-and-look-humble submission which to this day is considered necessary among soldiers. They were to give implicit obedience, and masters accustomed to implicit obedience and absolute submission are apt to become arbitrary. And the scourge, when it is in use, recommends itself strongly to those who use it. The system could not but be evil. Then, after some years, wages of £9 per annum were required from the masters for each man—out of which the men found their own clothes. This was a great improvement in the condition of the convicts, as they were thus enabled to own property and to exercise some of the rights of free men. At the same time they had awarded to them the privilege of leaving their masters if they chose, and of going on to the public works. This was a privilege which was but seldom exercised, as private work and private rations and private discipline were always better than the work and rations and discipline of the public gangs. But it was something for a man who could not endure a master to be able to shake that master's yoke from his neck. . . .

The system of transportation as carried on in Van Diemen's Land no doubt was bad. It was bad to stain with the crime of so many criminals a community which must necessarily be in itself so small. It could never have been hoped that the population of Van Diemen's Land could swallow up so large a body of English criminals as would be sent thither, without becoming a people especially noted for its convict element. And yet it was never intended that Van Diemen's Land should be devoted to convicts, as was Norfolk Island, and as is the little spot of land called Spike Island in the Cove of Cork. And the portioning out of convicts to settlers to be employed as labourers was bad; for it created a taste for slavery which has not yet lost its relish on the palate of many Tasmanians. A certain amount of harshness and bitter suffering was, no doubt, incidental to it. But I do not believe that men became fiends under its working. The fiends came out ready made, from England, and were on the whole treated with no undue severity. Of course there were exceptions— and the exceptions have reached the public ear much more readily than has the true history. Nevertheless the people rebelled against the system—or rather repudiated it with such strength, that the government at home was at last forced to give way. (II, 1)

• • •

New South Wales was taken up by Great Britain as a convict depôt, and grew as such till the free inhabitants who had followed and surrounded the convicts became numerous and strong enough to declare that they would have no more such neighbours sent among them. . . . Moreton Bay was still part of New South Wales when New South Wales refused to be any longer regarded as an English prison, and Van Diemen's Land did for herself that which New South Wales had done before. . . . In this way all the now existing Australian colonies, except South Australia, have either owed their origin to convicts, or have been at one period of their existence fostered by convict labour. (II, 9)

• • •

In telling the early tale of New South Wales I have endeavoured to explain how great was the struggle to maintain life on the first settlement; and the struggle was made only because it was necessary to Great Britain that she should find a distant home for her criminal exiles. The convicts were sent; and the attendants on the convicts, with convict assistance, made a new world. (II, 5)

The "horrors" Trollope refers to were perpetrated in significant part by Sir Ralph Darling (1775–1858), who became governor of New South Wales in 1825. He wanted a severe, undeviating standard of punishment for the convicts, regardless of merits in particular cases, and, as Hughes puts it, "The basis of this standard was the cat-o'-nine tails, whose whistle and dull crack were as much a part of the aural background to Australian life as the kookaburra's laugh" (RH 427). Hughes gives us a table summarizing corporal punishment inflicted in New South Wales from 1830 to 1837:

year	no. of floggings	total of lashes	avg lashes per flogging	male convict population
1830	2,985	124,333	41	18,571
1831	3,163	186,017	58	21,825
1832	3,816	164,001	43	24,154
1833	5,824	242,865	41	23,357
1834	6,328	243,292	38	25,200
1835	7,103	332,810	46	27,340
1836	6,904	304,327	44	29,406
1837	5,916	268,013	45	32,102

QUESTIONS AND TOPICS FOR DISCUSSION

1. We are fortunate to have an eyewitness account of conditions on the hulks, though it comes from a prisoner of war. Why do you think we have none from former convicts?

2. Magwitch and Compeyson endured horrendous conditions and treatment in their hulk and, very probably, on the way to and in Australia. The one, having earned his ticket of leave, worked and prospered. The other we are told little of, except that his hatred of his former partner was so great that he devoted all his time to watching, following, and informing upon him, returning the favor Magwitch dealt him in the marshes near the churchyard. Discuss and reflect on these two men and their different fates.

SUGGESTED READINGS AND WORKS CITED

Bateson, Charles. *The Convict Ships, 1787–1868*. Glasgow: Brown, Son & Ferguson, 1969.

Chapman, Don. *1788, The People of the First Fleet*. North Ryde, NSW: Cassell Australia, 1981.

Clarke, Marcus. *For the Term of His Natural Life* (1874). Stephen Murray-Smith, ed. London: Penguin Books, 1970.

Evans, Lloyd, ed. *Convicts and Colonial Society, 1788–1853*. Stanmore, NSW: Cassell Australia, 1976.

Frost, Alan. *Convicts and Empire: A Naval Question 1776–1811*. Melbourne: Oxford University Press, 1980.

Gibbings, Robert. *John Graham, Convict 1824: An Historical Narrative*. London: Faber and Faber, 1937.

Griffiths, Arthur. *The History and Romance of Crime from the Earliest Times to the Present Day*. London: The Grolier Society, n.d. (prior to 1915).

Hasluck, Alexandra. *Unwilling Immigrants: A Study of the Convict Period in Western Australia*. Melbourne: Oxford University Press, 1959.

Hughes, Robert. *The Fatal Shore: The Epic of Australia's Founding*. New York: Vintage Books, a div. of Random House, 1988.

Mortlock, Jon F. *Experiences of a Convict Transported for Twenty-One Years*. (London, 1864) Reprint, G. A. Wilkes and A. G. Mitchell, eds. Sydney: N.p., 1965.

Parker, Henry Walter. *The Rise, Progress, and Present State of Van Dieman's Land with Advice to Emigrants. Also, a Chapter on Convicts, Showing the Efficacy of Transportation as a Secondary Punishment*. London: J. Cross and Simpkin and Marshall, 1833.

Rudé, George. *Protest and Punishment: The Story of the Social and Political Protesters Transported to Australia, 1788–1868*. Oxford: Oxford University Press, 1978.

Shaw, A.G.L. *Convicts and the Colonies: A Study of Penal Transportation from Great Britain and Ireland to Australia and Other Parts of the British Empire*. London: Faber, 1966.

Trollope, Anthony. *Australia*. 2 vols. paperback. Gloucester: Alan Sutton Publishing, 1987 (abstracting the Australian sections from *Australia and New Zealand*. London: Chapman & Hall, 1873).

Weidenhofer, Margaret. *The Convict Years: Transportation and the Penal System 1788–1868*. Melbourne: Lansdowne, 1973.

7

Australia: Making a Fortune in the Outback

How did Magwitch do it? Before Pip learns that he is the beneficiary, he asks a polite question.

> "How are you living?" I asked him.
> "I've been a sheep-farmer, stock-breeder, other trades besides, away in the new world," said he: "many a thousand mile of stormy water off from this. . . .
> "I've done wonderful well. There's others went out alonger me as has done well too, but no man has done nigh as well as me. I'm famous for it. . . .
> "When I was a hired-out shepherd in a solitary hut, not seeing no faces but faces of sheep till I half forgot wot men's and women's faces wos like, I see yourn . . . 'but wot, if I gets liberty and money, I'll make that boy a gentleman!' And I done it. . . .
> "I got money left me by my master (which died, and had been the same as me), and got my liberty and went for myself. . . . It all prospered wonderful. As I giv' you to understand just now, I'm famous for it. It was the money left me, and the gains of the first few year, wot I sent home to Mr Jaggers." (39)

A transportee, once in Australia, was bound to remain there for his term of sentence. In Magwitch's case, evidently, his sentence mandated his remaining there for life. This sort of prisoner had

only three ways to gain his freedom. He could be pardoned absolutely by the governor, which meant he had all his rights restored
including that to return home; he could be pardoned condition-
ally, which gave him colonial citizenship but no right of return;
and, most common, he could earn and retain a "ticket of leave."
This gave him freedom to work for whom he would, including
himself, as long as he stayed in the colony. A ticket lasted for a
year and had to be renewed. It could be revoked at any time. Many
of these people became farmers, and some achieved prosperity. In
this society, "tides of men and women were constantly flowing
from servitude into citizenhood and responsibility, from bitter poverty to new-found wealth" (RH 322).

Australia was a frontier society. It rewarded hard work in a way
unimaginable back in England. This was especially true of the ignorant and unskilled, for they came from a country where there
was no chance at all, to one in which hope, effort, and luck could
propel them to great things.

The "squatter," despite his undignified name, was the aristocrat
of the outback: the great husbandman and fortune-maker, who
struggled against climate, vermin, and his less fortunate, or less
diligent, fellow men. He would take over tens of thousands of acres
to run sheep. The wool produced was the original staple of the
Australian economy and critical to its viability in the early years.
But he did not own the land, and he was not allowed to buy it. It
was retained by the government on behalf of all the people of the
colony and was to be sold or leased as would be best for the public
advantage. The squatter's run, when he took it up and drove his
sheep or his cattle on it, had previously known no other occupant
than the aborigine. In the very early days of squatting some attempts were made to connect this occupation with possession, but
this was refused by the Crown. When independent government
was conceded to the Australian colonies, its right of ultimate ownership became the right of the people. Squatters knew that they
held their runs simply as tenants under the government acting for
all the people.

It is important to note that, since they did not buy their land,
squatters could get started on a modest investment. Their energy
and the scale of the land available could, with good luck in weather
and the market for wool, give them substantial incomes. Magwitch's master was probably of this sort. Magwitch tells us he was

a former prisoner who achieved great results. In time, Magwitch inherited the land, or "station," he was operating when he died, as well as whatever capital he had amassed. This was the stake Magwitch held as he looked back to England and the boy he vividly remembered for his humanity in that far-away churchyard.

Anthony Trollope went to Australia in 1871, having made a contract with his publishers for a travel book. He was, as always, very thorough and very diligent. He was much more interested in people than in scenery, and very interested in statistics, and he had a keen eye for detail. Included below are extracts discussing the opportunities and pitfalls for the working man and the struggles of the squatters, one of whom Magwitch seems to have become. Note the extract under "Apprenticeship" which describes a possible mode of life for the younger Magwitch. Headings have been added.

FROM ANTHONY TROLLOPE, *AUSTRALIA* (1873)
(Reprint from *Australia and New Zealand*. London: Dawson's of Pall Mall, 1968)

THE WORKER

If we may take 17s.6d. as the average money wages of a labouring man, he will receive in the year something over £45, besides his food. It must be understood also that in most of the occupations specified shelter is afforded—a place, that is, in which to cook, to sleep, and to eat. The man brings his own blankets, but he has a bunk on which he can lie, and the use of a hut. If, therefore, a man be unmarried and really careful, he can very quickly save enough money to enable himself to start as a buyer of land. I now presume myself to be addressing some young English labourer; and the young English labourer is doubtless certain that, when the circumstances described become his own, he will be prudent. I hope he may. There is no reason whatever why he should not. Those among whom he works will respect and even like him the better for it— and those for whom he works will of course do so. He will have every facility for saving his money, which will be paid to him in comparatively large sums, by cheques.

Perhaps he will do so. I am bound to tell him that I have my doubts about it. I shall very much respect him if he does; but, judging from the habits of others of his class, and from the experience of those who know the colony, I think that he will take his cheque to a public-house, give it to the publican, get drunk, and remain so till the publican tells him that the cheque has been consumed. The publican will probably let him eat and drink for a fortnight, and will then turn him out penniless, to begin again. He will begin again, and repeat the same folly time after time, till he will teach himself to think that it is the normal condition of his life.

A Queensland gentleman told me the story of a certain shearer who had shorn for him year after year, and had always gone through the same process of "knocking down his cheque", as the work is technically called. He liked the man, and on one occasion remonstrated with him as he handed him the paper, explaining to him the madness of the proceeding. Would he not on that occasion be content to get drunk only on a portion of his money, and put the remainder into a savings-bank? No; the man said that when he had earned his money he liked to feel that he could do what he pleased with it.

So he took his cheque—and started for the nearest town. On the following day he returned—to the astonishment of his employer, who knew that the knocking down of so substantial a cheque should have occupied perhaps three weeks—and told his story. Having a little silver in his pocket, and having thought much of what had been said to him, he had "planted" his cheque when he found himself near the town. In the language of the colonies, to plant a thing is to hide it. He had planted his cheque, and gone on to the publican with his silver.

To set to work to get drunk was a matter of course. He did get drunk— but the publican seemed to have had some doubt as to the propriety of supplying him freely. Why had not the man brought out his cheque in the usual manly way at once, instead of paying with loose silver for a few "nobblers" for himself and the company? The publican put him to bed drunk—stretching him out on some bunk or board in the customary hospitable manner; but he had his suspicions. Could it be that his old friend should have no cheque after shearing? It behoved him, at any rate, to know. The knocking down of an imaginary cheque would be dreadful to the publican.

So the publican stripped him and examined all his clothing, looked into his boots, and felt well through the possible secrets of every garment. The man, though drunk and drugged, was not so drunk or drugged but what he knew and understood the proceeding. He had not paid enough for a sufficient amount of drugs and liquor to make him absolutely senseless. The cheque had been securely planted, and nothing was found. On the next morning he was turned out ignominiously by the justly indignant owner of the house; but in the tree by the roadside he found his cheque, and returned with it to the station a wiser and a better man. (I,9)

• • •

The labourer who can live and save his money, who can refrain from knocking down his cheque, may no doubt in Queensland become the real lord of all around him and dwell on his own land in actual independence. As far as I have seen the lives of such men, they never want for food—are never without abundance of food. Meat and tea and bread they always have in their houses. The houses themselves are often rough—sheds at first made of bark till the free-selecter can with his own hands put up some stronger and more endurable edifice; but they are never so squalid as are many of our cottages at home. For a labouring man, such as I have described, life in Queensland is infinitely better than life at home. It is sometimes very rough, and must sometimes be very solitary. And Queensland is very hot. But there is plenty to eat and drink; —work is well remunerated;—and the working man, if he can refrain from drink, may hold his own in Queensland, and may enjoy as much independence as is given to any man in this world. (I,9)

THE SHEEPHERDER

When the stranger asks whence came these country gentlemen, whom he sees occasionally at the clubs and dinner-tables in Melbourne, exactly as he finds those in England up in London during the winter frosts, or in the month of May, he is invariably told that they or their fathers made their own fortunes. This man and that and the other came over perhaps from Tasmania, in the early days, joint owners of a small flock of sheep. They generally claim to have suffered every adversity with which Providence and unjust legislators could inflict a wretched victim; and, as the result, each owns so many thousand horned cattle, so many tens of thousand sheep, so many square miles of country, and so many thousands a year. Most of them have, I think, originally come out of Scotland. When you hear an absent acquaintance spoken of as "Mac", you will not at all know who is meant, but you may safely conclude that it is some prosperous individual. Some were butchers, drovers, or shepherds themselves but a few years since. But they now form an established aristocracy, with very conservative feelings, and are quickly becoming as firm a country party as that which is formed by our squirearchy at home. (I, 30)

• • •

Undoubtedly the staple of Australian wealth is wool, and the growers and buyers and sellers of Australian wool are the chief men of the colonies. In Queensland, when I was there, six out of the seven ministers of the Crown were squatters, men owning runs for sheep or cattle. The cattle are reared chiefly for home consumption. The wool is all exported. As wool goes up or down in the London markets, so does the prosperity of Australia vacillate. Any panic in commercial matters of Europe which brings down the price of wool—as panics have done most cruelly—half ruins the colonies. Sheep sink in value from 10s. and 7s. 6d. a head to

4*s*. Squatters' runs become valueless and unsaleable, and the smaller squatters, who are almost invariably in debt to the merchants, have to vanish. Then, when trade becomes steady again and wool rises, sheep again resume their former value, and the rich men who during the panic have taken up almost deserted sheep-walks become richer and richer.

The great drawback to the squatter's prosperity is to be found in the fact that a large proportion of them commence a great business with very insufficient capital. A man with £5,000 undertakes to pay £30,000 for a run, and finds himself enabled to enter in upon the possession of perhaps forty thousand sheep and the head station or house which has been built. To all outward appearance he is the owner. He manages everything. He employs and pays the various hands. He puts up fences and erects washpools. He buys and sells flocks. He makes great bales of wool, which he sends to Sydney, to Melbourne, or to London, as he pleases. Any rise in the price of wool is his good fortune, any fall is his calamity. But still he is little more than the manager for others. He has probably bought his run from a bank or from a merchant's house which has held a mortgage on it before, and the mortgage is continued. He has simply paid away the £5,000 to make the security of the mortgage commercially safe. At home when we speak of mortgaged property we allude as a rule to some real estate in land or houses. The squatter's real estate is generally very small—and, as I shall explain presently, the smaller the better. The property mortgaged consists of the squatter's sheep—and of his precarious right to feed his flocks on certain large tracts of land, which are the property of the public, and which are for the most part open to purchase. He is not therefore in reality left to himself in the management of his business, as would be a landowner in England who had mortgaged the land which he either farmed himself or let to a tenant. In such case the security of the mortgage would rest on the land, and the farmer would conduct his farming operations without let or hindrance.

It is far otherwise with the squatter. The security he has given rests on his wool, and the price of his wool therefore must pass through the hands of the merchant to whom the debt is due. Nor can he lessen his stock of sheep without accounting to the merchant for the price of the sheep sold. The merchant is of course bound to see that the security on which his money has been advanced is not impaired. Consequently the whole produce of the run goes into the merchant's hands. When the wool is sent off—say direct to London—an estimated sum on account of its value is placed to the squatter's credit. When the wool has been sold the balance is also placed to his credit. But the money does not come into his hands. The same rule prevails very generally in regard to sheep sold. Consequently the squatter's produce all goes from him, and he is driven to draw upon the merchant for the money necessary to maintain his station, to pay his wages, and to live.

It would appear at first sight as though the squatter could lose nothing by such an arrangement. As soon as the merchant receives the money for the wool, the squatter ceases to be charged with interest for so much. And when a sum is advanced to him, he again pays interest for so much—according to the terms which may exist between him and the merchant. The rate of interest may be eight, nine, or ten per cent., according to the value of the original security. But in addition to this the merchant adds a commission of two and a half per cent. on every new advance—so that the squatter in giving up his produce pays off a debt bearing say eight per cent interest, and in drawing money to defray his expenses incurs fresh debt at say ten and a half per cent. interest.

If things go well with him, he may no doubt free himself even at this rate. If he can sell his wool and sheep every year for £6,000, and carry on his station for £3,000, he will gradually—but very slowly—lessen his debt in spite of the interest which he pays. And he will live and the merchant will probably not disturb him. If everything should go well with him—if his ewes be prolific, if diseases do not decimate his flock, if neither droughts nor floods oppress him, if wool maintain its price, if he cling to his work and be able to deny himself the recreation of long absences from his station, he may succeed in working himself free.

But against a man so circumstanced the chances are very strong. Sheep are subject to diseases. Lambing is not always prosperous. Drought and floods do prevail in Australia. And the price of wool vacillates wonderfully—very wonderfully to the eyes of a noncommercial man who observes that whatever happens in the world men still wear coats and trousers. And when these misfortunes come they fall altogether on the squatter who has begun by owning only one-sixth of the property, and not at all on the merchant who has owned the other five-sixths. At such periods—when misfortune comes—the squatter's debt begins to swell instead of dwindle. The produce will not pay for the expenses and the ever-running interest. The thousands down in the book begin to augment, and the merchant begins to see that he must secure himself. Then the station passes into other hands—into the hands probably of some huge station-owner, who, having commenced life as a shepherd or a drover, has now stations of his own all over the colonies, and money to advance on all such properties—and our friend with his £5,000 vanishes away, or becomes perhaps the manager with a fixed salary of the very sheep which he used to consider his own.

For a squatter of the true commercial kind not to owe money to his merchant or his banker is an unusual circumstance—unless he be one who has stuck to his work till he is able to lend instead of borrow. The normal, and I may almost say the proper, condition of a squatter is indebtedness to some amount. The business of squatting would be very restricted, country life in Australia very different from what it is, the amount of wool produced for the benefit of the world woefully diminished, and the extension of enterprise over new lands altogether checked, if no capital were to be invested in the pursuit of squatting except that owned by the squatters themselves. No doubt this, the greatest interest of Australia, has been created and fostered by the combination of squatters and merchants. If the squatter commencing business can do so owing no more than half the value of his run he will probably do well, and in time pay off his debt. If the man with £5,000 will content himself with 12,000 sheep instead of 40,000 and will borrow another £5,000 instead of £25,000, he will find that there is something like a fair partnership between himself and the merchant, and that gradually his partner will be unnecessary to him. His partner, while the partnership lasts, will be getting at least ten per cent. for his money, but in such a condition of things the squatter will get twenty per cent. for his money. No doubt there will still be risks, from which the town partner will be comparatively free—but unless there come heavy misfortunes indeed these risks will not break the squatter's back if his burden be no heavier than that above described.

The amount of debt in some stations is enormous, and the total interest paid, including bank charges, commission, and what not, frequently amounts to twenty per cent. When this state of things arises, the nominal squatter enjoys a certain security arising from the ambitious importance of his indebtedness—due even to his own absolute insolvency. Were the merchant to sell him up and get rid of him, more than half the debt must be written off as absolutely bad. In such cases it may be better to maintain the squatter, on condition that he will work at the station. The squatter is maintained—and lives like other squatters a jolly life. The rate at which his house is kept will depend rather on the number of the sheep to be shorn than on his own income. He has no income, but the station is maintained, and among the expenses of the station are his wife's dresses and his own brandy and water.

I don't know that there can be a much happier life than that of a squatter, if the man be fairly prosperous, and have natural aptitudes for country occupations. He should be able to ride and to shoot—and to sit in a buggy all day without inconvenience. He should be social—for he must entertain often and be entertained by other squatters; but he must be indifferent to society, for he will live away from towns and be often alone with his family. He must be able to command men, and must do so in a frank and easy fashion—not arrogating to himself any great superiority, but with full power to let those around him know that he is master. He must prefer plenty to luxury, and be content to have things about him a little rough. He must be able to brave troubles—for a squatter has many troubles. Sheep will go amiss. Lambs will die. Shearers will sometimes drink. And the bullocks with the most needed supplies will not always arrive as soon as they are expected. And, above all things, the squatter should like mutton.

In squatters' houses plenty always prevails, but that plenty often depends upon the sheep-fold. If a man have these gifts, and be young and energetic when he begins the work, he will not have chosen badly in becoming a squatter. The sense of ownership and mastery, the conviction that he is the head and chief of what is going on around; the absence of any necessity of asking leave or submitting to others—these things in themselves add a charm to life. The squatter owes obedience to none, and allegiance only to the merchant—who asks no questions so long as the debt be reduced or not increased. He gets up when he pleases and goes to bed when he likes. Though he should not own an acre of the land around him, he may do what he pleases with all that he sees. He may put up fences and knock them down. He probably lives in the middle of a forest—his life is always called life in the bush—and he may cut down any tree that he fancies. He has always horses to ride, and a buggy to sit in, and birds to shoot at, and kangaroos to ride after. He goes where he likes, and nobody questions him. There is probably no one so big as himself within twenty miles of him, and he is proud of the conviction that he knows how to wash sheep better than any squatter in the colony. But the joy that mostly endears his life to him is the joy that he need not dress for dinner. (I, 5)

• • •

It was a very pleasant life that I led at these stations. I like tobacco and brandy and water, with an easy-chair out on a verandah, and my slippers on my feet. And I like men who are energetic and stand up for themselves and their own properties. I like having horses to ride and kangaroos to hunt, and sheep became quite a fascination to me as a subject of conversation. And I liked that roaming from one house to another—with a perfect conviction that five minutes would make me intimate with the next batch of strangers. Men in these Colonies are never ashamed of their poverty; nor are they often proud of their wealth. In all country life in Australia there is an absence of any ostentation or striving after effect—which is delightful. Such as their life is, the squatters share it with you, giving you, as is fitting for a stranger, the best they have to give. (I, 5, 6)

APPRENTICESHIP
Attached to the station there is always a second home called the barracks, or the cottage, in which the young men have their rooms. There

are frequently one or two such young men attached to a sheep-station, either learning their business or earning salaries as superintendents. According to the terms of intimacy existing, or to the arrangements made, these men live with the squatter's family or have a separate table of their own. They live a life of plenty, freedom, and hard work, but one which is not surrounded by the comforts which young men require at home. Two or three share the same room, and the washing apparatus is chiefly supplied by the neighbouring creek. Tubs are scarce among them, but bathing is almost a rule of life. They are up and generally on horseback by daylight, and spend their time in riding about after sheep.

The general idyllic idea of Arcadian shepherd-life, which teaches us to believe that Tityrus lies under a beech-tree most of his hours, playing on his reed and "spooning" Phyllis, is very unlike the truth in Australian pastures. Corin is nearer the mark when he tells Touchstone of his greasy hands. It is a life, even for the upper shepherd of gentle birth and sufficient means, of unremitting labour amidst dust and grease, amidst fleeces and carcasses. The working squatter, or the squatter's working assistant, must be a man capable of ignoring the delicacies of a soft way of living. He must endure clouds of dust, and be not averse to touch tar and oil, wool, and skins. He should be able to catch a sheep and handle him almost as a nurse does a baby. He should learn to kill a sheep, and wash a sheep, and shear a sheep. He should tell a sheep's age by his mouth— almost by his look. He should know his breeding, and the quality of his wool. He should be able to muster sheep—collect them in together from the vast pastures on which they feed, and above all he should be able to count them.

He must be handy with horses—doing anything which has to be done for himself. He must catch his own horse—for the horses live on grass, turned out in paddocks—and saddle him. The animal probably is never shod, never groomed, and is ignorant of corn. And the young man must be able to sit his horse—which perhaps is more than most young men could do in England—for it may be that the sportive beast will buck with the young man, jumping up into the air with his head between his legs, giving his rider as he does so such a blow by the contraction of his loins as will make any but an Australian young man sore all over for a week, even if he be not made sore for much longer time by being sent far over the brute's head.

This young man on a station must have many accomplishments, much knowledge, great capability; and in return for these things he gets his rations, and perhaps £100 per annum, perhaps £50, and perhaps nothing. But he lives a free, pleasant life in the open air. He has the scolding of many men, which is always pleasant; and nobody scolds him, which is pleasanter. He has plenty and no care about it. He is never driven to calculate whether he can afford himself a dinner—as is often done by young men at home who have dress coats to wear and polished leather boots for happy occasions. He has always a horse to ride, or two or three, if he needs them. His salary is small, but he has nothing to buy—except moleskin trousers and flannel shirts. He lives in the open air, has a good digestion, and sleeps the sleep of the just. After a time he probably works himself up into some partnership—and has always before him the hope that the day will come in which he too will be a master squatter. (I, 6)

Trollope extensively discusses gold in Australia, which made the fortunes of a great many men over time, beginning after the 1849 discoveries in California. The story is a fascinating one, and it is tempting to wonder whether Magwitch could have struck it rich in that way: he says he did things other than sheepherding. But the chronology we believe applies in analyzing *Great Expectations* would have had Magwitch returning to England in the late 1830s, well before this aspect of the Australian economy began to develop.

Trollope's splendid novel, *John Caldigate* (1879), tells of a fortune made in Australian gold.

QUESTIONS AND TOPICS FOR DISCUSSION

1. Note the pitfalls of life for the worker in Australia. A shepherd was considered the lowest form of human existence, and Magwitch testifies to many hours alone in a shepherd's hut. How do these facts influence your appraisal of Magwitch as a man?

2. Compeyson evidently never lost track of Magwitch and was ready to follow him back to England on short notice. Given the enormous size of the Australian region they were in, how might you account for his ability to keep up with his colleague?

3. Why is it important for the reader to appreciate how Magwitch came to have money?

SUGGESTED READINGS AND WORKS CITED

Atkinson, James. *An Account of the State of Agriculture and Grazing in New South Wales*. London: J. Cross, 1826.

Breton, William H. *Excursions in New South Wales, Western Australia and Van Diemen's Land, 1830–33*. London: R. Bentley, 1833.

Clark, C. Manning H. *A History of Australia*. Michael Cathcart, abr. Melbourne: University Press; New York: Specialized Book Service, 1993.

Collins, David. *An Account of the English Colony in New South Wales* (1798, 1802), 2 vols. Adelaide: Libraries Board of South Australia, 1971, reprint.

Griffiths, Arthur. *The History and Romance of Crime from the Earliest Times to the Present Day*. London: The Grolier Society, n.d., prior to 1915.

Harris, Alexander. *The Emigrant Family: or, The Story of an Australian Settler*. London: n.p., 1849; W. S. Ramson, ed., Canberra: Australia National University Press, 1967, reprint.

———. *Settlers and Convicts, or Recollections of Sixteen Years' Labour in the Australian Backwoods*. London: n.p., 1847; C.M.H. Clark, ed., Carlton, Victoria: University Press, 1977, reprint.

Haygarth, Henry W. *Recollections of Bush Life in Australia, During a Residence of Eight Years in the Interior*. London: J. Murray, 1861.

Hughes, Robert. *The Fatal Shore: The Epic of Australia's Founding*. New York: Vintage Books, a div. of Random House, 1988.

Parker, Henry Walter. *The Rise, Progress, and Present State of Van Dieman's Land with Advice to Emigrants. Also, a Chapter on Convicts, Showing the Efficacy of Transportation as a Secondary Punishment*. London: J Cross and Simpkin and Marshall, 1833.

Trollope, Anthony. *Australia*. 2 vols. paperback. Gloucester: Alan Sutton Publishing, 1987 (abstracting the Australian sections from *Australia and New Zealand*. London: Chapman & Hall, 1873). Reprint from *Australia and New Zealand* (1873); London: Dawson's of Pall Mall, 1968.
———. *John Caldigate*. London: Chapman & Hall, 1879.

8

The Bow Street Police

At the time period in which *Great Expectations* is set, England had no effective, centralized police force. An impetus for its organization came from the notorious Gordon Riots of 1780, when several thousand people invaded London, ostensibly to protest proposals to reduce legal strictures on Roman Catholics, and caused a great deal of damage before the army militia was called out to deal with them. When they did, several hundred lives were lost. The story is told in detail in Dickens's *Barnaby Rudge*.

At last, London got professional police when Sir Robert Peel obtained passage of the Police Act of June 1829. For long after, members of the new uniformed force were called "Peelers," and they are still called "Bobbys." Until then, most law enforcement came from the parish watchmen known as "Charlies." Advanced in age and likely to be feeble, their deterrence of crime was modest at best. So, the magistrates relied on a class of informers and private bounty hunters, known as "thief-takers." (Chapter 5 includes a passage describing a successful thief-taker's efforts to apprehend a coiner.) There was one "bright" spot: the red-coats of the little police force stationed at and operating out of the Bow Street Police-Office. They were, at any rate, full-time professionals, though their methods for detecting and solving crimes and apprehending criminals were rudimentary compared with what followed.

We cannot assume there was no adequate police in England before 1829, of course: someone captured Magwitch and Compeyson before the story in *Great Expectations* began; someone caught Estella's mother Molly and brought her to trial; someone was on the spot to apprehend the criminals who came in desperation to seek the aid of lawyer Jaggers. But Dickens stresses the "Bow Street boys," and they are worth pausing to consider briefly.

Dickens pictures these early policemen, not very flatteringly, when they come to investigate the assault on Mrs. Joe:

> [They] did pretty much what I have heard and read of like authorities doing in other such cases. They took up several obviously wrong people, and they ran their heads very hard against wrong ideas, and persisted in trying to fit the circumstances to the ideas, instead of trying to extract ideas from the circumstances. Also, they stood about the door of the Jolly Bargemen, with knowing and reserved looks that filled the whole neighbourhood with admiration; and they had a mysterious manner of taking their drink, that was almost as good as taking the culprit. But not quite, for they never did it. (16)

Dickens had exposed his readers to the Bow Street Office long before, in his second novel, *Oliver Twist*, written when the Office was still in being. The police in this case seem competent, though their mission is frustrated by a signal lack of cooperation by the gentry and manifold confusion on the part of the servants. Bill Sikes has brought Oliver along on a burglary attempt in Chertsey, a London suburb. It has been foiled by servants in the house, and Oliver, wounded, has been brought in and put to bed. The sound of wheels is heard. "It's the runners!"

FROM CHARLES DICKENS, *OLIVER TWIST*
(London: Bentley, 1836)

"Open the door," replied a man outside; "it's the officers from Bow Street, as was sent to, to-day." . . .

The man who had knocked at the door, was a stout personage of middle height, aged about fifty: with shiny black hair, cropped pretty close; half-whiskers, a round face, and sharp eyes. The other was a red-headed, bony man, in top-boots; with a rather ill-favoured countenance, and a turned-up, sinister-looking nose. . . .

Mr Blathers made a bow. Being desired to sit down, he put his hat on the floor, and taking a chair, motioned Duff to do the same. The latter gentleman, who did not appear quite so much accustomed to good society, or quite so much at his ease in it—one of the two—seated himself, after undergoing several muscular affections of the limbs, and forced the head of his stick into his mouth, with some embarrassment. . . .

"Now, what is this, about this here boy that the servants are a-talking on?" said Blathers.

"Nothing at all," replied the doctor. "One of the frightened servants chose to take it into his head, that he had something to do with this attempt to break into the house; but it's nonsense: sheer absurdity."

"Wery easy disposed of, if it is," remarked Duff.

"What he says is quite correct," observed Blathers, nodding his head in a confirmatory way, and playing carelessly with the handcuffs, as if they were a pair of castanets. "Who is the boy? What account does he give of himself? Where did he come from? He didn't drop out of the clouds, did he, master?"

"Of course not," replied the doctor, with a nervous glance at the two ladies. "I know his whole history: but we can talk about that presently. You would like, first, to see the place where the thieves made their attempt, I suppose?"

"Certainly," rejoined Mr Blathers. "We had better inspect the premises first, and examine the servants arterwards. That's the usual way of doing business."

Lights were then procured; and Messrs Blathers and Duff, attended by the native constable, Brittles, Giles, and everybody else in short, went into the little room at the end of the passage and looked out at the window; and afterwards went round by way of the lawn, and looked in at the window; and after that, had a candle handed out to inspect the shutter with; and after that, a lantern to trace the footsteps with; and after that, a pitchfork to poke the bushes with. This done, amidst the breathless interest of all beholders, they came in again; and Mr Giles and Brittles were put through a melodramatic representation of their share in the previous night's adventures: which they performed some six times over: contradicting each other, in not more than one important respect, the first time, and in not more than a dozen the last. This consummation being arrived at, Blathers and Duff cleared the room, and held a long council together, compared with which, for secrecy and solemnity, a consultation of great doctors on the knottiest point in medicine, would be mere child's play. . . .

"Well, master," said Blathers, entering the room followed by his colleague, and making the door fast, before he said any more. "This warn't a put-up thing."

"And what the devil's a put-up thing?" demanded the doctor, impatiently.

"We call it a put-up robbery, ladies," said Blathers, turning to them, as if he pitied their ignorance, but had a contempt for the doctor's, "when the servants is in it."

"Nobody suspected them, in this case," said Mrs Maylie.

"Wery likely not, ma'am," replied Blathers; "but they might have been in it, for all that."

"More likely on that wery account," said Duff.

"We find it was a town hand," said Blathers, continuing his report; "for the style of work is first-rate."

"Wery pretty indeed it is," remarked Duff, in an undertone.

"There was two of 'em in it," continued Blathers; "and they had a boy with 'em' that's plain from the size of the window. That's all to be said at present." (31)

Percy Fitzgerald combines a survey of the theater district (see Chapter 9) with a picture of Bow Street police activity. Some of the latter was foreshadowed by Dickens in his "The Prisoners' Van" in *Sketches by Boz*. The depictions, in both cases, are of the kinds of unfortunates who had failed to achieve legal representation by the redoubtable Jaggers and had been sentenced to a term in Newgate.

FROM PERCY FITZGERALD, *CHRONICLES OF BOW STREET POLICE-OFFICE*
(London: Chapman & Hall, 1888)

But there is a large section of the community for which none of these things [in the theater district] offer so much interest as does an important building which has lately been reared opposite Covent Garden Theatre. For such a class the "Bow Street" office suggests strange and painful associations—an interest that is extended often to the respectable workingman's family. In such is commonly found some misguided youth, whom bad company or bad connections has brought to sad acquaintance with the initial processes of the law as established at Bow Street.

A few years ago there used to be a painful and not undramatic scene witnessed every afternoon in the street, which furnished a sort of excitement for the motley and uncleanly crowd which never failed to attend.

This was the arrival of the funereal-looking prison-van in front of the straitened little office door. Clustered round it, could be seen patiently waiting as strange a miscellany as could be conceived. It was then that the curious observer could study the habitual criminal "type," and note how mysteriously habits of crime seemed to impress revealing marks and tokens on face, expression, bearing, manner, dress. In older followers this evidence was not so conspicuous; but there was in the juvenile section, in the youths and girls—a strange and revolting air of precocity—a hardened air that would strike even the most careless.

When at length the moment arrived, the circle narrowed, and the draggled procession began to emerge, each item having a separate display of his own. Then passed by, with an assumed bearing that was almost dramatic, the reckless prisoners, each being saluted with encouraging cries from the friends who had, with a touching loyalty, come to see him "off." Some "danced out," and tripped into the van with a familiar air; others, who had not recovered from the surprise of their sentence, passed on with a sturdy scowl.

More painful was the shame of the decently-dressed first offender—victim, it might be, of circumstances, who shrank from the unclean, but really indifferent, gaze of the throng. For *them* even the shelter of the van was a relief. Almost as characteristic was the stolid *insouciant* bearing of the police in charge, who attended each prisoner forth with a carelessness that came of strength and security. The last guardian—the necessary blue papers in his hand—closed the strange defile, and locked himself in with the rest. Then came the strange cries of comfort and farewell from their "pals," those of experience uttering their words under the very floor of the van, and receiving some sort of response. And thus "Black Maria," heavily laden, and drawn by powerful steeds, reels off and sways as she moves, to discharge her load at one of the great prisons.

This strange and indecent scene had, until a few years ago, been repeated daily from the beginning of the century. It seems to have been an agreeable break in the day. Yet it was doing its part in the wholesale education in crime. It made familiar and recognized what ought to have been mysterious and unknown. Instead of being a vulgar show to be lightened by the encouragement of friends and "pals," it would have been far more wholesome that the criminal on sentence should have sunk out of view and have been at once lost to society. Happily, with the opening of new Bow Street offices in 1881, this salutary principle was recognized, and the degrading scene is no longer witnessed. (2–5)

SUGGESTED READINGS AND WORKS CITED

Armitage, G. *The History of the Bow Street Runners 1729–1829*. London: Wishart & Co., 1932.

Colquhoun, Patrick. *A Treatise on the Police of the Metropolis*. London: H. Fry for C. Dilly, 1797.

Dickens, Charles. "Criminal Courts," "A Visit to Newgate," and "The Prisoners' Van" in *Sketches by Boz*. London: Macrone, 1836; Michael Slater, ed. London: J. M. Dent, 1994, reprint.

———. *Oliver Twist*. London: Bentley, 1836.

———. *Barnaby Rudge*. London: Bentley, 1841.

Ewens, William Thomas. *Thirty Years at Bow Street Police Court*. London: T. Werner Laurie, 1924.

Fielding, Henry. *An Enquiry into the Causes of the Late Increase of Robbers*. London: A. Millar, 1751.

Fielding, John. *A Plan for Preventing Robberies within Twenty Miles of London*. London: A. Millar, 1755.

Fitzgerald, Percy. *Chronicles of Bow Street Police-Office*. London: Chapman & Hall, 1888.

Hodder, George. *Sketches of Life and Character: Taken at the Police Court. [Bow Street]*. London: Sherwood and Bowyer, 1845.

Sadleir, John. *Recollections of a Victorian Police Officer*. Melbourne: G. Robertson, 1913.

9

English Private Theaters in the Early Nineteenth Century

In the early nineteenth century, English drama was in decline. There were no great actors on the boards to keep vivid the tradition of David Garrick and Edmund Kean. A clear distinction was made between "legitimate" theater—a term that has come down to us as a loose characterization of "serious" theatrical effort, usually not musical—and "illegitimate" theater. Originally, the legitimate article was performed only in the three theaters holding a royal patent: Covent Garden, Drury Lane, and, in the summer, the Haymarket. Illegimate performances occurred in a number of minor theaters all across London, which catered to popular taste. These latter theaters were not allowed to perform straight plays. They circumvented the restriction by adding music and spectacle. "Melodrama," drama with music, became highly popular. For the literati, Shakespeare and Richard Brinsley Sheridan were the iconic playwrights of the day.

Serious drama in London did not fill the enormous patent theaters. The taste of the time inclined more towards spectaculars, pantomimes, animal acts, and melodrama, the latter appreciated for its straightforward, simple moral line that pitted good against evil and always saw the triumph of the good. A typical theater evening would include melodrama, a farce, a juggler, and so on, and seats could be had at half price after 9 P.M. The atmosphere in the houses was likely to be disorderly. Audiences voiced their pleasure and their disapprobation vociferously. Acting styles had to be flamboyant and large-scale for the actors to be heard at all.

There were three seating areas in the theaters: the cheap and noisy gallery, the upper-scale boxes whose occupants could come and go as they chose and who mostly stayed away because of the disreputable character of most of what went on; and the pit, later known as the stalls, for the middle class, youth, and the slightly raffish literary and artistic denizens of the city. In these times, the auditorium remained illuminated. Only later in the century, when theaters were smaller and more orderly, did audiences sit in the dark to watch the lit-up stage.

Outside London, there were provincial patent theaters, called Theatres Royal. These had been granted licenses to be in business—letters patent—after the Restoration in 1660. There were also troupes of strolling players, like the Crummles company in Dickens's *Nicholas Nickleby*.

A major change occurred in 1843, when the Theatre Regulation Act was passed, adopting recommendations of a Royal Commission appointed in 1832 to inquire into the state of the drama in England. The act broke the patented theaters' monopoly and allowed all kinds of houses to present all kinds of plays and attractions. The Lord Chamberlain's jurisdiction to approve performances was strengthened, and an expectation of theatrical revival began to spread. But it did not come at once: only in the 1850s and 1860s did greater stage realism and refurbished and more elegant houses begin to win back fastidious audiences. The pastiche of an earlier year was replaced by a single play, which often had a "run" of consecutive performances, sometimes a long one. Near the end of the century, exceptional dramatists began to appear, Arthur Pinero, Oscar Wilde, George Bernard Shaw, and W. S. Gilbert among them. The great Henrik Ibsen's influence began to be strongly felt.

Dickens was himself an accomplished actor. But for the accident of a serious cold the day he was to audition, he might have gone on the stage instead of establishing a writing career. His love of the life endured all his days, and he frequently directed, produced, and starred in plays, some of them the classics of Shakespeare, Congreve, Sheridan, and the like, and some newly created by colleagues like Wilkie Collins and Mark Lemon. In his early days, when he worked as a newspaper reporter, he reviewed many dramatic presentations, usually with sympathy. These reviews are assembled in abridged form in the author's *Everyone in Dickens*.

Authentic original material on the little theaters of London like the one where Wopsle/Waldengarver tried out his *Hamlet* is rare. These little theaters were run by speculators trading on the susceptibility of stage-struck youngsters and fatuous old hands, who were willing to pay hard cash for the opportunity to go onstage in a famous part. The houses were not liked by the authorities: in July 1829, the Mansion House magistrate's court heard evidence from a policeman who had observed "romping and very indecent conduct" among the patrons of the Catherine Street Theatre. Although there are plenty of performance reviews in papers like John Forster's *Examiner* and *The Morning Chronicle*, there is no one to take us backstage except Dickens himself. Michael Slater, introducing Dickens's sketch of the backstage at Catherine Street, calls our attention to its "harsh and scornful tone," which Slater thought "may result from a determination to distance himself from a less than reputable aspect of his own recent past. . . . Dickens may have acted in private theatres" (MS 120).

Wopsle, of course, is no stage-struck youngster, but stage-struck he clearly seems always to have been. His frustration during service as a church clerk who longed for the limelight is a highlight of his early characterization during Christmas Dinner at the Gargerys':

> Mr Wopsle, united to a Roman nose and a large shining bald forehead, had a deep voice which he was uncommonly proud of; indeed it was understood among his acquaintance that if you could only give him his head, he would read the clergyman into fits; he himself confessed that if the Church was "thrown open," meaning to competition, he would not despair of making his mark in it. The Church not being "thrown open," he was, as I have said, our clerk. But he punished the Amens tremendously; and when he gave out the psalm—always giving the whole verse—he looked all around the congregation first, as much as to say, "You have heard our friend overhead; oblige me with your opinion of this style!" (4)

THE TYPICAL LONDON PRIVATE THEATER

The sketch extracted below appeared in London's *The Evening Chronicle* of August 11, 1835, as one of its "Sketches of London," the writer's name being given as "Boz." It was subsequently included as one of a series of "Scenes" in the one-volume edition of *Sketches by Boz*. "Boz" is now known to the world as Charles Dickens. The picture presented is factual: Dickens was a fanatically punctilious reporter, and we can be confident that what he depicted is what he saw on his visit to Catherine Street. Clues in *Great Expectations*, like the dresser who accosts Pip and Herbert, tell us that the following piece closely resembles his idea of what happened backstage at the Waldengarver *Hamlet*.

FROM CHARLES DICKENS, *SKETCHES BY BOZ*
(London: Macrone, 1836)

PRIVATE THEATRES
"Richard the Third.—Duke of Glo'ster, *2l*; Earl of Richmond, *1l*; Duke of Buckingham, *15s*; Catesby, *12s*; Tressel, *10s. 6d.*; Lord Stanley, *5s*; Lord Mayor of London, *2s. 6d.*"

Such are the written placards wafered up in the gentlemen's dressing room, or the green room (where there is any), at a private theatre; and such are the sums extracted from the shop till, or overcharged in the office expenditure, by the donkeys who are prevailed upon to pay for permission to exhibit their lamentable ignorance and boobyism on the stage of a private theatre. This they do, in proportion to the scope afforded by the character for the display of their imbecility. For instance, the Duke of Glo'ster is well worth two pounds, because he has it all to himself; he must wear a real sword, and what is better still, he must draw it several times in the course of the piece. The soliloquies alone are well worth fifteen shillings; then there is the stabbing King Henry—decidedly cheap at three-and-sixpence, that's eighteen-and-sixpence; bullying the coffin bearers—say eighteen-pence, though it's worth much more—that's a pound. Then the love scene with Lady Ann, and the bustle of the fourth act can't be dear at ten shillings more—that's only one pound ten, including the "off with his head!"—which is sure to bring down the applause, and it is very easy to do—"Orf with his ed" (very quick and loud; —then slow and sneeringly)—"So much for Bu-u-u-uckingham!" Lay the emphasis on the "uck"; get yourself gradually into a corner, and work with your right hand, while you're saying it, as if you were feeling your way, and it's sure to do. The tent scene is confessedly worth half-a-sovereign, and so you have the fight in, gratis, and everybody knows what an effect may be produced by a good combat. One—two—three—four—over; then, one—two—three—four—under; then thrust; then dodge and slide about; then fall down on one knee; then fight upon it, and then get up again and stagger. You may keep on doing this, as long as it seems to take—say ten minutes—and then fall down (backwards, if you can manage it without hurting yourself), and die game: nothing like it for producing an effect. They always do it at Astley's and Sadler's Wells, and if they don't know how to do this sort of thing, who in the world does? A small child, or a female in white, increases the interest of a combat materially—indeed, we are not aware that a regular legitimate terrific broadsword combat could be done without; but it would be rather diffi-cult, and somewhat unusual, to introduce this effect in the last scene of Richard the Third, so the only thing to be done is, just to make the best of a bad bargain, and be as long as possible fighting it out.

The principal patrons of private theatres are dirty boys, low copying clerks in attorneys' offices, capacious-headed youths from city counting houses, Jews whose business, as lenders of fancy dresses, is a sure pass-port to the amateur stage, shopboys who now and then mistake their masters' money for their own; and a choice miscellany of idle vagabonds. The proprietor of a private theatre may be an ex-scene-painter, a low coffee house keeper, a disappointed eighth-rate actor, a retired smuggler, or uncertificated bankrupt. The theatre itself may be in Catherine Street, Strand, the purlieus of the city, the neighbourhood of Gray's Inn Lane, or the vicinity of Sadler's Wells; or it may, perhaps, form the chief nui-sance of some shabby street, on the Surrey side of Waterloo Bridge.

The lady performers pay nothing for their characters, and it is needless to add, are usually selected from one class of society; the audiences are necessarily of much the same character as the performers, who receive, in return for their contributions to the management, tickets to the amount of the money they pay.

All the minor theatres in London, especially the lowest, constitute the centre of a little stage-struck neighbourhood. Each of them has an audi-ence exclusively its own; and at any you will see dropping into the pit at half price, or swaggering into the back of a box, if the price of admission be a reduced one, divers boys of from fifteen to twenty-one years of age, who throw back their coat and turn up their wristbands, after the por-traits of Count D'Orsay, hum tunes and whistle when the curtain is down, by way of persuading the people near them, that they are not at all anx-ious to have it up again, and speak familiarly of the inferior performers as Bill Such-a-one, and Ned So-and-so, or tell each other how a new piece called *The Unknown Bandit of the Invisible Cavern*, is in rehearsal; how Mister Palmer is to play *The Unknown Bandit*; how Charley Scarton is to take the part of an English sailor, and fight a broadsword combat with six unknown bandits, at one and the same time (one theatrical sailor is always equal to half a dozen men at least); how Mister Palmer and Charley Scarton are to go through a double hornpipe in fetters in the second act; how the interior of the invisible cavern is to occupy the whole extent of the stage; and other town-surprising theatrical announcements. These gentlemen are the amateurs—the *Richards, Shylocks, Beverleys*, and *Othellos*—the *Young Dorntons, Rovers, Captain Absolutes*, and *Charles Surfaces*—of a private theatre.

See them at the neighbouring public house or the theatrical coffee shop! They are the kings of the place, supposing no real performers to be present; and roll about, hats on one side, and arms akimbo, as if they had actually come into possession of eighteen shillings a week, and a share of a ticket night. If one of them does but know an Astley's super-numerary he is a happy fellow. The mingled air of envy and admiration with which his companions will regard him, as he converses familiarly with some mouldy-looking man in a fancy neckerchief, whose partially corked eyebrows, and half-rouged face, testify to the fact of his having just left the stage or the circle, sufficiently shows in what high admiration these public characters are held.

With the double view of guarding against the discovery of friends or employers, and enhancing the interest of an assumed character, by attach-ing a high-sounding name to its representative, these geniuses assume fictitious names, which are not the least amusing part of the play-bill of a private theatre. Belville, Melville, Treville, Berkeley, Randolph, Byron, St Clair, and so forth, are among the humblest; and the less imposing titles of Jenkins, Walker, Thomson, Barker, Solomons, &c., are completely laid aside. There is something imposing in this, and it is an excellent apology for shabbiness into the bargain. A shrunken, faded coat, a de-cayed hat, a patched and soiled pair of trousers—nay, even a very dirty shirt (and none of these appearances are very uncommon among the members of the *corps dramatique*), may be worn for the purpose of disguise, and to prevent any troublesome inquiries or explanations about employment and pursuits; everybody is a gentleman at large, for the occa-sion, and there are none of those unpleasant and unnecessary distinc-tions to which even genius must occasionally succumb elsewhere. As to the ladies (God bless them), they are quite above any formal absurdities; the mere circumstance of your being behind the scenes is a sufficient introduction to their society—for of course they know that none but strictly respectable persons would be admitted into that close fellowship with them, which acting engenders. They place implicit reliance on the manager, no doubt; and as to the manager, he is all affability when he knows you well,—or, in other words, when he has pocketed your money once, and entertains confident hopes of doing so again.

A quarter before eight—there will be a full house tonight—six parties in the boxes, already; four little boys and a woman in the pit; and two fiddles and a flute in the orchestra, who have got through five overtures since seven o'clock (the hour fixed for the commencement of the performances), and have just begun the sixth. There will be plenty of it, though, when it does begin, for there is enough in the bill to last six hours at least.

That gentleman in the white hat and checked shirt, brown coat and brass buttons, lounging behind the stage box on the O.P. side, is Mr Horatio St Julien, alias Jem Larkins. His line is genteel comedy—his father's, coal and potato. He *does* Alfred Highflier in the last piece, and very well he'll do it—at the price. The party of gentlemen in the opposite box, to whom he has just nodded, are friends and supporters of Mr Beverley (otherwise Loggins), the *Macbeth* of the night. You observe their attempts to appear easy and gentlemanly, each member of the party, with his feet cocked upon the cushion in front of the box! They let them do these things here, upon the same humane principle which permits poor people's children to knock double knocks at the door of an empty house—because they can't do it anywhere else. The two stout men in the centre box, with an opera glass ostentatiously placed before them, are friends of the proprietor—opulent country managers, as he confidentially informs every individual among the crew behind the curtain—opulent country managers looking out for recruits; a representation which Mr Nathan, the dresser, who is in the manager's interest, and has just arrived with the costumes, offers to confirm upon oath if required—corroborative evidence, however, is quite unnecessary for the gulls believe it at once.

The stout Jewess who has just entered is the mother of the pale bony little girl, with the necklace of blue glass beads, sitting by her; she is being brought up to "the profession." Pantomime is to be her line, and she is coming out tonight, in a hornpipe after the tragedy. The short thin man beside Mr St Julien, whose white face is so deeply seared with the small-pox, and whose dirty shirt-front is inlaid with open-work, and embossed with coral studs like ladybirds, is the low comedian and comic singer of the establishment. The remainder of the audience—a tolerably numerous one by this time—are a motley group of dupes and blackguards.

The footlights have just made their appearance: the wicks of the six little oil lamps round the only tier of boxes are being turned up, and the additional light thus afforded serves to show the presence of dirt, and absence of paint, which forms a prominent feature in the audience part of the house. As these preparations, however, announce the speedy commencement of the play, let us take a peep "behind", previous to the ringing up.

The little narrow passages beneath the stage are neither especially clean nor too brilliantly lighted; and the absence of any flooring, together with the damp mildewy smell which pervades the place, does not conduce in any great degree to their comfortable appearance. Don't fall over this plate basket—it's one of the "properties"—the caldron for the witches' cave; and the three uncouth-looking figures, with broken clothes-props in their hands, who are drinking gin and water out of a pint pot, are the weird sisters. This miserable room, lighted by candles in sconces placed at lengthened intervals round the wall, is the dressing room, common to the gentlemen performers, and the square hole in the ceiling is *the* trap door of the stage above. You will observe that the ceiling is ornamented with the beams that support the boards, and tastefully hung with cobwebs.

The characters in the tragedy are all dressed, and their own clothes are scattered in hurried confusion over the wooden dresser which surrounds the room. That snuff-shop-looking figure, in front of the glass, is *Banquo*: and the young lady with the liberal display of legs, who is kindly painting his face with a hare's foot, is dressed for *Fleance*. The large woman, who is consulting the stage directions in Cumberland's edition of *Macbeth*, is the *Lady Macbeth* of the night; she is always selected to play the part, because she is tall and stout, and *looks* a little like Mrs Siddons—at a considerable distance. That stupid-looking milksop, with light hair and bow legs—a kind of man whom you can warrant town-made—is fresh caught; he plays *Malcolm* tonight, just to accustom himself to an audience. He will get on better by degrees; he will play *Othello* in a month, and in a month more, will very probably be apprehended on a charge of embezzlement. The black-eyed female with whom he is talking so earnestly, is dressed for the "gentlewoman." It is *her* first appearance, too— in that character. The boy of fourteen who is having his eyebrows smeared with soap and whitening, is *Duncan*, King of Scotland; and the two dirty men with the corked countenances, in very old green tunics, and dirty drab boots, are the "army."

"Look sharp below there, gents," exclaims the dresser, a red-headed and red-whiskered Jew, calling through the trap, "they're a-going to ring up. The flute says he'll be blowed if he plays any more, and they're getting precious noisy in front." A general rush immediately takes place to the half dozen little steep steps leading to the stage, and the heterogeneous group are soon assembled at the side scenes, in breathless anxiety and motley confusion.

"Now," cries the manager, consulting the written list which hangs behind the first P.S. wing. "Scene 1, open country—lamps down—thunder
and lightning—all ready, White?" [This is addressed to one of the army.]
"All ready."—"Very well. Scene 2, front chamber. Is the front chamber
down?"—"Yes."—"Very well."—"Jones" [to the other army who is up in
the flies], "Hallo!"—"Wind up the open country when we ring up."—"I'll
take care."—"Scene 3, back perspective with practical bridge. Bridge
ready, White? Got the tressels there?"—"All right."

"Very well. Clear the stage;" cries the manager, hastily packing every
member of the company into the little space there is between the wings
and the wall, and one wing and another. "Places, places. Now then,
Witches—Duncan—Malcolm—bleeding officer—where's the bleeding officer?"—"Here!" replies the officer, who has been rose pinking for the
character. "Get ready, then; now, White, ring the second music bell." The
actors who are to be discovered, are hastily arranged, and the actors who
are not to be discovered place themselves, in their anxiety to peep at the
house; just where the audience can see them. The bell rings, and the orchestra, in acknowledgment of the call, play three distinct chords. The
bell rings—the tragedy (!) opens—and our description closes. (120–26)

The theater district of nineteenth-century London was a colorful,
earthy, disreputable arena, combining as it did activities in the legitimate theaters and those in the borderline emporia such as Dickens describes above, with the seedy riffraff and sad criminality
associated with the Bow Street Police-Station (discussed more fully
in Chapter 8). The flavor of the scene is well captured by one of
London's veteran observers and Dickens fanciers, Percy Fitzgerald.

FROM PERCY FITZGERALD, *CHRONICLES OF BOW STREET
POLICE-OFFICE*
(London: Chapman & Hall, 1888)

At the top of Wellington Street, and close to the more crowded portion
of the busy Strand, is to be found one of the most interesting spots in
London, where exciting dramas of real life and passion, as well as their
mimic reproduction, are daily played. This characteristic quarter has been
always the centre of criminal as well as of theatrical life. The eyes of the
actor, as well as those of the rogue, often turn to it with an almost painful
interest; and there is hardly an hour of the day during which members

of both communities may not be seen lounging opposite the buildings where their respective interests are concerned in some critical issue.

Here, within a small area, are clustered the great theatres of Drury Lane and Covent Garden, with the Lyceum, and the costumiers, as also the newspaper in which players put forward their wants, and often their merits. Close by are the greater journals in which the merits and defects of the players are dealt with, and the favourite houses of resort and refreshment—the taverns and wine-shops, which are never without the cluster of professionals, busy discussing their hopes and grievances. In short, the quarter offers as distinctly marked and interesting characteristics of its own, as do others which the metropolis offers in plenty—such as the French quarter in Soho, the Banking district in the City, the Jew quarter, and others.

Here, we come upon the entrance to the great Flower Market, lately the luckless Floral Hall, which was tried as a concert-room with equal lack of success. It has just reverted to its original purpose, and, at midnight, when the theatres have discharged their audiences, throws open its gates and begins its performance. Then the wains and carts draw up and begin unloading their fragrant burdens—all through the night the heavily laden vehicles are heard rumbling by, and by dawn every adjoining street is blocked—an extraordinary spectacle of business and industry, literally unknown to, and perhaps unthought of, by the lazy Londoner who rises late. . . .

It is just half-past five, and the grey dawn is struggling in the east to diffuse a few faint rays over the western portion of the horizon. There are but few wanderers in the street at this early hour. St Paul's, Covent Garden, chimes the hour of *six*, and the rumbling of market-carts laden with flowers and vegetables, now begins to disturb the tranquillity of the street. *Seven*, and blinds begin to be drawn up. . . . *Eleven*, and actors, who had a call for a ten o'clock rehearsal, begin to bustle into the theatre with evident symptoms of perturbation and anxiety; managers look glum, and machinists nervous, whilst the prompter glances hatchets and tomahawks at those unlucky supers who have been three minutes behind time.

Now do ladies, with pink parasols and sky-blue bonnets, hasten to Kenneth's, the dramatic agency office, for an engagement; the theatrical generally leading to a matrimonial one. *Twelve*, and Harris's shop gets thronged with votaries of the sock and buskin. Papers are read, notes are written, and criticisms spoken of. During that dreary interval invariably occurring at rehearsals, this is the spot where actors "most do congregate," and this is the tribunal where disputes, appertaining to the mimic art, are referred for decision. *One*, and the steaming vapour that exhales from the *cuisine* of the *Globe* begins to assail the nostrils of the peckish passenger. Collarless coves, with long frock coats, buttoned tight up to the throat to conceal the want of a waistcoat, now supply the cravings of nature by eagerly inhaling the savoury steam that indicates the kind of preparation going on below, thus making one sense relieve the privations of the other.

And now the business of Bow Street labours under an interregnum of several hours' duration; a dread *hiatus* occurs in its proceeding, and, with the exception of Saturday, when the treasury delays their departure, scarcely an actor can at this time be observed in this previously Thespian-thronged throughfare. The first signs of returning animation are seen in the arrival of crowds and carriages at the Covent Garden portico, waiting for the opening of the doors. On every side rings the well-known cry of "Bill of the play, gentle*men*;" the last syllable receiving, from a habit, a double allowance of emphasis. Now comes the withdrawal of bolts; the rush of many feet and the crowd disappears, a few stragglers alone remaining undecided in the avenue.

Crossing over the way to the tobacconists, we find a group of mingled amateurs and professionals chatting together at the door, or else seated upon diminutive casks, in the most theatrical and picturesque manner, imbibing the fumes of the choice cigar. Attentively perusing the playbills that decorate one side of the wall, is a tall, thin young man, with a pale countenance and dark brown hair, falling in savage profusion over his coat collar. That is the *Hamlet* of the preceding night, a would-be aspirant to dramatic fame, and who, having *once* smelt the lamps at a minor theatre, will rest not until he has succeeded in getting an engagement at one of the theatres royal. Next to him stands one who played *Laertes* on the same night, and this very day week they play *Richard* and *Richmond* together, with the combat most awfully protracted, for that night only.

But the performances have concluded, and the rumbling of carriages, hackney-coaches, and cabs is heard once more. The cry of "Ham-sandwiches, only a penny," blends most harmoniously with "Coach un-hired." Some of the company wend their way to the Coal-hole, others to the Wrekin, whilst many, with visions of rump-steaks and stout before their eyes, cross over to the Garrick. At the head of the table is Mr Fly, the chairman, an eminent hand at the bass, often going down so low that it takes him half-an-hour to get up again. To the right is the tenor, Mr Gorgon; at his elbow sits Mr Tart, a very staid individual, who always seems as if he were going to laugh and *couldn't*. Listen to what emanates from the chair. "Now, gentlemen, with your kind permission, we will attempt a glee." Loud cries of "Hear, hear," and "Bravo" resound throughout the room, and the glee is forthwith attempted. A capital glee it is, too, with plenty of ha! ha's! and clipping of monosyllables.

Bow Street, according to an old writer, took the name from its shape "running in the shape of a bent bow," as may be seen to this hour, on one side. The other side seems to have been somewhat straightened when the Opera House was built. It was once an exceedingly fashionable district, and, at its northern portion, was quite close to the country fields. About one hundred and twenty years ago it was almost as *recherché* as St James's Street and the quarter about it now. Interesting, too, are the many historical associations which make the whole area "sacred ground." What a history would be that of Covent Garden Theatre alone, with its traditions of manager Rich, Peg Woffington, Garrick, Kemble, and the terrible "O.P." Riots, down to the fatal March 5, 1856, when it was burnt to the ground, under the vulgar patronage of a "Wizard of the North."

Some amateur had a souvenir made out of the charred remains, some four inches long by two and a half broad, its massives sides of highly-polished oak giving it an imposing look. Its edges are of the orthodox dull red, its back of morocco. The title is "Theatrical Ashes," and its wooden walls were cut from a partially burnt log of oak taken from the ruins of Covent Garden Theatre, after an orgie snobbishly called a *bal masqué*. There are many amateurs at this moment busy collecting all the facts and cuttings that bear on the history of Bow Street and the adjoining Covent Garden—on "the Hummums," lately rebuilt and rejuvenated, the Bedford Head, Inigo Jones's Church, Tom Davies' shop, and the curious and eccentric beings that "hung loose" upon the society of the district.

The old antiquarian associations have been retailed at length in the innumerable topographical works on London, and scarcely concern us here. Wycherly, the dramatist, after his marriage with the Countess of Drogheda, was, according to an oft-told tale, so harassed at his fireside, that he often retired, for peace' sake, to the tavern opposite, but he was ordered to keep the windows open so that his lady might see with what company he was engaged.

The old police-office, it is believed, stood upon the site of Waller the poet's house. It is curious to think that the well-known "ham-and-beef" shop at the corner, which still displays its old tiled roof, was once "Will's Coffee House," to which the most famous wits used to resort. And in Russell Street the house still stands where Boswell was introduced to Dr Johnson. The vivacious O'Keeffe, when he first came to town, was deeply impressed by these recollections, and used to recall the speech in the "Constant Couple" where Beau Clincher talks of his going to the jubilee at Rome:—"Supposing the corner of a street—suppose it Russell Street here," &c. "Well, thought I," he adds in his natural way, "here am I at last, standing at the corner of Russell Street!"

William Lewis, the comedian, lived in the very house in Bow Street that belonged to Wilkes, the original Sir Harry Wildair in the "Constant Couple" and used the same private passage from it into Covent Garden Theatre. This Wilkes was an Irishman. Lewis also lived in another celebrated house: it was in Great Queen Street, on the right hand going to Lincoln's Inn Fields. In Queen Anne's reign it belonged to Dr Radcliffe. Sir James Thornhill, the painter, lived in the next house, and I saw the very door the subject of Dr Radcliffe's severe sarcasm against Thornhill. *"I don't care what he does with the door, so he does not paint it."*

The older Bow Street office, a "squeezed" building, which had witnessed so many dramatic scenes, having lost its purpose, was allowed to linger on for some half a dozen years. It fell into the occupation of Stinchcombe, a well-known theatrical *costumier* and wig provider, who here carried on his duties till the middle of the year 1887. About September the Duke of Bedford was busy restoring the Floral Hall close by to its original function of a flower-market. The old-fashioned Bedford Hotel, which had once flourished under Inigo Jones' cheerful Piazzas—having been abandoned and reduced to being a warehouse for the sale of potatoes and other vegetables, was clearly on its way to demolition. There was a tract of valuable space between the hotel and the police office, for both were *dos-à-dos*. In October, as was to be expected, the *costumier* Stinchcombe had gone, hoardings had been put up, and in a few weeks not a vestige of old Bow Street office was left. (PF 5–12)

SUGGESTED READINGS AND WORKS CITED

Booth, Michael. *English Melodrama*. London: H. Jenkins, 1965.

———. *Theatre in the Victorian Age*. Cambridge: Cambridge University Press, 1991.

Brooks, Peter. *The Melodramatic Imagination*. New Haven: Yale University Press, 1976, 1995.

Dickens, Charles. "Private Theatres," "Astley's," "Greenwich Fair," "Vauxhall Gardens," and "Mrs Joseph Porter," in *Sketches by Boz*. London: Macrone, 1836; Michael Slater, ed. London: J. M. Dent, 1994, reprint.

———. "Two Views of a Cheap Theatre." In *All the Year Round*, February 25, 1860. Collected in *The Uncommercial Traveller*. New York: Oxford University Press (Oxford Illustrated Dickens), 1987.

Fitzgerald, Percy. *Chronicles of Bow Street Police-Office*. London: Chapman & Hall, 1888.

———. *The World Behind the Scenes*. London: Chapman & Hall, 1889.

Jackson, Russell, ed. *Victorian Drama*. London: Black (New Mermaid Series), 1989.

Jenkins, Anthony. *The Making of Victorian Drama*. Cambridge: Cambridge University Press, 1991.

Johnson, Edgar, and Eleanor Johnson, eds. *The Dickens Theatrical Reader*. London: V. Gollancz, 1964.

MacKay, Carol Hanbery, ed. *Dramatic Dickens*. Basingstoke: Macmillan, 1989.

Mayhew, Augustus. *Paved With Gold, or The Romance and Reality of the London Streets*. London: Chapman & Hall, 1858.

Newlin, George, comp. and ed. *Everyone in Dickens*. Westport, CT: Greenwood Press, 1995.

Reynolds, G.W.M. *The Mysteries of London*. Trefor Thomas, ed. London: Keele, 1966.

Slater, Michael, ed. *The Dent Uniform Edition of Dickens' Journalism*, Vol. 1. London: J. M. Dent, 1994.

Vlock, Deborah. *Dickens, Novel Reading and the Victorian Popular Theatre*. Cambridge: Cambridge University Press, 1998.

Watson, Ernest Bradles. *Sheridan to Robertson, a Study of the Nineteenth-Century London Stage*. Cambridge, MA: Harvard University Press, 1926.

Williams, Anthony Ronald. "Dramatic Interpretations of the Metropolis, 1821–1881." Unpublished Ph.D. dissertation, Birkbeck College, University of London, 1998.

10

The Marsh Country and the River

Charles Dickens routinely used actual places and topographical features in his works, usually changing their names but leaving them entirely recognisable in description. Much pleasurable research on the ground has been done over the years to track and mark these elements, and no one has been more thorough than Colonel W. Laurence Gadd, whose *The Great Expectations Country* (1929) is a mine of useful discoveries and connections. As we read extracts from this work, we find the devoted concentration to Dickens, word by word, touching and inspiring. It is the beginning of serious literary criticism, however rudimentary, for it respects the facts.

THE MARSH COUNTRY

The marshes in *Great Expectations* are those of the Hoo peninsula between the Thames and the Medway Rivers in the County of Kent. From his house at Gad's Hill, Dickens had them in good view. They extend roughly between the towns of Higham and Yantlett, and are at least one mile and sometimes nearly three miles in width. "Broad, open breezy expanses, with the tang of the sea in the air," they are everywhere intersected by wide, deep ditches of water and soft mud, "so that, although they appear from a distance to form a great flat plain, covered with coarse grass and reeds, it is almost impossible to cross them without a guide, or local knowledge of the practicable way" (WLG 5).

There is a mud sea wall, constructed originally by Dutch engineers who were expert in building dikes. From above the wall, ships' masts, funnels, and sails can be seen with the illusion that they are growing out of the marshes.

The marsh country begins at Chalk, on the old Dover Road, about one and a half miles from Gravesend going toward Rochester.

Though there are proponents for Cooling, the consensus of opinion seems to be that the town where Mr. Pumblechook and his tradesmen colleagues lives was Lower Higham, on the flat inshore, one mile from the church and almost exactly four miles from Rochester. The old Chequers Inn was the original for the Three Jolly Bargemen.

The church where Pip and Magwitch had their first encounter was St. Mary the Virgin, Dickens's parish church when he was at Gad's Hill. It has a quaint timber steeple, shingled with tiles and "looking like an old-fashioned candle extinguisher" (WLG 21). Nearly all the other churches in the area have square stone towers.

The lozenge-shaped tombstones of Pip's five brothers have their originals at Cooling, where there are thirteen such bearing the family names of Comport and Baker. These little ones all died of ague, which was then prevalent in the marsh country. Dickens often walked friends over to Cooling (then Cowling) to look at them.

The original of Joe Gargery's forge stood at the corner of the Dover Road and a little lane leading toward Singlewell and Cobham, within the precincts of the hamlet of Chalk. Dickens transported it to Lower Higham. W. Laurence Gadd, who surveyed the countryside for his book, reports that he visited the forge. He describes it, noting that the garden was gone.

Miss Havisham's Satis House was a house in Rochester known as Restoration House because Charles II stayed there the night before he was officially restored to the throne in 1660.

On the Kent (southern) side of the Thames the river is very shallow. There are mud flats called the Blyth Sands. There were only three places where hulks could be moored: at the mouths of the Higham and Cliffe creeks in the Lower Hope, and at Egypt Bay, a small inlet north of High Halstow, in Sea Reach. Dickens chose Egypt Bay. There was a hulk there—a coast guard vessel—which

Dickens converted to a prison ship, but at least until 1823, when Dickens was a boy in Chatham, there were three convict ships moored in the Medway off Upnor Castle. They were the *Euryalus* and the *Canada*, old wooden frigates, and the *Hercules*, a prison hospital.

THE RIVER

Dickens's first and perhaps greatest biographer, John Forster, illustrates the author's thoroughness in preparing himself to write the critical scenes on the Thames when Pip and Herbert plan and try to effect Magwitch's escape:

> At the opening of the story there had been an exciting scene of the wretched man's chase and recapture among the marshes, and this has its parallel at the close in his chase and recapture on the river while poor Pip is helping to get him off. To make himself sure of the actual course of a boat in such circumstances, and what possible incidents the adventure might have, Dickens hired a steamer for the day from Blackwall to Southend. Eight or nine friends and three or four members of his family were on board, and he seemed to have no care, the whole of that summer day (22nd of May 1861), except to enjoy their enjoyment and entertain them with his own in shape of a thousand whims and fancies; but his sleepless observation was at work all the time, and nothing had escaped his keen vision on either side of the river. The fifteenth chapter of the third volume [chapter 54] is a masterpiece. (JF, III, 332–33)

Pip tells the story as Dickens has prepared it from this research:

> Our plan was this. The tide, beginning to run down at nine, and being with us until three, we intended still to creep on after it had turned, and row against it until dark. We should then be well in those long reaches below Gravesend, between Kent and Essex, where the river is broad and solitary, where the water-side inhabitants are very few, and where lone public-houses are scattered here and there, of which we could choose one for a resting-place. There, we meant to lie by, all night. The steamer for Hamburg, and the steamer for Rotterdam, would start from London at about nine on Thursday morning. We should know at what time to expect them, according to where we were, and would hail the first; so that if by

any accident we were not taken aboard, we should have another chance. We knew the distinguishing marks of each vessel. (54)

FROM W. LAURENCE GADD, *THE GREAT EXPECTATIONS COUNTRY*
(London: Cecil Palmer, 1929)

THE RIVER JOURNEY

It was about half-past eight on a March morning, when the sun shines hot and the wind blows cold, that the three friends, Pip, Herbert and Startop, went down to the Temple Stairs and embarked upon the expedition that was to end in the recapture of Magwitch. It was just about high-tide, and they dropped easily down on the slack water, to London Bridge—Old London Bridge in those days, although the houses had been removed and the heads of traitors had long ceased to be exposed on pikes over the south gate. At certain states of the tide there was a dangerous race of water between the starlings of the old bridge, but Pip had already learned how to negotiate the passage. . . .

London Bridge was soon passed, and Billingsgate market, with its oyster boats and Dutchmen. . . .

Pip had sometimes left his boat at the Custom House, to be afterwards brought up to the Temple, when he had been as far down the river as Erith; and now this, and the White Tower and Traitor's Gate, and Quilp's Wharf on the Surrey side, were passed in quick succession, and the friends were among the steamers and barges, and colliers discharging their freights at the various wharves on both sides of the river. They were now among the tiers of shipping in the Pool, and, noting the Rotterdam and Hamburg steamers due to sail on the morrow, passed under the bowsprit of one of them.

To the three friends in the boat, the river would appear to be much wider than when viewed from the bank, or from the deck of a ship, and the boat itself a relatively very small object, especially when passing close to the tall and rusty iron sides of some moored steamer. A seaman possibly peering down at them from the apparently immense height of her bridge, would be much more remote from their concern than the great links of the anchor cable, splitting the tide into two bubbling lines of foam. And now, Pip, sitting in the stern, could see Mill Pond Bank and Mill Pond Stairs close ahead.

Mill Pond Bank was at Rotherhithe, on the Surrey side of the Lower Pool, and west of the Surrey Commercial Docks. The district has been much altered, but, in the early part of the last century, an elongated sheet of water called "Mill Pond," lay in the region north of the present Southwark Park, its lower end being separated from the Thames only by the thoroughfare known as Rotherhithe or Redriff. On the west side, its approaches were by Jamaica Row (now Jamaica Road), and Blue Anchor Lane; on the east were Love Land and the Old and New Paradise Streets. According to Wemmick, Mill Pond Bank was "by the river side, down the Pool there, between Limehouse and Greenwich," and was a fresh kind of place, where the wind from the river had room to turn itself round. Not far from the pond, was a thoroughfare called Rope-walk, and a little nearer to London Bridge there were four actual rope walks, but I cannot take upon myself to say which of these (all now vanished), was the "Old Green Copper."

The house with the bow window was evidently on the Rotherhithe and facing the river, for Provis used to pull down the blind of a window facing east, to shew that all was well, when Pip occasionally rowed down to Erith, prior to the actual expedition; and old Bill Barley spent most of his time with one eye at a telescope, which was fitted on his bed for the convenience of sweeping the river. Also, Provis was to come down to some stairs "hard by the house" when the time came for him to be taken into the boat.

There were several stairs along the Redriff near Mill Pond, but none named Mill Pond Stairs. From west to east, they were Fountain Stairs; Cherry Garden Stairs . . . West Lane Stairs; Redriff Stairs, and King's Stairs. Perhaps Mill Pond *Bank* was the Rotherhithe itself, but the stairs nearest to the Mill Pond were the West Lane and the Redriff Stairs. From one of these stairs Provis probably stepped into the boat, as its progress was arrested there for a moment.

There is only one difficulty about this identification, which, otherwise, fits in with the story perfectly well. Wemmick said "down the Pool there, between Limehouse and Greenwich." Between these two places lies the whole length of Limehouse Reach, trending southwards, while the Lower Pool trends northwards. In Limehouse Reach, the only district in which Chinks's Basin could be situated is Deptford, and I can find nothing there corresponding to Mill Pond Bank. Moreover, it would be quite impossible for Pip to see any stairs on the Surrey side of Limehouse Reach from the Lower Pool where his boat appears to have been when he sighted the stairs; so I am obliged to get over the difficulty by assuming that Mr. Wemmick made a mistake. . . .

I must not linger here any longer, for by this time, the falling tide is running down more strongly and our boat is making good headway down Greenwich Reach. . . .

On the opposite side of the river is the Isle of Dogs, now a populous dock district, but in Pip's day a barren marsh, on which several gibbets, with the bodies of pirates suspended from them, were erected along the muddy shore. At the end of the eighteenth century and the beginning of the nineteenth, there were sometimes three or four blackened carcases swinging there at one time, and the boatmen of Greenwich reaped a small harvest by making a charge for the privilege of viewing the distant pirates through the telescope.

At the lower end of Greenwich Reach is Blackwall Reach, and here we pass the Trinity House Wharf, with rows of parti-coloured buoys ready to be sent to any part of the coast, as required; and keeping in the run of the ebb tide, we round Blackwall point on Bugsby's Marsh. . . .

Beyond Woolwich Reach, which need not detain us, we gain Gallions, where the water deepens to twenty feet or more at low tide; and, at night, we see ahead of us a light, flashing at four-second intervals, on Tripcock Point.

Before this, our boat party would have been free of the tiers of shipping, past the "John of Sutherland," and the "Betsy of Yarmouth," and would be moving in a less congested stream, where ships could shake out their sails, and ships' boys need no longer fish in troubled waters with fenders. At that time, the country hereabouts was more open, and where we now see warehouses and factories, chimneys, and streets of houses, Pip saw only marshland and muddy creeks. On the Kentish side of Gallions and Barking Reaches, wide tracts of the Plumstead and Erith marshes yet remain, backed by the distant hills and woods about Shooter's Hill and Belevedere. On the Essex side, the country is flat, from about Dagenham, but broken here and there by huge mounds of refuse, that have been raised on the marshes. . . . At Crossness and Jenningtree Points, on the Kentish side, are occulting lights for the guidance of pilots and ship-masters.

At Crossness Point we pass a number of decayed and blackened stakes and timbers; all that remains of a derelict pier or landing stage, the one-time purpose of which is beyond my ken. The locality is merely a dismal swamp, as dismal now as when Pip saw it; but there is a public house there, known as the Half-Way House, and I suppose it must be half-way to somewhere. . . .

Another bend in the river brings us into Erith Rands, with the town of Erith in the bend, opposite the light on Cold-Harbour Point.

Erith is very drab and uninteresting, but the parish church there is ancient and quaint in design. Pip would see its squat spire from the river, as his boat passed what was then a mere village. . . .

The Greenhithe that Pip saw, on his river journey, was a little riverside village of one street, backed by green and wooded hills of some altitude. It was here that our boat party landed at a little stone causeway, to purchase some bottled beer, Provis remaining quietly in the boat.

I am pretty sure that the "White Hart" Inn at Greenhithe supplied the bottled beer, because it is easily the most likely of the two or three Inns, between London Bridge and Gravesend, that conform to the necessary conditions. . . .

The first part of the boat journey, down to the inn where the bottled beer was obtained, is not described in Chapter 54 of *Great Expectations* with sufficient detail to enable me to follow the actual course taken, but in the account of the later portion of the run, below Gravesend, the references are quite clear enough to indicate the movements of the boat without the slightest doubt, and, in this part of the river, it is unquestionable that Dickens caused the party to follow the proper and only practicable route against a flood tide. Anyone with experience of rowing on a tidal stream will appreciate the difficulty of pulling for ten or twelve miles against a tide running at five or six knots per hour, and Dickens rightly ascertained the route by which a rowing boat could make headway, keeping in slack water all the way. I, therefore, give him credit for having been as accurate with regard to the portion of river above Gravesend as with the portion below that town.

Dickens's observation must indeed have been marvellously exact, and his memory most retentive if his account of the river journey was based upon a single day's run from Blackwall to Southend [as recounted by John Forster]. I think it evinces a much closer acquaintance with the river than that; although I imagine he did ascertain on that trip the right and proper course for a boat, coming down on the ebb tide as far as Gravesend and then against the tide to the journey's end. On this I base the identification of the "White Hart" at Greenhithe.

The ebb tide, in passing from one Reach to another, between London and Gravesend, sets generally towards the shore immediately facing it, and not smoothly round the intervening points of land. This produces the eddies and whirlpools already mentioned, which a rowing boat is compelled to avoid. There is thus a particular course which Pip's boat should have followed all the way down, and this would depend upon the varying state of the tide throughout the day. The tide was with the party until they reached Gravesend, at about three o'clock in the afternoon, from which information it is not difficult to compute the route followed down the different Reaches.

I consider that the inn, where the party went ashore to buy bottled beer, must have been close to the riverside, visible from the water, and on the proper side for a landing in the particular Reach. It is also certain that, under the circumstances, some quiet, out-of-the-way place would be chosen, it being imperative to avoid chance meetings with Customs or other officials, and to give rise to no suspicion as to the object of the journey. As already stated, there are very few taverns, between London and Gravesend, that satisfy these conditions, and of these few, the "White

Hart" at Greenhithe, is the only one free from objection, on one ground or another. I have no doubt that Dickens spotted the inn, and its stone causeway, on his trip down the river in 1861. . . .

The "White Hart" faces the river, and has its own little stone causeway, at which our party landed. . . .

Leaving Greenhithe, we continue our journey down Saint Clement's Reach, with marsh land on both sides of the river. On the Essex side, the square tower of Saint Clement's Church is seen close to the river bank; and near it a beacon, one of the few yet remaining on the riverside.

Saint Clement's Church is an ancient edifice, built upon the foundations of an older Saxon church, and is the parish church of West Thorrock—a name supposed to have been derived from "Thor's Oak." In mediaeval times it was the last church at which pilgrims from East Anglia rested before crossing the river, on their way to Canterbury. A causeway over the Swanscombe marshes, on the Kentish side, then led to Galley Hill and to Watling Street. The lane from the marshes (now concreted to carry the heavy traffic connected with the Swanscombe cement factory), is still called the Pilgrim's Way.

Opposite Broadness, at the end of Saint Clement's Reach, is a dangerous shoal known as the Black Shelf; and in the bend between Saint Clement's Reach and Northfleet Hope lies the town of Grays, off which is moored the training ship "Exmouth". . . .

From Broadness Point, on which is a light, we pass down the west side of Northfleet Hope with marsh land on both sides, and so into Gravesend Reach. . . .

Gravesend Reach extends from Tilbury Ness to Coal House Point a distance of four nautical miles. This is the busiest part of the river, Gravesend being the entrance to the Port of London; and the official anchorage for shipping is just below the town. Here, ships take up or drop their pilots, whose headquarters are at the Terrace Pier. . . .

The surface of the stream is dotted with barges tacking up against the wind, their rich brown sails . . . adding to the colour scheme; whilst tramp steamers pass up and down, and fussy steam-tugs cleave their powerful way through the water in every direction. The graceful sailing ships of Pip's day are rarely to be seen. . . .

Viewed from the river, the town of Gravesend has rather a picturesque appearance, the jumble of houses by the riverside being dominated by the tower of Saint George's Church. The narrow High Street running uphill from the Town Pier, and presenting a veritable avenue of sign boards overhanging the pavements, is part of the older town, which was originally all down by the river.

Beyond the town, the land rises to the south in a series of green and wooded hills to the top of the North Downs, ten miles away.

Pip and his companions in the boat reached Gravesend at about three o'clock in the afternoon, when the last of the ebb tide was still with them, Pip purposely steering close in to the Custom House boat and out into the stream again.

The tide now began to slacken and to turn, and the craft at anchor to swing, so Pip steered for the Essex side in order to find easy water; and, as that is the correct course for a rowing boat against the flood tide, we follow him. Dickens does not say the boat went across to the north side, but there is no doubt about it, because Pip states that the ships taking advantage of the new tide crowded upon him in a fleet; and ships must come up on the north side of a line drawn from Northfleet Beacon to a point west of Shornmead Fort, whilst vessels about to anchor must do so south of that line. At night, the light on Northfleet Beacon shews red over the anchorage and white over the fairway.

Following Pip's boat, we keep close to the north shore, passing Tilbury Fort (with its rivergate built by Charles the Second), and a little tavern with the rather unusual sign of "The World's End". . . .

At Coalhouse Point, three or four miles below Gravesend, a spit or tongue of mud runs out to the centre of the river and forms the southern extremity of the extensive Mucking Flats. The spit is marked by a black conical buoy carrying an occulting gaslight and, at low tide, boats of even shallow draught must round this buoy to clear the shoal water.

This spit is the "low shallow and mudbank" which Pip carefully avoided, after creeping along the shore to keep out of the tideway.

We are now in the Lower Hope, a stretch of river running almost due north, whereas, the Reach we have just left runs practically west to east. On our left hand stretch the Mucking Flats, occupying one-third of the river's breadth, but covered with shallow water at high tide. The slack water in the Lower Hope, as also the deep water channel, is on the eastern side, so we continue beyond the Ovens buoy to that side of the river, passing the mouths of Higham and Cliffe creeks, and close under the concrete walls of Cliffe Fort. The marshes on our right hand are Pip's own marshes, and on his boat journey he passed close to the old battery and the beacon of his childhood. . . .

After passing the old beacon at the mouth of Cliffe creek our boat party continued to hug the shore nearly as far as Lower Hope Point, whence they struck across to the Essex side to find the slack water in Sea Reach. Here they landed; and we will follow their example. . . .

The slippery stones upon which we land form a stony spit, running out anglewise from the shore into the mud of Mucking Flats, a little to the west of the lighthouse. It is the only spot hereabouts, and for some distance in either direction, upon which Pip and his party could possibly have landed, the shores elsewhere being composed of very soft and treacherous mud.

Close by is a number of slimy black stakes, sticking up out of the mud, and known to pilots and watermen as the "Farmer's Teeth." Whether these stakes are the remains of an ancient and forgotten landing place of some kind I know not, but they have been on the spot as long as the oldest Gravesend waterman can remember.

To the west and south of the spit of loose and slippery stones stretch the Mucking Flats, at low tide a broad expanse of soft mud in which a man would sink to his waist . . . and along the cant edge of which lie at anchor certain powder hulks, roofed and mastless, sometimes afloat and sometimes stranded, according to the state of the tide. . . .

Eastwards, Sea Reach stretches for thirteen miles to the Nore Lightship, and close to us is Mucking Flat Lighthouse, the little squat shoal lighthouse of the story. It is a curious little iron structure on open piles, built in 1851, and originally connected with the shore, where the keepers' dwellings were, by a footbridge now partly broken down. An errant schooner carried away a portion of the latter one dark night when half a gale of wind was blowing. . . .

Opposite to the lighthouse, and about half-way across the river, the black and white chequered West Blyth buoy twists round and round in the current. It is moored in two and a quarter fathoms and marks the western edge of the Blyth sands, a vast shoal stretching all the way down the Kentish side to beyond Grain Island, and in places covering fully one half of the total width of the river. With field glasses, you may see the Middle Blyth buoy opposite Hole Haven and in line with Egypt Bay where Pip's convict hulk was. This is a black and white buoy with vertical stripes. Much farther off, the East Blyth, another chequered buoy, warns the mariner of the same dangerous shoal.

Behind us are the flat and dreary Essex marshes, with a distant horizon formed by the Laindon Hills to the north. Although not Pip's own marshes, they are, as he says, very like them in character; a flat region of reeds and coarse grass, with many muddy creeks and ditches; and even twenty years ago with hardly a building of any kind upon it.

I think it would be about five o'clock in the evening of that March day when Pip's boat party pushed off from the stony spit near Mucking lighthouse, and continued their journey. It was harder work now, for the young tide was growing lusty and strong, and the rowers would need to keep well into the Essex side in order to make any headway.

So they rowed and rowed until the sun went down. The rising tide had by this time lifted the boat a little, and Pip could see the red sun setting on the low level of the solitary flat marsh. This is another clear indication that the boat was following the correct course, and was close to the north shore of the river. From the Kentish side, the setting sun would have been seen over the water, and not over the Stanford-le-Hope or Mucking marshes, as Pip saw it.

I calculate that the sun went down at between five-thirty and six-thirty p.m. Shortly afterwards the night fell fast, and presently it became as dark as it would be until morning; but still Herbert and Startop held on steadily for "four or five dull miles," until Pip descried a light and a roof, which was shortly discovered to be the light and roof of a solitary tavern, by the side of a little stone causeway, at which the party landed.

This was the "Lobster Smack" Inn at Hole Haven on Canvey Island, a little wooden hostelry with a tiled roof. Approaching it by water, as Pip did, only the roof and one window can be seen, on account of the high sea-wall in front.

The stone causeway, a slippery landing place now but little used, juts out into Hole Haven, a creek or indentation on the west side of Canvey Island. This creek is navigable for small craft from half flood to half ebb, and offers good shelter from all but southerly winds. The channel runs along the east side, so, if you wish to enter the haven when the tide is not at the full, you should not turn into the creek until nearly in line with the sea-wall on that side, or you may run aground on the spit.

Canvey Island is rather difficult of access except by water, and even then you may get wet, when landing or embarking, if a south-westerly breeze is blowing and there is a bit of a sea on. It was a much more isolated place at the time when Pip landed on the stone causeway, although the "Lobster Smack" is still, probably, the most solitary tavern on the lower Thames. . . .

The "Lobster Smack" Inn is a building of two stories, and from its upper windows there is a clear view over the marshes and the estuary towards the Nore lightship which bears south-east by east, half east; its light at night being plainly visible. Hence, looking from his bedroom window, Pip could see the two strangers, who had examined his boat, striking across the marshes in the direction of the Nore.

The upper windows are those of two or three old-fashioned bedrooms (containing Dutch four-poster double beds) all reached from the kitchen by a narrow crooked staircase ending in a long passage. The largest of the upper rooms is now used as a dining room, the west window (that seen when approaching by water), having been converted into an entrance, on the level of the sea-wall, with a little wooden bridge or gangway connecting the two.

Dickens described the interior of the tavern as being a dirty place enough, probably not unknown to smuggling adventures. I daresay the smuggling adventures were true enough, but whatever the condition may have been then, the inn does not now deserve any censure on the score of cleanliness, and Mr Went is a very obliging host. The inn is a favourite week-end resort of Thames yachtsmen.

I do not know that Dickens ever actually visted the Lobster Smack Inn on Canvey Island, but his reference to the double-bedded rooms is sufficiently correct to suggest that he may have derived his information from the skipper of the steamboat in which he made his voyage of investigation. The inn was probably well-known to the skipper, as it is to most people who regularly use the Thames to-day.

The deep water channel for steamers lies close to Canvey Island, and it was an easy matter to put off from Hole Haven and get into the track of the Hamburg steamer. It could not have been done from the south side of the river, as the extensive Blyth sands stretch all the way from Lower Hope point to the sea; and a boat would have had to put off from the Kentish side more than an hour before the steamer left London, and then hang about in the channel, against the strong ebb tide, for four or five hours until the ship arrived. So Dickens made good use of his observations and enquiries in May, 1861, and placed the "Ship Inn" of the story on the proper side of the river for the purpose in view.

The easiest way to reach Canvey Island from Gravesend or Tilbury is by motor launch or sailing boat, but I have rowed over that stretch of four or five dull miles, from the squat shoal lighthouse to Hole Haven, under conditions very similar to those in *Great Expectations*; that is, at night and against the flood tide. . . .

Being the lighter weight, I took the bow oar, but the dinghy was such a cockleshell of a boat that even my modest mass sufficed to depress the prow so that we shipped a good deal of salt water, most of which I caught on the back of my neck. The easterly breeze was also decidedly chilly, and a sopping wet sweater was not the ideal garment under the circumstances.

I do not remember how long it took us to reach Canvey Island, but I know it was a long stiff pull against the tide, although we kept close into the shore in order to find the easiest water . . . there was nothing to be seen except the flat solitary marshes, with no life upon them, for the whole of the way. The shore was broken by a succession of creeks and muddy headlands, against which the tide flapped dismally. In the half light, which seemed to come from the water rather than the sky, the river appeared to be immensely wide, and our boat the only speck upon it, save when the sailing lights and the ghostly shadow of some distant vessel glided silently by.

However, we eventually rounded the low headland that forms the western end of Hole Haven, and saw the light of the "Lobster Smack" Inn about half a mile ahead. Inside the Haven, we were sheltered from the wind, but as there were then no wooden landing steps, we had to get ashore on the lee side of the slippery and sea-weedy stone causeway. Of course, I had no sooner jumped out, and grasped the gunwale to steady the boat, than a swell rolled along the hard and swamped me up to the knees; but this was so much in the nature of the day's work as to excite no comment, humorous or otherwise.

We found a good fire in the inn kitchen, and yarned with the landlord for a short spell, before departing with our precious provisions; and the run back on the tide was mere child's play.

East of Canvey Island, the Chapman Light—another shoal lighthouse—marks the edge of the extensive Leigh Sands, behind which are the towns of Leigh and Southend, both calling themselves "On Sea." The low point of land from behind which Pip saw the four-oared police galley shoot out, just as he and Provis were saying "good-bye" to Herbert Pocket and Startop, was probably Deadman's Point, a mile or more east of Hole Haven. The advent of that police galley put an end to the expedition by the capture of Magwitch, and the death of his accuser, Compeyson. . . .

Returning to Hole Haven from this little excursion inland, we again take to our boat, for, if we are to follow the river journey of *Great Expectations* to its conclusion, we must row out again into the channel and watch for the Hamburg or the Rotterdam steamer coming down from London.

As we drift a little, and paddle a little, to keep our station in the fairway, a short distance from the shore, we look back over our course of yesterday towards the west, and watch for the steamer's smoke. At length we see it, travelling down the Lower Hope, but "by reason of the bend and wind of the river" we see, as yet, only the smoke (and perhaps the masts of the vessel), over a stretch of the Higham Marshes.

But now, the steamer rounds Lower Hope Point and comes towards us head on, and presently we make her out to be one of the "Batavier" boats, bound for Rotterdam; so the Rotterdam boat has arrived first.

Whatever might have been done a hundred and more years ago, the chances of the "Batavier" stopping her way to pick up a passenger in Sea Reach are, in this age, very remote, so as we have no wish to follow Pip's boat to the very end, and to go to the bottom of the river, we had better get out of the steamer's way. Her pilot evidently thinks so too, for he gives a hoarse warning blast from the steam whistle.

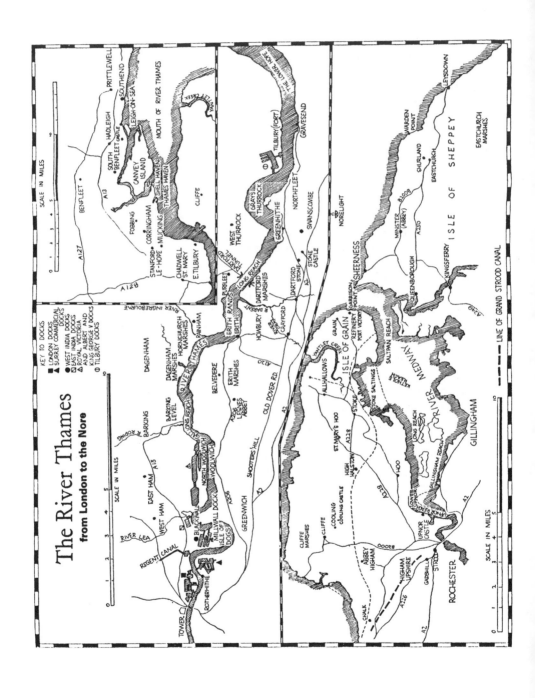

SUGGESTED READINGS AND WORKS CITED

Forster, John. *The Life of Charles Dickens*. 3 vols. London: Chapman and Hall, 1872–74.

Fox Smith, C. *Anchor Lane*. London: Methuen & Co. Ltd., 1933.

Gadd, W. Laurence. *The Great Expectations Country*. London: Cecil Palmer, 1929.

Goodsall, Robert Harold. *The Widening Thames*. London: Constable, 1965.

The River Thames, the Highway of the Port of London: Commercial Guide to the River Thames. London: Wm. Cory & Son Ltd., n.d.; mid-twentieth century.

Index

About the Author

GEORGE NEWLIN is an independent scholar who manages to combine his background in the legal profession with his passion for the arts and literature. He is the author of *Understanding A Tale of Two Cities* (1998) for the Greenwood Press "Literature in Context" series. He is the compiler and editor of the three-volume *Everyone in Dickens* (Greenwood, 1995), and *Everything in Dickens* (Greenwood, 1996).

The Greenwood Press "Literature in Context" Series
Student Casebooks to Issues, Sources, and Historical Documents